Codeless Deep Learning with KNIME

Build, train, and deploy various deep neural network architectures using KNIME Analytics Platform

Kathrin Melcher

Rosaria Silipo

BIRMINGHAM—MUMBAI

Codeless Deep Learning with KNIME

Commissioning Editor: Sunith Shetty
Acquisition Editor: Reshma Raman
Senior Editor: David Sugarman
Content Development Editor: Nathanya Dias
Technical Editor: Sonam Pandey
Copy Editor: Safis Editing
Project Coordinator: Aishwarya Mohan
Proofreader: Safis Editing
Indexer: Tejal Daruwale Soni
Production Designer: Nilesh Mohite

First published: November 2020
Production reference: 1251120

Published by Packt Publishing Ltd.
Livery Place
35 Livery Street
Birmingham
B3 2PB, UK.

ISBN 978-1-80056-661-3

www.packt.com

Packt.com

Subscribe to our online digital library for full access to over 7,000 books and videos, as well as industry leading tools to help you plan your personal development and advance your career. For more information, please visit our website.

Why subscribe?

- Spend less time learning and more time coding with practical eBooks and videos from over 4,000 industry professionals

- Improve your learning with skill plans tailored especially for you

- Get a free eBook or video every month

- Fully searchable for easy access to vital information

- Copy and paste, print, and bookmark content

Did you know that Packt offers eBook versions of every book published, with PDF and ePub files available? You can upgrade to the eBook version at packt.com and, as a print book customer, you are entitled to a discount on the eBook copy. Get in touch with us at customercare@packtpub.com for more details.

At www.packt.com, you can also read a collection of free technical articles, sign up for a range of free newsletters, and receive exclusive discounts and offers on Packt books and eBooks.

Contributors

About the authors

Kathrin Melcher is a data scientist at KNIME. She holds a master's degree in mathematics from the University of Konstanz, Germany. She joined the evangelism team at KNIME in 2017 and has a strong interest in data science and machine learning algorithms. She enjoys teaching and sharing her data science knowledge with the community, for example, in the book *From Excel to KNIME*, as well as on various blog posts and at training courses, workshops, and conference presentations.

Rosaria Silipo has been working in data analytics since 1992. Currently, she is a principal data scientist at KNIME. In the past, she has held senior positions with Siemens, Viseca AG, and Nuance Communications, and worked as a consultant in a number of data science projects. She holds a Ph.D. in bioengineering from the Politecnico di Milano and a master's degree in electrical engineering from the University of Florence (Italy). She is the author of more than 50 scientific publications, many scientific white papers, and a number of books for data science practitioners.

There are so many people to thank! We would like to thank Corey Weisinger for the Demand Prediction workflow in Chapter 6, and Jon Fuller for the image classification workflow in Chapter 9; Marcel Wiedenmann, Christian Dietz, and Benjamin Wilhelm, from the KNIME development team, for the great Keras integration and the many deep learning nodes; and finally, Paolo Tamagnini and Maarit Widmann, from the components team at KNIME, for the shared components we used in this book.

About the reviewers

Corey Weisinger is a data scientist at KNIME in Austin, Texas. He studied mathematics at Michigan State University, focusing on actuarial techniques and functional analysis. Prior to KNIME, he worked as an analytics consultant for the auto industry in Detroit, Michigan. He currently focuses on signal processing and numeric prediction techniques, teaches a time series course on KNIME, and is the author of the guidebook, *From Alteryx to KNIME*.

Adrian Nembach has a master's degree in computer science from the University of Konstanz. During his master's, he focused on deep learning for computer vision, including generative adversarial networks for semi-supervised classification of cell images and depth extraction from light field images. Alongside his studies, he also worked as a working student at KNIME, where he was involved in the development of various machine learning-related nodes and extensions, including integrations for Keras, XGBoost, and a rewrite of KNIME's native logistic regression and random forest nodes. After completing his degree, he started as a software engineer at KNIME, developing nodes for machine learning interpretability, active learning, and weak supervision.

Barbora Stetinova is experienced in the data science and business intelligence spheres. She started her career, after obtaining her MA and MBA degrees from university, at WITTE Automotive. Her data journey began in the controlling department as a data analyst, and she currently works in the IT department, where she is responsible for data science and business intelligence projects. Parallel to this, Barbora is engaged as a business analyst consultant for different industries at Leadership Synergy Community. To help others on their data science journey, she publishes her own data science e-learning courses. All of this led her to cooperate with Packt on data science projects as an e-learning trainer and technical reviewer, and with KNIME AG on a data visualization course.

Packt is searching for authors like you

If you're interested in becoming an author for Packt, please visit authors. packtpub.com and apply today. We have worked with thousands of developers and tech professionals, just like you, to help them share their insight with the global tech community. You can make a general application, apply for a specific hot topic that we are recruiting an author for, or submit your own idea.

Table of Contents

3

Getting Started with Neural Networks

4

Building and Training a Feedforward Neural Network

Section 2: Deep Learning Networks

5

Autoencoder for Fraud Detection

6

Recurrent Neural Networks for Demand Prediction

7

Implementing NLP Applications

8

Neural Machine Translation

9
Convolutional Neural Networks for Image Classification

Section 3: Deployment and Productionizing

10
Deploying a Deep Learning Network

11
Best Practices and Other Deployment Options

Other Books You May Enjoy

Index

Preface

This book aims to introduce you to the concepts and practices of deep learning networks. A number of case studies based on deep learning solutions are studied. In each case study, a neural architecture is explained and implemented through the codeless KNIME Analytics Platform tool. We start with a brief introduction to the basic concepts of deep learning and the visual programming KNIME Analytics Platform tool. Once the basic concepts are clear, we continue on with case studies on the usage of deep learning architectures to solve specific tasks: a neural autoencoder for fraud detection, recurrent neural networks for demand prediction and natural language processing, an encoder-decoder architecture for neural machine translation, and a convolutional neural network for image classification. The book concludes by describing the deployment options of trained networks and offering a few tips and tricks to train and successfully apply a deep learning network.

Who this book is for

If you have always wanted to develop solutions based on deep learning networks but you have not wanted to invest the time in learning how to code, this book is for you. It teaches you the basics of the algorithms behind deep learning and how to practically and codelessly build, train, and evaluate deep learning networks. While a codeless tool reduces the entrance barrier considerably, the complexity behind deep learning networks remains. A math background is required to understand the data shaping and operations as well as the math behind the algorithms.

What this book covers

Chapter 1, Introduction to Deep Learning with KNIME Analytics Platform, is a preparation chapter to get you familiar with the tool and the recent popularity of deep learning techniques.

Chapter 2, Data Access and Preprocessing with KNIME Analytics Platform, dives a bit deeper into the basic and advanced functionalities of KNIME Analytics Platform: from data access to workflow parameterization.

Chapter 3, Getting Started with Neural Networks, is the only theoretical chapter of the book. It paints an overview of the basic concepts around neural and deep learning networks and the algorithms used to train them.

Chapter 4, Building and Training a Feedforward Neural Network, is where we put into practice what we describe in *Chapter 3, Getting Started with Neural Networks*; we will build, train, and evaluate our first simple feedforward networks for classification tasks.

Chapter 5, Autoencoder for Fraud Detection, is where, with a neural autoencoder to solve the problem of fraud detection in credit card transactions, we start the series of case studies based on deep learning solutions.

Chapter 6, Recurrent Neural Networks for Demand Prediction, is where we introduce **Long Short-Term Memory** (**LSTM**) models in recurrent neural networks. Indeed, with their dynamic behavior, they are particularly effective in solving time series problems, such as a classic demand prediction problem.

Chapter 7, Implementing NLP Applications, covers how LSTM-based recurrent neural networks are often also used to implement solutions for natural language processing tasks. In this chapter, we cover a few case studies for free text generation, free name generation, and sentiment analysis.

Chapter 8, Neural Machine Translation, looks at an encoder-decoder architecture for automatic translations.

Chapter 9, Convolutional Neural Networks for Image Classification, covers a case study on image classification, which we could not miss. We classify histopathology images into cancer diagnoses using a convolutional neural network.

Chapter 10, Deploying a Deep Learning Network, starts describing the deployment phase. A simple example of the deployment workflow is explained in detail.

Chapter 11, Best Practices and Other Deployment Options, extends the previous chapter dedicated to deployment with more deployment options, such as web applications and REST services, and we conclude the book with a few tips and tricks.

To get the most out of this book

KNIME Analytics Platform is a very easy-to-use tool. No previous coding knowledge is necessary.

Some previous math knowledge, however, is necessary to deal with the data transformations and understand the training algorithms.

Software covered in the book	OS requirements
KNIME Analytics Platform	Windows, macOS X, and Linux (any)
KNIME Server (optional)	Windows, macOS X, and Linux (any)

KNIME Analytics Platform is open source and can be downloaded, installed, and used for free. Download it from `https://www.knime.com/downloads`.

KNIME Server is only needed in *Chapter 11, Best Practices and Other Deployment Options*, to run the trained network within a REST service or a web application. KNIME Server is not open source and cannot be used for free but requires a yearly license. For a test license, please fill in the contact form at `https://www.knime.com/contact`.

Download the example workflows

You can download the example workflows for this book from KNIME Hub at `https://hub.knime.com/kathrin/spaces/Codeless%20Deep%20Learning%20with%20KNIME/latest/`, or from GitHub, at `https://github.com/PacktPublishing/Codeless-Deep-Learning-with-KNIME`. If there's an update to the workflows, it will be updated on the existing KNIME Hub and GitHub repositories.

We also have other code bundles from our rich catalog of books and videos available at `https://github.com/PacktPublishing/`. Check them out!

Download the color images

We also provide a PDF file that has color images of the screenshots/diagrams used in this book. You can download it here: `https://static.packt-cdn.com/downloads/9781800566613_ColorImages.pdf`.

Conventions used

There are a number of text conventions used throughout this book.

`Code in text`: Indicates code words in text, database table names, folder names, filenames, file extensions, pathnames, dummy URLs, user input, and Twitter handles. Here is an example: " We drag and drop the `Demographics.csv` file from `Example Workflows/TheData/Misc` into the workflow editor."

Bold: Indicates a new term, an important word, or words that you see onscreen. For example, words in menus or dialog boxes appear in the text like this. Here is an example: "After configuration is complete, we click **OK**; the node state moves to yellow and the node can now be executed."

> **Tips or important notes**
> The automatic creation of the node and the configuration of its settings by file drag and drop works only for specific file extensions: `.csv` for a File Reader, `.table` for a Table Reader, `.xls` and .xlsx for an Excel Reader, and so on.

Get in touch

Feedback from our readers is always welcome.

General feedback: If you have questions about any aspect of this book, mention the book title in the subject of your message and email us at `customercare@packtpub.com`.

Errata: Although we have taken every care to ensure the accuracy of our content, mistakes do happen. If you have found a mistake in this book, we would be grateful if you would report this to us. Please visit `www.packtpub.com/support/errata`, selecting your book, clicking on the Errata Submission Form link, and entering the details.

Piracy: If you come across any illegal copies of our works in any form on the Internet, we would be grateful if you would provide us with the location address or website name. Please contact us at `copyright@packt.com` with a link to the material.

If you are interested in becoming an author: If there is a topic that you have expertise in and you are interested in either writing or contributing to a book, please visit `authors.packtpub.com`.

Reviews

Please leave a review. Once you have read and used this book, why not leave a review on the site that you purchased it from? Potential readers can then see and use your unbiased opinion to make purchase decisions, we at Packt can understand what you think about our products, and our authors can see your feedback on their book. Thank you!

For more information about Packt, please visit `packt.com`.

Section 1: Feedforward Neural Networks and KNIME Deep Learning Extension

This section is introductory. It is here to ease you into the world of neural networks and the tool at hand, KNIME Analytics Platform.

This section comprises the following chapters:

- *Chapter 1, Introduction to Deep Learning with KNIME Analytics Platform*
- *Chapter 2, Data Access and Preprocessing with KNIME Analytics Platform*
- *Chapter 3, Getting Started with Neural Networks*
- *Chapter 4, Building and Training a Feedforward Neural Network*

1
Introduction to Deep Learning with KNIME Analytics Platform

We'll start our journey of exploring **Deep Learning** (DL) paradigms by looking at KNIME Analytics Platform. If you have always been drawn to neural networks and deep learning architectures and have always thought that the coding part would be an obstacle to you developing a quick learning curve, then this is the book for you.

Deep learning can be quite complex, and we must make sure that the journey is worth the result. Thus, we'll start this chapter by stating, once again, the relevance of deep learning techniques when it comes to successfully implementing applications for data science.

We will continue by providing a quick overview of the tool of choice for this book – KNIME Software – and focus on how it complements both KNIME Analytics Platform and KNIME Server.

The work we'll be doing throughout this book will be implemented in KNIME Analytics Platform, which is open source and available for free. We will dedicate a full section to how to download, install, and use KNIME Analytics Platform, even though more details will be provided in the chapters to follow.

Among the benefits of KNIME Analytics Platform is, of course, its codeless Deep Learning - Keras Integration extension, which we will be making extensive use of throughout this book. In this chapter, we will just focus on the basic concepts and requirements for this KNIME extension.

Finally, we will conclude this chapter by stating the goal and structure of this book. We wanted to give it a practical flavor, so most of the chapters will revolve around a practical case study that includes real-world data. In each chapter, we will take the chance to dig deeper into the required neural architecture, data preparation, deployment, and other aspects necessary to make the case study at hand a success.

In this chapter, we will cover the following topics:

- The Importance of Deep Learning
- Exploring KNIME Software
- Exploring KNIME Analytics Platform
- Installing KNIME Deep Learning – Keras Integration
- Goals and Structure of this Book

We'll start by stating the importance of deep learning when it comes to successful data science applications.

The Importance of Deep Learning

If you have been working in the field of **data science** – or **Artificial Intelligence (AI)**, as it is called nowadays – for a few years, you might have noticed the recent sudden explosion of scholarly and practitioner articles about successful solutions based on deep learning techniques.

The big breakthrough happened in 2012 when the deep learning-based AlexNet network won the ImageNet challenge by an unprecedented margin. This victory kicked off a surge in the usage of deep learning networks. Since then, these have expanded to many different domains and tasks.

So, what are we referring to exactly when we talk about deep learning? Deep learning covers a subset of **Machine Learning (ML)** algorithms, most of which stem from neural networks. Deep learning is indeed the modern evolution of traditional neural networks. Apart from the classic feedforward, fully connected, backpropagation-trained, and multilayer perceptron architectures, *deeper* architectures have been added. Deeper indicates more hidden layers and a few new additional neural paradigms, including **Recurrent Neural Networks (RNNs)**, **Long-Short Term Memory (LSTM)**, **Convolutional Neural Networks (CNNs)**, **Generative Adversarial Networks (GANs)**, and more.

The recent success of these new types of neural networks is due to several reasons. First, the increased computational power in modern machines has favored the introduction and development of new paradigms and more complex neural architectures. Training a complex neural network in minutes leaves space for more experimentation compared to training the same network for hours or days. Another reason is due to their flexibility. Neural networks are universal function approximators, which means that they can approximate almost anything, provided that their architecture is sufficiently complex.

Having mathematical knowledge of these algorithms, experience with the most effective paradigms and architectures, and domain wisdom are all basic, important, and necessary ingredients for the success of any data science project. However, there are other, more contingent factors – such as ease of learning, speed of prototyping, options for debugging and testing to ensure the correctness of the solution, flexibility to experiment, availability of help from external experts, and automation and security capabilities – that also influence the final result of the project.

In this book, we'll present deep learning solutions that can be implemented with the open source, visual programming-based, free-to-use tool known as KNIME Analytics Platform. The deployment phases for some of these solutions also use a few features provided by KNIME Server.

Next, we will learn about how KNIME Analytics Platform and KNIME Server complement each other, as well as which tasks both should be used for.

Exploring KNIME Software

We will mainly be working with two KNIME products: KNIME Analytics Platform and KNIME Server. KNIME Analytics Platform includes ML and deep learning algorithms and data operations needed for data science projects. KNIME Server, on the other hand, provides the IT infrastructure for easy and secure deployment, as well as model monitoring over time.

We'll concentrate on KNIME Analytics Platform first and provide an overview of what it can accomplish.

KNIME Analytics Platform

KNIME Analytics Platform is an open source piece of software for all your data needs. It is free to download from the KNIME website (`https://www.knime.com/downloads`) and free to use. It covers all the main data wrangling and machine learning techniques available at the time of writing, and it is based on visual programming.

Visual programming is a key feature of KNIME Analytics Platform for quick prototyping. It makes the tool very easy to use. In visual programming, a **Graphical User Interface (GUI)** guides you through all the necessary steps for building a pipeline (workflow) of dedicated blocks (nodes). Each node implements a given task; each workflow of nodes takes your data from the beginning to the end of the designed journey. A workflow substitutes a script; a node substitutes one or more script lines.

Without extensive coverage when it comes to commonly used data wrangling techniques, machine learning algorithms, and data types and formats, and without integration with most common database software, data sources, reporting tools, external scripts, and programming languages, the software's ease of use would be limited. For this reason, KNIME Analytics Platform has been designed to be open to different data formats, data types, data sources, and data platforms, as well as external tools such as Python and R.

We'll start by looking at a few ML algorithms. KNIME Analytics Platform covers most machine learning algorithms: from decision trees to random forest and gradient boosted trees, from recommendation engines to a number of clustering techniques, from Naïve Bayes to linear and logistic regression, from neural networks to deep learning. Most of these algorithms are native to KNIME Analytics Platform, though some can be integrated from other open source tools such as Python and R.

To train different deep learning architectures, such as RNNs, autoencoders, and CNNs, KNIME Analytics Platform has integrated the **Keras** deep learning library through the **KNIME Deep Learning - Keras Integration** extension (`https://www.knime.com/deeplearning/keras`). Through this extension, it is possible to drag and drop nodes to define complex neural architectures and train the final network without necessarily writing any code.

However, defining the network is just one of the many steps that must be taken. Ensuring the data is in the right form to train the network is another crucial step. For this, a very large number of nodes are available so that we can implement a myriad of **Data Wrangling** techniques. By combining nodes dedicated to small tasks, you can implement very complex data transformation operations.

KNIME Analytics Platform also connects to most of the required data sources: from databases to cloud repositories, from big data platforms to files.

But what if all of this is not enough? What if you need a specific procedure for a specific domain? What if you need a specific network manipulation function from Python? Where KNIME Analytics Platform and its extensions cannot reach, you can integrate with other scripting and programming languages, such as **Python**, **R**, **Java**, and **Javascript**, just to mention a few. In addition, KNIME Analytics Platform has seamless integration with BIRT, a business intelligence and reporting tool. Integrations with other reporting platforms such as Tableau, QlickView, PowerBI, and Spotfire are also available.

Several JavaScript-based nodes are dedicated to implementing data visualization plots and charts: from a simple scatter plot to a more complex sunburst chart, from a simple histogram to a parallel coordinate plot, and more. These nodes seem simple but are potentially quite powerful. If you combine them within a **component**, you can interactively select data points across multiple charts. By doing this, the component inherits and combines all the views from the contained nodes and connects them in a way that, if the points are selected and visualized in one chart, they can also be selected and visualized in the other charts of the component's composite view.

Figure 1.1 shows an example of a composite view:

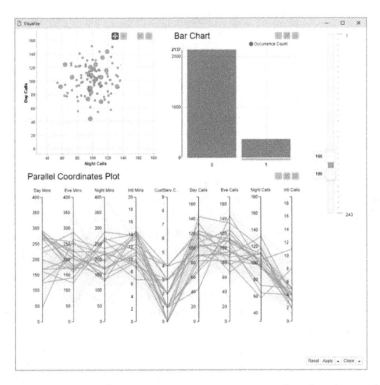

Figure 1.1 – Composite view of a component containing a scatter plot, a bar chart, and a parallel coordinate plot

Figure 1.1 shows the composite view of a component containing a scatter plot, a bar chart, and a parallel coordinate plot. The three plots visualize the same data and are connected in a way that, by selecting data in the bar chart, it selects and optionally visualizes the data that's been selected in the other two charts.

When it comes to creating a data science solution, KNIME Analytics Platform provides everything you need. However, KNIME Server offers a few additional features to ease your job when it comes to moving the solution to production.

KNIME Server for the Enterprise

The last step in any data science cycle is to deploy the solution to production – and in the case of an enterprise, providing an easy, comfortable, and secure deployment.

This process of moving the application into the real world is called *moving into production*. The process of including the trained model in this final application is called **deployment**. Both phases are deeply connected and can be quite problematic since all the errors that occurred in the application design show up at this stage.

It is possible, though limited, to move an application into production using KNIME Analytics Platform. If you, as a lone data scientist or a data science student, do not regularly deploy applications and models, KNIME Analytics Platform is probably enough for your needs. However, if you are just a bit more involved in an enterprise environment, where scheduling, versioning, access rights, disaster recovery, web applications and REST services, and all the other typical functions of a production server are needed, then just using KNIME Analytics Platform for production can be cumbersome.

In this case, **KNIME Server**, which comes with an annual license fee, can make your life easier. First of all, it is going to fit the governance of the enterprise's IT environment better. It also offers a protected collaboration environment for your group and the entire data science lab. And of course, its main advantage consists of making model deployment and moving it into production easier and safer since it uses the *integrated deployment* feature and allows you to use *one-click deployment* into production. End users can then run the application from a KNIME Analytics Platform client or – even better – from a web browser.

Remember those composite views that offer interactive interconnected views of selected points? These become fully formed web pages when the application is executed on a web browser via **KNIME Server's WebPortal**.

Using the components as touchpoints within the workflow, we get a **Guided Analytics** (https://www.knime.com/blog/principles-of-guided-analytics) application within the web browser. Guided analytics inserts touchpoints to be consumed by the end user from a web browser within the flow of the application. The end user can take advantage of these touchpoints to insert knowledge or preferences and to steer the analysis in the desired direction.

Now, let's download KNIME Analytics Platform and give it a try!

Exploring KNIME Analytics Platform

To install KNIME Analytics Platform, follow these steps:

1. Go to http://www.knime.com/downloads.

2. Provide some details about yourself (step **1** in *Figure 1.2*).

3. Download the version that's suitable for your operating system (step **2** in *Figure 1.2*).

4. While you're waiting for the appropriate version to download, browse through the different steps to get started (step **3** in *Figure 1.2*):

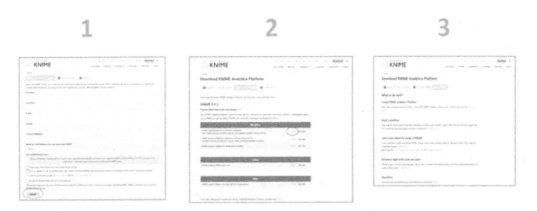

Figure 1.2 – Steps for downloading the KNIME Analytics Platform package

Once you've downloaded the package, locate it, start it, and follow the instructions that appear onscreen to install it in any directory that you have write permissions for.

Once it's been installed, locate your instance of KNIME Analytics Platform – from the appropriate folder, desktop link, application, or link in the start menu – and start it.

When the splash screen appears, a window will ask for the location of your workspace (*Figure 1.3*). This workspace is a folder on your machine that will host all your work. The default workspace folder is called `knime-workspace`:

Figure 1.3 – The KNIME Analytics Platform Launcher window asking for the workspace folder

After clicking **Launch**, the workbench for **KNIME Analytics Platform** will open.

The workbench of KNIME Analytics Platform is organized as depicted in *Figure 1.4*:

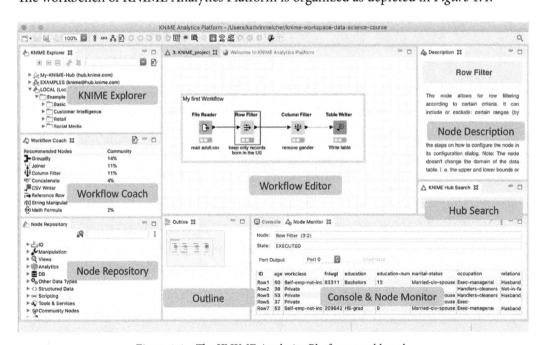

Figure 1.4 – The KNIME Analytics Platform workbench

The KNIME workbench consists of different panels that can be resized, removed by clicking the **X** on their tab, or reinserted via the **View** menu. Let's take a look at these panels:

- **KNIME Explorer**: The **KNIME Explorer** panel in the upper-left corner displays all the workflows in the selected (**LOCAL**) workspace, possible connections to mounted KNIME servers, a connection to the **EXAMPLES** server, and a connection to the **My-KNIME-Hub** space.

  The **LOCAL** workspace displays all workflows, saved in the workspace folder that were selected when KNIME Analytics Platform was started. The very first time the platform is opened, the LOCAL workspace only contains workflows and data in the *Example Workflows* folder. These are example applications to be used as starting points for your projects.

  The **EXAMPLES** server is a read-only KNIME hosted server that contains many more example workflows, organized into categories. Just double-click it to be automatically logged in with read-only mode. Once you've done this, you can browse, open, explore, and download all available example workflows. Once you have located a workflow, double-click it to explore it or drag and drop it into **LOCAL** to create a local editable copy.

  My-KNIME-Hub provides access to the KNIME community shared repository (**KNIME Hub**), either in public or private mode. You can use **My-KNIME-Hub/ Public** to share your work with the KNIME community or **My-KNIME-Hub/ Private** as a space for your current work.

- **Workflow Coach**: **Workflow Coach** is a node recommendation engine that aids you when you're building workflows. Based on worldwide user statistics or your own private statistics, it will give you suggestions on which nodes you should use to complete your workflow.

- **Node Repository**: The **Node Repository** contains all the KNIME nodes you have currently installed, organized into categories. To help you with orientation, a search box is located at the top of the **Node Repository** panel. The magnifier lens on its left switches between the exact match and the fuzzy search option.

- **Workflow Editor**: The **Workflow Editor** is the canvas at the center of the page and is where you assemble workflows, configure and execute nodes, inspect results, and explore data. Nodes are added from the **Node Repository** panel to the workflow editor by drag and drop or double-click. Upon starting KNIME Analytics Platform, the Workflow Editor will open on the **Welcome Page** panel, which includes a number of useful tips on where to find help, courses, events, and the latest news about the software.

- **Outline**: The **Outline** view displays the entire workflow, even if only a small part is visible in the workflow editor. This part is marked in gray in the **Outline** view. Moving the gray rectangle in the **Outline** view changes the portion of the workflow that's visible in the Workflow Editor.

- **Console** and **Node Monitor**: The **Console** and the **Node Monitor** share one panel with two tabs. The **Console** tab prints out possible error and warning messages. The same information is written to a log file, located in the workspace directory. The **Node Monitor** tab shows you the data that's available at the output ports of the selected executed node in the Workflow Editor. If a node has multiple output ports, you can select the data of interest from a dropdown menu. By default, the data at the top output port is shown.

- **KNIME Hub**: The **KNIME Hub** (`https://hub.knime.com/`) is an external space where KNIME users can share their work. This panel allows you to search for workflows, nodes, and components shared by members of the KNIME community.

- **Description**: The **Description** panel displays information about the selected node or category. In particular, for nodes, it explains the node's task, the algorithm behind it (if any), the dialog options, the available views, the expected input data, and the resulting output data. For categories, it displays all contained nodes.

Finally, at the very top, you can find the **Top Menu**, which includes menus for file management and preference settings, workflow editing options, additional views, node commands, and help documentation.

Besides the core software, KNIME Analytics Platform benefits from external **extensions** provided by the KNIME community. The **install KNIME extensions** and **update KNIME** commands, available in the **File** menu, allow you to expand your current instance with external extensions or update it to a newer version.

Under the top menu, a **toolbar** is available. When a workflow is open, the toolbar offers commands for workflow editing, node execution, and customization.

A **workflow** can be built by dragging and dropping nodes from the **Node Repository** panel onto the **Workflow Editor** window or by just double-clicking them. Nodes are the basic processing units of any workflow. Each **node** has several input and/or output ports. **Data** flows over a connection from an **output port** to the **input port**(s) of other nodes. Two nodes are connected – and the data flow is established – by clicking the mouse at the output port of the first node and releasing the mouse at the input port of the next node. A pipeline of such nodes makes a workflow.

In *Figure 1.5*, under each node, you will see a **status light**: red, yellow, or green:

Figure 1.5 – Node structure and status lights

When a new node is created, the status light is usually red, which means that the node's settings still need to be configured for the node to be able to execute its task.

To configure a node, right-click it and select **Configure** or just double-click it. Then, adjust the necessary settings in the node's dialog. When the dialog is closed by pressing the **OK** button, the node is configured, and the status light changes to yellow; this means that the node is ready to be executed. Right-clicking on the node again shows an enabled **Execute** option; pressing it will execute the node.

The ports on the left are input ports, where the data from the outport of the predecessor node is fed into the node. Ports on the right are outgoing ports. The result of the node's operation on the data is provided by the output port of the successor nodes. When you hover over the port, a tooltip will provide information about the output dimension of the node.

> **Important note**
> Only ports of the same type can be connected!

Data ports (black triangles) are the most common type of node ports and transfer flat data tables from node to node. **Database ports** (brown squares) transfer SQL queries from node to node. Many more node ports exist and transfer different objects from one node to the next.

After successful execution, the status light of the node turns green, indicating that the processed data is now available on the outports. The result(s) can be inspected by exploring the outport view(s): the last entries in the context menu open them.

With that, we have completed our quick tour of the workbench in KNIME Analytics Platform.

Now, let's take a look at where we can find starting examples and help.

Useful Links and Materials

At this point, we have already looked at the **KNIME Hub** already. The KNIME Hub (`https://hub.knime.com/`) is a very useful public repository for applications, extensions, examples, and tutorials provided by the KNIME community. Here, you can share your workflows and download workflows that have been created by other KNIME users. Just type in some keywords and you will get a list of related workflows, components, extensions, and more. For example, just type in `read file` and you will get a list of example workflows illustrating how to read CSV files, `.table` files, Excel files, and so on. (*Figure 1.6*):

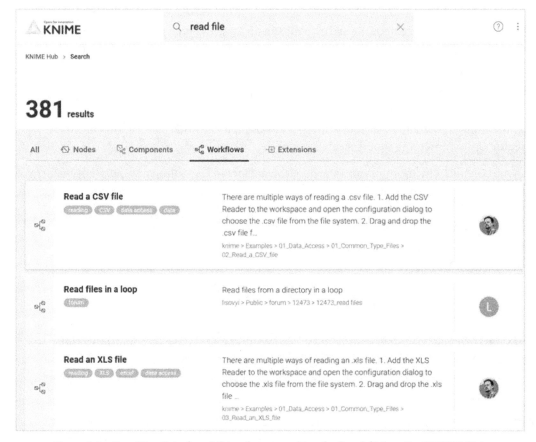

Figure 1.6 – Resulting list of workflows from searching for "read file" on the KNIME Hub

All workflows described in this book are also available on the KNIME Hub for you: `https://hub.knime.com/kathrin/spaces/Codeless%20Deep%20 Learning%20with%20KNIME/latest/`.

Once you've isolated the workflow you are interested in, click on it to open its page, and then download it or open it in KNIME Analytics Platform to customize it to your own needs.

On the other hand, to share your work on the KNIME Hub, just copy your workflows from your local workspace into the *My-KNIME-Hub/Public* folder in the **KNIME Explorer** panel within the KNIME workbench. It will be automatically available to all members of thé KNIME community.

The KNIME community is also very active, with tips and tricks available on the **KNIME Forum** (`https://forum.knime.com/`). Here, you can ask questions or search for answers.

Finally, contributions from the community are available as posts on the **KNIME Blog** (`https://www.knime.com/blog`), as books via **KNIME Press** (`https://www.knime.com/knimepress`), and as videos via the **KNIME TV** (`https://www.youtube.com/user/KNIMETV`) channel on YouTube.

The two books *KNIME Beginner's Luck* and *KNIME Advanced Luck* provide tutorials for those users who are starting out in data science with KNIME Analytics Platform.

Now, let's build our first workflow, shall we?

Build and Execute Your First Workflow

In this section, we'll build our first, simple, small workflow. We'll start with something basic: reading data from an ASCII file, performing some filtering, and displaying the results in a bar chart.

In KNIME Explorer, do the following:

1. Create a new empty folder by doing the following:

    a) Right-click **LOCAL** (or anywhere you want your folder to be).

    b) Select **New Workflow Group...** (as shown in *Figure 1.7*), and, in the window that opens, name it `Chapter 1`.

2. Click **Finish**. You should then see a new folder with that name in the **KNIME Explorer** panel.

> **Important note**
> Folders in KNIME Explorer are called **Workflow Groups**.

Similarly, you can create a new workflow, as follows:

1. Create a new workflow by doing the following:

    a) Right-click the `Chapter 1` folder (or anywhere you want your workflow to be).

b) Select **New KNIME Workflow** (as shown in *Figure 1.7*) and, in the window that opens, name it `My_first_workflow`.

2. Click **Finish**. You should then see a new workflow with that name in the **KNIME Explorer** panel.

After clicking **Finish**, the Workflow Editor will open the canvas for the empty workflow.

> **Tip**
> By default, the canvas for a new workflow opens with the grid on; to turn it off, click the **Open the settings dialog for the workflow editor** button (the button before the last one) in the toolbar. This button opens a window where you can customize the workflow's appearance (for example, allowing curved connections) and perform editing (turn the grid on/off).

Figure 1.7 shows the **New Workflow Group...** option in the KNIME Explorer's context menu. It allows you to create a new, empty folder:

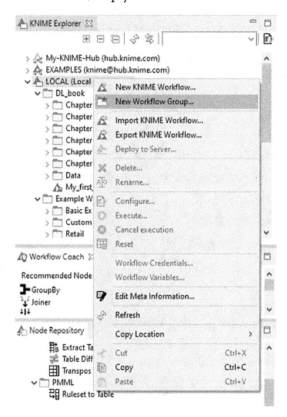

Figure 1.7 – Context menu for creating a new folder and a new workflow in KNIME Explorer

The first thing we need to do in our workflow is read an ASCII file with the data. Let's read the *adult.csv* file that comes with the installation of KNIME Analytics Platform. This can be found under **Example Workflows/The Data/Basics**. adult.csv is a US Census public file that describes 30K people by age, gender, origin, and professional and private life.

Let's **create** the node so that we can read the *adult.csv* ASCII file:

a) In the **Node Repository**, search for the **File Reader** node (it is actually located in the **IO/Read** category).

b) Drag and drop the **File Reader** node onto the **Workflow Editor** panel.

c) Alternatively, just double-click the **File Reader** node in the **Node Repository**; this will automatically create it in the **Workflow Editor** panel.

In *Figure 1.8*, see the **File Reader** node located in the **Node Repository**:

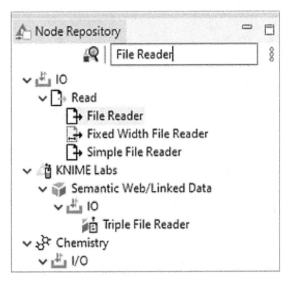

Figure 1.8 – The File Reader node under IO/Read in the Node Repository

Now, let's **configure** the node so that it reads the *adult.csv* file. Double-click the newly created **File Reader** node in the Workflow Editor and manually configure it with the file path to the *adult.csv* file. Alternatively, just drag and drop the *adult.csv* file from the **KNIME Explorer** panel (or from anywhere on your machine) onto the **Workflow Editor** window. You can see this action in *Figure 1.9*:

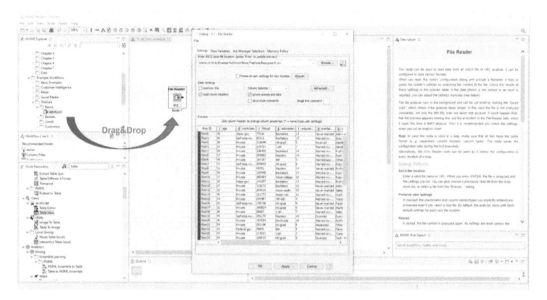

Figure 1.9 – Dragging and dropping the adult.csv file onto the Workflow Editor panel.

This automatically generates a File Reader node that contains most of the correct configuration settings for reading the file.

Tip

The **Advanced** button in the File Reader configuration window leads you to additional advanced settings: reading files with special characters, such as quotes; allowing lines with different lengths; using different encodings; and so on.

To execute this node, just right-click it and from the context menu, select **Execute**; alternatively, click on the **Execute** buttons (single and double white arrows on a green background) that are available in the toolbar.

To inspect the output data table that's produced by this node's execution, right-click on the node and select the last option available in the context menu. This opens the data table that appears as a result of reading the *adult.csv* file. You will notice columns such as **Age**, **Workclass**, and so on.

> **Important note**
>
> Data in KNIME Analytics Platform is organized into tables. Each cell is uniquely identified via the **column header** and the **row ID**. Therefore, column headers and row IDs need to have unique values.

fnlwgt is one column for which we were never sure of what it meant. So, let's remove it from further analysis by using the **Column Filter** node.

To do this, search for **Column Filter** in the search box above the Node Repository, then drag and drop it onto the Workflow Editor and connect the output of the **File Reader** node to the input of the **Column Filter** node. Alternatively, we can select the **File Reader** node in the **Workflow Editor** panel and then double-click the **Column Filter** node in the Node Repository. This automatically creates a node and its connections in the Workflow Editor.

The **Column Filter** node and its configuration window are shown in *Figure 1.10*:

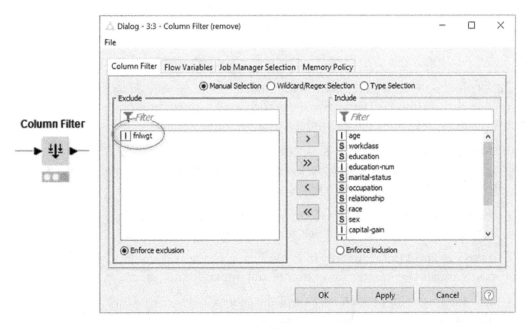

Figure 1.10 – Configuring the Column Filter node to remove the column named fnlwgt
from the input data table

Again, double-click or right-click the node and then select **Configure** to configure it. This configuration window contains three options that can be selected via three radio buttons: **Manual Selection**, **Wildcard/Regex Selection**, and **Type Selection**. Let's take a look at these in more detail:

- **Manual Selection** offers an Include/Exclude framework so that you can manually transfer columns from the **Include** set into the **Exclude** set and vice versa.

- **Wildcard/Regex Selection** extracts the columns you wish to keep, based on a wildcard (using * as the wildcard) or regex expression.

- **Type Selection** keeps the columns based on the data types they carry.

Since this is our first workflow, we'll go for the easiest approach; that is, Manual Selection. Go to the **Manual Selection** tab and transfer the fnlwgt column to the **Exclude** set via the buttons in-between the two frames (these can be seen in *Figure 1.10*).

After executing the Column Filter node, if we inspect the output data table (right-click and select the last option in the context menu), we'll see a table that doesn't contain the fnlwgt column.

Now, let's extract all the records of people who work more than 20 hours/week. hours-per-week is the column that contains the data of interest.

For this, we need to create a Row Filter node and implement the required condition:

```
IF hours-per-week  > 20     THEN Keep data row.
```

Again, let's locate the **Row Filter** node in the Node Repository panel, drag and drop it (or double-click it) into the Workflow Editor, connect the output port of the Column Filter node to its input port, and open its configuration window.

In the configuration window of the Row Filter node (*Figure 1.11*), we'll find three default filtering criteria: **use pattern matching**, **use range checking**, and **only missing values match**. Let's take a look at what they do:

- **use pattern matching** matches the given pattern to the content of the selected column in the **Column to test** field and keeps the matching rows.

- **use range checking** keeps only those data rows whose value in the **Column to test** columns falls between the **lower bound** and **upper bound** values.

- **only missing values match** only keeps the data rows where a missing value is present in the selected column.

The default behavior is to include the matching data rows in the output data table. However, this can be changed by enabling **Exclude rows by attribute value** via the radio buttons on the left-hand side of the configuration window.

Alternative filtering criteria can be done by row number or by row ID. This can also be enabled via the radio buttons on the left-hand side of the configuration window:

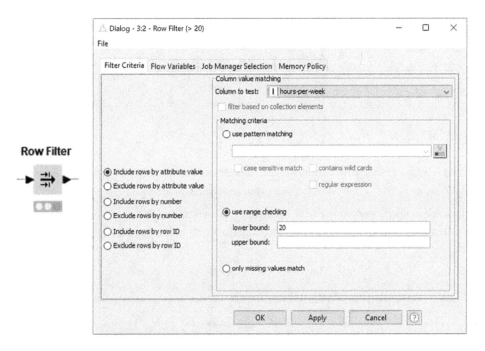

Figure 1.11 – Configuring the Row Filter node to keep only rows with hours-per-week > 20 in the input data table

After execution, upon opening the output data table (*Figure 1.12*), no data rows with *hours-per-week < 20* should be present:

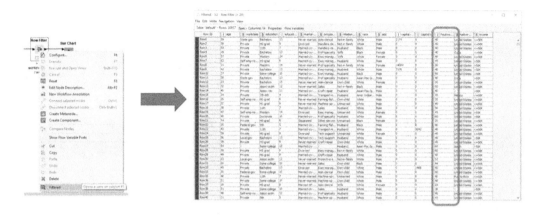

Figure 1.12 – Right-clicking a successfully executed node and selecting the last option shows the data table that was produced by the node

Now, let's look at some very basic visualization. Let's visualize the number of men versus women in this dataset, which contains people who work more than 20 hours/week:

Figure 1.13 – The Bar Chart node and its configuration window

To do this, locate the **Bar Chart** node in the Node Repository, create an instance in the workflow, connect it to receive input from the **Row Filter** node, and open its configuration window (*Figure 1.13*). Here, there are four tabs we can use for configuration purposes. **Options** covers all data settings, **General Plot Options** covers all plot settings, **Control Options** covers all control options, and **Interactivity** covers all subscription events when it comes to interacting with other plots, views, and charts when they've been assembled to create a component. Again, since this is just a beginner's workflow, we'll adopt all the default settings and just set the following:

- From the **Options** tab, set **Category Column** to sex, ensuring it appears on the *x* axis. Then, select **Occurrence Count** in order to count the number of rows by sex.

- From the **General Plot Options** tab, set a title, a subtitle, and the axis labels.

This node does not produce data, but rather a view of the bar chart. So, to inspect the results produced by this node after its execution, right-click it and select the central option; that is, **Interactive View: Group Bar Chart** (*Figure 1.14*):

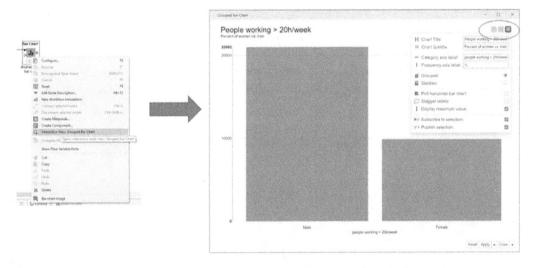

Figure 1.14 – Right-clicking a successfully executed visualization node and selecting the Interactive View: Grouped Bar Chart option to see the chart/plot that has been produced

Notice the three buttons in the top-right corner of the view on the right of *Figure 1.14*. These three buttons enable **zooming**, **toggling to full screen**, and **node settings**, respectively. From the view itself, you can explore how the chart would look if different settings were to be selected, such as a different category column or a different title.

> **Important note**
>
> Most data visualization nodes produce a view and not a data table. To see the respective view, right-click the successfully executed node and select the **Interactive View: ...** option.

The second lower input port of the **Bar Chart** node is optional (a white triangle) and is used to read a color map so that you can color the bars in the bar chart.

> **Important note**
>
> Note that a number of different data visualization nodes are available in the Node Repository: JavaScript, Local(Swing), Plotly, and so on. **JavaScript** and **Plotly** nodes offer the highest level of interactivity and the most polished graphics. We used the **Bar Chart** node from the JavaScript category in the **Node Repository** panel here.

Now, we'll add a few comments to document the workflow. You can add comments at the node level or at the general workflow level.

Each node in the workflow is created with a default label of *Node xx* under it. Upon double-clicking it, the node label editor appears. This allows you to customize the text, the font, the color, the background, and other similar properties of the node (*Figure 1.15*). We need to write a little comment under each node to make it clear what tasks they are implementing:

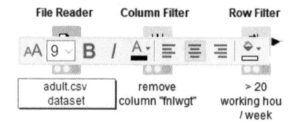

Figure 1.15 – Editor for customizing the labels under each node

You can also write annotations at the workflow level. Just right-click anywhere in the Workflow Editor and select **New Workflow Annotation**. A yellow frame will appear in editing mode. Here, you can add text and customize it, as well as its frame. To close the annotation editor, just click anywhere else in the Workflow Editor. To reopen the annotation editor, double-click in the top-left corner of the annotation (*Figure 1.16*):

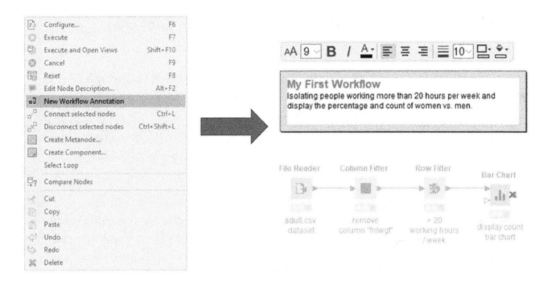

Figure 1.16 – Creating and editing workflow annotations

Congratulations! You have just built your first workflow with KNIME Analytics Platform. It should look something like the one in *Figure 1.17*:

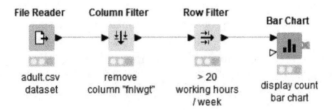

Figure 1.17 – My_first_Workflow

That was a quick introduction to how to use KNIME Analytics Platform.

Now, let's make sure we have KNIME Deep Learning – Keras Integration installed and functioning.

Installing KNIME Deep Learning – Keras Integration

In this section, you will learn how to install and set up **KNIME Deep Learning - Keras Integration** in order to train neural networks in KNIME Analytics Platform.

KNIME Analytics Platform consists of a software core and several provided extensions and integrations. Such extensions and integrations are provided by the KNIME community and extend the original software core through a variety of data science functionalities, including advanced algorithms for AI.

The KNIME extension of interest here is called **KNIME Deep Learning – Keras Integration**. It offers a codeless GUI-based integration of the Keras library, while using TensorFlow as its backend. This means that a number of functions from Keras libraries have been wrapped into KNIME nodes, within KNIME's classic, easy-to-use visual dialog window. Due to this integration, you can read, write, create, train, and execute deep learning networks without writing code.

Another deep learning integration that's available is called **KNIME Deep Learning - TensorFlow Integration**. This extension allows you to convert **Keras** models into **TensorFlow** models, as well as read, execute, and write TensorFlow models.

TensorFlow is an open source library provided by Google that includes a number of deep learning paradigms. TensorFlow functions can run on single devices, as well as on multiple CPUs and multiple GPUs. This parallel calculation feature is the key to speeding up the computationally intensive training that's required for deep learning networks.

However, using the TensorFlow library within Python can prove quite complicated, even for an expert Python programmer or a deep learning pro. Thus, a number of simplified interfaces have been developed on top of TensorFlow that expose a subset of its functions and parameters. The most successful of such TensorFlow-based libraries is Keras. However, even Keras still requires some programming skills. The KNIME Deep Learning – Keras Integration puts the KNIME GUI on top of the Keras libraries that are available, mostly eliminating the need to code.

To make the KNIME Deep Learning – Keras Integration work, a few pieces of the puzzle need to be installed:

- The Keras and TensorFlow nodes
- The Python environment

Let's start with the first piece: installing the Keras and TensorFlow nodes.

Installing the Keras and TensorFlow Nodes

To add nodes to the Node Repository, you must install a few extensions and integrations.

You can install them from within KNIME Analytics Platform by clicking on **File** from the top menu and selecting **Install KNIME Extension…**. This opens the dialog shown in *Figure 1.18*:

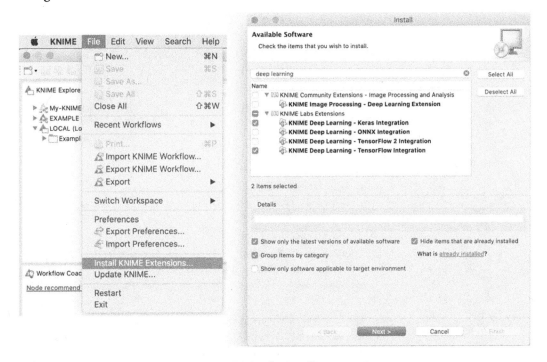

Figure 1.18 – Dialog for installing extensions

From this new dialog, you can select the extensions and integrations you want to install. Using the search bar at the top is helpful for filtering the available extensions and integrations.

> **Tip**
> Another way you can install extensions is by dragging and dropping them from the KNIME Hub.

To install the Keras and TensorFlow nodes that will be used in the case studies described in this book, you need to select the following:

- **KNIME Deep Learning – Keras Integration**
- **KNIME Deep Learning – TensorFlow Integration**

Then, press the **Next** button, accept the terms and conditions, and click **Finish**. Once the installation is done, you need to restart KNIME Analytics Platform.

At this point, you should have the Keras and TensorFlow nodes in your Node Repository (*Figure 1.19*):

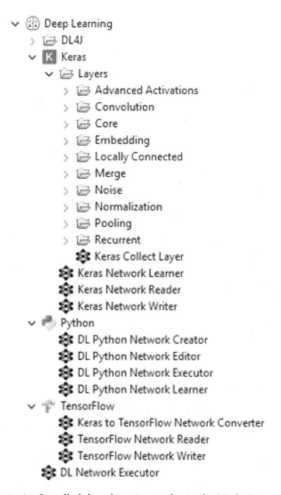

Figure 1.19 – Installed deep learning nodes in the Node Repository

A large number of nodes implement neural layers: the nodes for input and dropout layers can be found in the **Core** sub-category, the nodes for LSTM layers can be found in **Recurrent**, and the nodes for embedding layers can be found in **Embedding**. Then, there are the Learner, Reader, and Writer nodes, which can be used to train, load, and store a network, respectively. All these nodes have a configuration window and don't require any coding. The Python deep learning nodes allow you to define, train, execute, and edit networks using Python code. The last subcategory contains TensorFlow-based nodes.

Next, we need to set up the Python environment.

Setting up the Python Environment

The KNIME Keras Integration and the KNIME TensorFlow Integration depend on an existing **Python** installation, which requires certain Python dependencies to be installed.

Similar to the KNIME Python Integration, the KNIME Deep Learning Integration uses **Anaconda** to manage Python environments. If you have already installed Anaconda for, for example, the KNIME Python Integration, you can skip the first step.

Let's get started:

1. First, get and install the latest Anaconda version (Anaconda ≥ 2019.03, conda ≥ 4.6.2) from `https://www.anaconda.com/products/individual`. On the Anaconda download page, you can choose between Anaconda with Python 3.x or Python 2.x. Either one should work (if you're not sure, we suggest selecting Python 3).

2. Next, we need to create an environment with the correct libraries installed. To do so, from within KNIME Analytics Platform, open the Python Deep Learning preferences. From here, do the following:

3. First, select **File -> Preferences** from the top menu. This will open a new dialog with a list on the left.

4.   From the dialog, select **KNIME -> Python Deep Learning**.

You should now see a dialog like that in *Figure 1.20*:

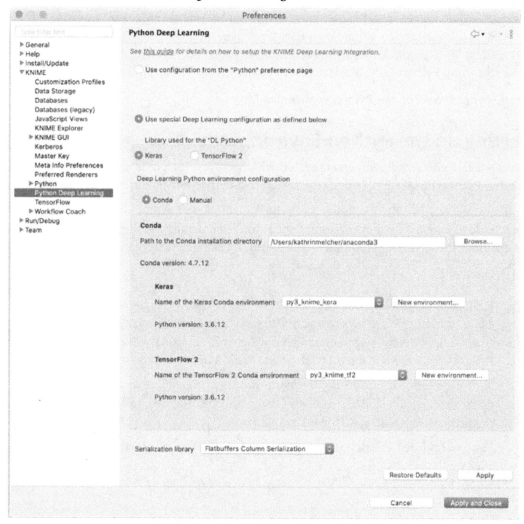

Figure 1.20 – Python Deep Learning preference page

From this page, create some Conda environments with the correct packages installed for Keras or TensorFlow 2. For the case studies in this book, it will be sufficient to set up an environment for Keras.

5. To create and set up a new environment, enable **Use special Deep Learning configuration** and set **Keras** to **Library used for DL Python**. Next, enable **Conda** and provide the path to your Conda installation directory.

6. In addition, to create a new environment for Keras, click on the **New environment…** button in the Keras framework.

   This opens a new dialog, as in *Figure 1.21*, where you can set the new environment's name:

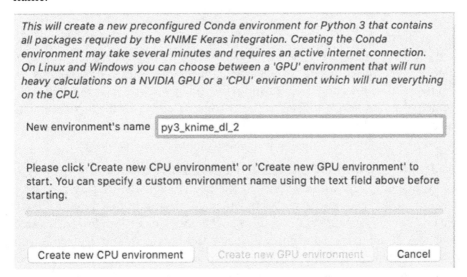

   This will create a new preconfigured Conda environment for Python 3 that contains all packages required by the KNIME Keras integration. Creating the Conda environment may take several minutes and requires an active internet connection. On Linux and Windows you can choose between a 'GPU' environment that will run heavy calculations on a NVIDIA GPU or a 'CPU' environment which will run everything on the CPU.

   New environment's name   py3_knime_dl_2

   Please click 'Create new CPU environment' or 'Create new GPU environment' to start. You can specify a custom environment name using the text field above before starting.

   Create new CPU environment   Create new GPU environment   Cancel

Figure 1.21 – Dialog for setting the new environment's name

7. Click on the **Create new CPU environment** or **Create new GPU environment** button to create a new environment for using either a CPU or GPU, if available.

Now, you can get started. In this section, you were introduced to the most convenient way of setting up a Python environment. Other options can be found in the KNIME documentation: `https://docs.knime.com/2019-06/deep_learning_installation_guide/index.html#keras-integration`.

Goal and Structure of this Book

In this book, our aim is to provide you with a strong theoretical basis about deep learning architectures and training paradigms, as well as some detailed codeless experience of their implementations for solving practical case studies based on real-world data.

For this journey, we have adopted the codeless tool, KNIME Analytics Platform. KNIME Analytics Platform is based on visual programming and exploits a user-friendly GUI to make data analytics a more affordable task without the barrier of coding. As with many other external extensions, KNIME Analytics Platform has integrated the Keras libraries under this same GUI, thus including deep learning as part of its list of codeless extensions. From within KNIME Analytics Platform, you can build, train, and test a deep learning architecture with just a few drag and drops and a few clicks of the mouse. We provided a little introduction to the tool in this chapter, but we will provide more detailed information about it in *Chapter 2, Data Access and Preprocessing with KNIME Analytics Platform*.

After that, in *Chapter 3, Getting Started with Neural Networks*, we will provide a quick overview of the basic concepts behind neural networks and deep learning. This chapter will by no means provide complete coverage of all the architectures and paradigms involved in neural networks and deep learning. Instead, it will provide a quick overview of them to help you familiarize yourself with the concept, either for the first time or again, before you continue implementing them. Please refer to more specialized literature if you want to know more about the mathematical background of deep learning.

As we stated previously, we decided to talk about deep learning techniques in a very practical way; that is, always with reference to real case studies where a particular deep learning technique had been successfully implemented. We'll start this trend in *Chapter 4, Building and Training a Feedforward Network*, where we'll describe a few basic example applications we can use to train and apply the basic concepts surrounding deep learning networks that we explored in *Chapter 3, Getting Started with Neural Networks*. Although these are simple toy examples, they are still useful for illustrating how to apply the theoretical concepts we described in the previous chapter.

With *Chapter 5, Autoencoder for Fraud Detection*, we'll start looking at real case studies. The first case study we'll describe in this chapter aims to prevent fraud detection in credit card transactions by firing an alarm every time a suspicious transaction is detected. To implement this subspecies of anomaly detection, we'll use an approach based on the autoencoder architecture, as well as the calculated distance between the output and the input values of the network.

With *Chapter 5, Autoencoder for Fraud Detection*, we are still in the realm of classic neural networks, including feedforward networks and those trained with backpropagation, albeit with an original architecture. In *Chapter 6, Recurrent Neural Networks for Demand Prediction*, we'll enter the realm of deep learning network with RNNs – specifically, with LSTMs. Here, the dynamic character of such networks and their capability to capture the time evolution of a signal will be exploited to solve a classic time series analysis problem: demand prediction.

Upon introducing RNNs, we will learn how to use them for **Natural Language Processing (NLP)** case studies. *Chapter 7, Implementing NLP Applications*, covers a few such NLP use cases: sentiment analysis, free text generation, and product name generation, to name a few. All such use cases are similar in the sense that they analyze streams of text. All of them are also slightly different in that they find a solution to a different problem: classification for sentiment analysis for the former case, and unconstrained generation of sequences of words or characters for the other two use cases. Nevertheless, data preparation techniques and RNN architectures are similar for all case studies, which is why they have been placed into one single chapter.

Chapter 8, Neural Machine Translation, describes a spin-off case of free text generation with RNNs. Here, a sequence of words will be generated at the output of the network as a response to a corresponding sequence of words in the input layer. The output sequence will be generated in the target language, while the input sequence will be provided in the source language.

Deep learning does not just come in the form of RNNs and text mining. Actually, the first examples of deep learning networks came from the field of image processing. *Chapter 9, Convolutional Neural Networks for Image Classification*, is dedicated to describing a case study where histopathology slide images must be classified as one of three different types of cancer. To do that, we will introduce CNNs. Training networks for image analysis is not a simple task in terms of time, the amount of data, and computational resources. Often, to train a neural network so that it recognizes images, we must rely on the benefits of transfer learning, as described in *Chapter 9, Convolutional Neural Networks for Image Classification*, as well.

Chapter 9, Convolutional Neural Networks for Image Classification, concludes our in-depth look into how deep learning techniques can be implemented for real case studies. We are aware of the fact that other deep learning paradigms have been used to produce solutions for other data science problems. However, here, we decided to only report the common paradigms in which we had real-life experiences.

After training a network, the deployment phase must take place. Deployment is often conveniently forgotten since this is the phase where all problems are put to the test. This includes errors in the application's design, in training the network, in accessing and preparing the data: all of them will show up here, during deployment. Due to this, the last two chapters of this book are dedicated to the deployment phase of trained deep learning networks.

Chapter 10, Deploying a Deep Learning Network, will show you how to build a deployment application, while *Chapter 11, Best Practices and Other Deployment Options*, will show you all the deployment options that are available (a web application or a REST service). It will also provide you with a few tips and tricks from our own experience.

Each chapter comes with its own set of questions so that you can test your understanding of the material that's been provided.

With that, please read on to discover the various deep learning architectures that can be applied to real use cases using KNIME Analytics Platform.

Summary

This first chapter aimed to prepare you for the content provided in this book.

Thus, we started this chapter by reminding you of the importance of deep learning, as well as the surge in popularity it garnered following the first deep learning success stories. Such a surge in popularity is probably what brought you here, with the desire to learn more about practical implementations of deep learning networks for real use cases.

Nowadays, the main barrier that we come across when learning about deep learning is the coding skills that are required. Here, we adopted KNIME software, and in particular the open source KNIME Analytics Platform, so that we can look at the case studies that will be proposed throughout this book. To do this, we described KNIME software and KNIME Analytics Platform in detail.

KNIME Analytics Platform also benefits from an extension known as KNIME Deep Learning – Keras Integration, which helps with integrating Keras deep learning libraries. It does this by wrapping Python-based libraries into the codeless KNIME GUI. We dedicated a full section to installing it.

Finally, we concluded this chapter by providing an overview of what the remaining chapters in this book will cover.

Before we dive into the math and applications of deep learning networks, we will use the next chapter to familiarize ourselves with the basic features of KNIME Analytics Platform.

2
Data Access and Preprocessing with KNIME Analytics Platform

Before deep-diving into neural networks and deep learning architectures, it might be a good idea to get familiar with KNIME Analytics Platform and its most important functions.

In this chapter, we will cover a few basic operations within KNIME Analytics Platform. Since every project needs data, we will first go through the basics of how to access data: from files or databases. In KNIME Analytics Platform, you can also access data from REST services, cloud repositories, specific industry formats, and more. We will leave the exploration of these other options to you.

Data comes in a number of shapes and types. In the *Data Types and Conversions* section, we will briefly investigate the tabular nature of the KNIME data representation, the basic types of data in a data table, and how to convert from one type to another.

At this point, after we have imported the data into a KNIME workflow, we will show some basic data operations, such as filtering, joining, concatenating, aggregating, and other commonly used data transformations.

The parameterization of a static workflow will conclude this very quick overview of the basic operations you can perform with KNIME Analytics Platform on your data.

This chapter will take you through the following topics:

- Accessing Data
- Data Types and Conversions
- Transforming Data
- Parameterizing the Workflow

Let's start with how to import data into a KNIME workflow.

Accessing Data

Before starting with examples of how to access and import data into a KNIME workflow, let's create the workflow:

1. Click on the **File** item in the top menu or right-click on a folder, such as **LOCAL**, for example, in **KNIME Explorer**.
2. Then, select the **New KNIME Workflow** option.
3. Give it a name – for example, `Ch2_Workflow_Examples` – and a destination.

   An empty canvas will open in the central part of the KNIME workbench: the workflow editor.

For this chapter, we will use toy data already available at installation. A set of workflows is installed together with the core KNIME Analytics Platform. You can find them in the `Example Workflows` folder (*Figure 2.1*) in the **KNIME Explorer** panel. Its `TheData` sub-folder contains some free toy datasets:

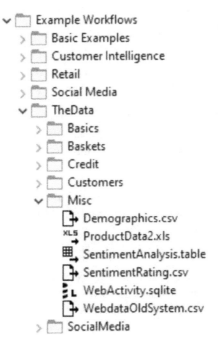

Figure 2.1 – Structure of the Example Workflows folder in the KNIME Explorer panel

We will mainly use the datasets in the `Misc` sub-folder.

> **Tip**
> In order to upload data to the **KNIME Explorer** panel, just copy it into a folder within the current workspace folder on your machine. The folder and its contents will then appear in **KNIME Explorer** in the list of workflows, servers, KNIME Hub spaces, and data available.

Reading Data from Files

Let's start with a classic: reading a **CSV-formatted** text file. To read a CSV-formatted text file, you need the **File Reader** node or its simplified version, the **CSV Reader** node. Let's focus on the File Reader node, which, though more complex, is also more powerful and flexible. There are now two ways to create and configure a File Reader node.

In the long way, you search for the File Reader node in the Node Repository; drag and drop it into the workflow editor; double-click it to open its configuration window, or alternatively, right-click it and then select **Configure**; and set the required settings, which at the very least require the file path via the **Browse** button (*Figure 2.2*).

In the short way, you just drag and drop your CSV-formatted file from the File Explorer panel into the workflow editor. This way automatically creates a File Reader node, fills up most of its configuration settings, including the file path, and keeps the configuration window open for further adjustments (*Figure 2.2*).

Under the file path, there are some basic settings: whether to read the first row as column headers and/or the first column as RowID, the column delimiter for general text files, and how to deal with spaces and tabs.

Notice two more things in this configuration window of the File Reader node: the data preview and the **Advanced** button. The data preview in the lower part of the window allows you to see whether the dataset is being read properly. The **Advanced** button takes you to more advanced settings, such as enabling shorter lines, character encoding, quotes, and other similar preferences.

When using the short way to create and configure a **File Reader** node, in the preview panel in the node configuration window (*Figure 2.2*), you can see whether the automatic settings were sufficient or whether additional customization is necessary:

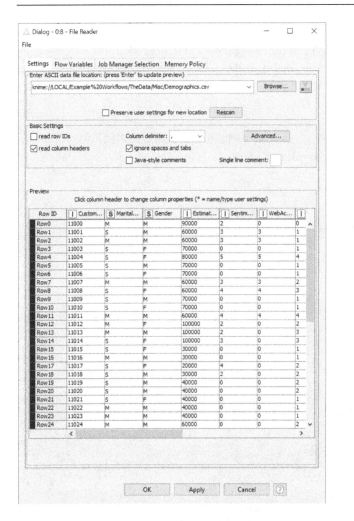

Figure 2.2 – The File Reader node and its configuration window

We drag and drop the Demographics.csv file from Example Workflows/
TheData/Misc into the workflow editor. In the configuration window of the File Reader
node, we see that the CustomerKey column is interpreted as the row ID of the data
rows, rather than its own column. We need to disable the **read Row IDs** option to read the
data properly. After the configuration is complete, we click **OK**; the node state moves to
yellow and the node can now be executed.

> **Tip**
>
> The automatic creation of the node and the configuration of its settings by file drag and drop works only for specific file extensions: `.csv` for a File Reader node, `.table` for a Table Reader node, `.xls` and `.xlsx` for an Excel Reader node, and so on.

Similarly, if we drag and drop the `ProductData2.xls` file from the KNIME Explorer panel to the workflow editor, an **Excel Reader (XLS)** node is created and automatically configured (*Figure 2.3*):

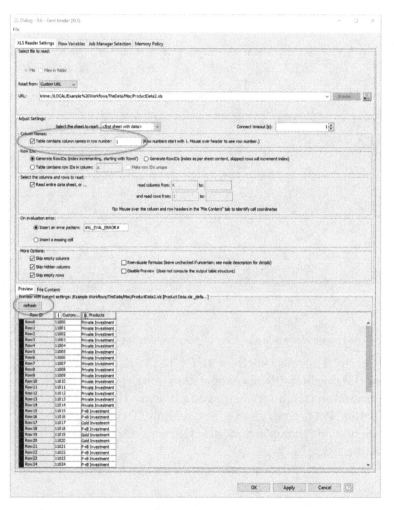

Figure 2.3 – The Excel Reader (XLS) node and its configuration window

The configuration window (*Figure 2.3*) is similar to the one of the **File Reader** node, but, of course, customized to deal with Excel files. Three items especially are different:

- The preview part is activated by a **refresh** button. You need to click on **refresh** to update the preview.

- Column headers and row IDs are extracted from spreadsheet cells, identified with an alphabet letter (the column with the row IDs) and a row number (the row with the column headers), according to the Excel standards.

- On top of the URL path, there is a menu with a default choice, **Custom URL**. This menu allows you to express the file path as an absolute path (**local file system**), as a path relative to a mountpoint (**Mountpoint**), as a path relative to one of the current locations (data, workflow, or mountpoint), or as a custom path (**Custom URL**). This feature will be soon extended to other reader nodes.

In our case, the automated configuration process does not include the column headers. We can see this from the preview segment. So, because we have the column headers in the first row, we adjust the **Table contains column names in row number** setting to 1, refresh the preview, and click **OK** to save the changes and close the window.

Next, let's read the `SentimentAnalysis.table` file. `.table` files contain binary content in a KNIME proprietary format optimized for speed and size. These files are read by the Table Reader node. Since all the information about the file is already included in the file itself, the configuration window of the **Table Reader** node just requires the file path and a few additional settings to limit the content to import. Again, dragging and dropping the `SentimentAnalysis.table` file automatically generates a Table Reader node with a pre-configured URL.

To conclude this section, let's read the last files, `SentimentRating.csv` and `WebDataOldSystem.csv`, with two more File Reader nodes; then, let's add the name of the file in the comment under each node. Then, finally, let's group all these reader nodes inside an annotation explaining **Reading data from files** (*Figure 2.9*).

`Demographics.csv` contains the demographics of a number of customers, such as age and gender. Each customer is identified via a `CustomerKey` value. `ProductData2.xls` contains the products purchased by each customer, again identified via the `CustomerKey` value. `SentimentAnalysis.table` contains the sentiment expressed as text by the customer toward the company and the product, again identified via the `CustomerKey` value. `SentimentRating.csv` contains the mapping between the sentiment rating and the sentiment text. Finally, `WebdataOldSystem.csv` contains the old activity index by each customer, as classified in the old web system, before migration.

Of course, if there is a dataset from before migration, we must have a newer dataset with data from the system after migration. This can be found in a database table in the `WebActivity.sqlite` SQLite database.

This leads us to the next section, where we will learn how to read data from a database.

Reading Data from Databases

In the Node Repository, there is a category named **DB**, dedicated to **database** operations. All database operations are performed according to the same sequence (*Figure 2.4*): connect to database, select the table to work on, build a SQL query, and import data according to the SQL query.

There are nodes for each of these steps, as shown in *Figure 2.4*:

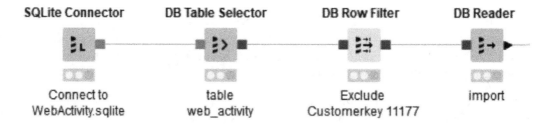

Figure 2.4 – Importing data from databases: connect, select, build SQL query, and import

Let's check these nodes one by one:

- **Connectors**: Connector nodes connect KNIME Analytics Platform to a database. The only generic connector is the **DB Connector** node. Besides that, there are many dedicated connectors. There is a SQLite connector, a MySQL connector, a Microsoft Access connector, and many other dedicated connectors. The SQLite connector is what we need to connect to the database contained in the `WebActivity.sqlite` file. The configuration window only requires the database file path since SQLite is a file-based database. All other settings have been preset in the node. Indeed, it is common to have some preset settings in dedicated connectors, and therefore dedicated connectors need fewer settings than the generic DB Connector node. A drag and drop of the `.sqlite` file automatically generates the **SQLite DB Connector** node with preloaded configuration settings.

- **Selecting the Table**: The **DB Table Selector** node allows you to select the table from the connected database to work on. If you are a SQL expert, the **Custom Query** flag allows you to create your own query for the subset of data to extract.

- **Build SQL Query**: If you are not a SQL expert, you can still build your SQL query to extract the subset of data. The DB nodes in the **DB/Query** category take a SQL query as input and add one more SQL queries on top of it. The node GUI is completely codeless and therefore there is no need to know any SQL code. So, for example, the configuration window of the **DB Row Filter** node presents a graphical editor on the right to build a row-filtering SQL query.

In the following screenshot (*Figure 2.5*), record(s) of **CustomerKey = 11177** have been excluded:

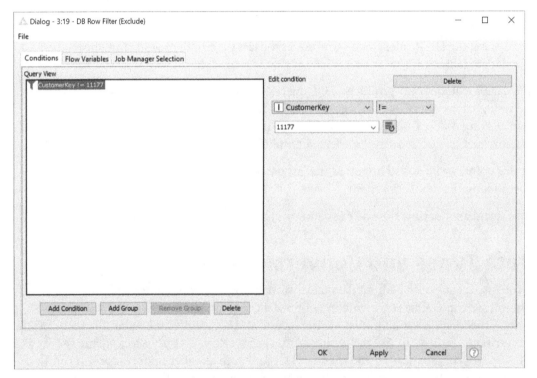

Figure 2.5 – The GUI of the DB Row Filter node. This node builds a SQL query to filter out records without using any SQL script

- **Import Data**: Finally, the **DB Reader** node imports the data from the database connection according to the input SQL query. The DB Reader node has no configuration window since all the required SQL settings to import the data are contained in the SQL query at its input port. There are many other nodes, besides the DB Reader node, to import data from a database at the end of such a sequence. They are all in the **DB/Read/Write** category in the Node Configuration panel.

> **Important note**
>
> Did you notice the node ports in *Figure 2.4*? We passed from the black triangle (data) to the red square (connection) to the brown square (SQL query). Only ports of the same type, transporting data of the same type, can be connected!

In order to inspect the results, after the successful execution of the DB Reader node, you can right-click the last node in the sequence – the one with a black triangle (data) port, in this case, the DB Reader node – and select the last item in the menu. This shows the output data table.

The database nodes only produce a SQL query. At the output port, you can still inspect the results of the query by right-clicking the node, selecting the last item in the menu, then clicking on the **Cache no of Rows** button in the **Table Preview** tab to temporarily visualize just the top rows in the selected number.

At this point, we have also imported the last dataset, including customer web activity after migration to the new web system.

Let's spend a bit of time now on the data structure and data types.

Data Types and Conversions

If you inspect any of the output data tables from any of the nodes described previously, you will see a table-like representation of the data. Here, each value is identified via RowID, the identification number for the record, and via a **column header**, the name of the attribute (*Figure 2.6*). So, the gender of CustomerKey 11000 is M, as identified via the Gender column header, and the row ID is Row0. In a reader node, the row ID and column header can be generated automatically or assigned from the values in a column or a row in the data.

The following is a screenshot of the data table output by the File Reader node:

File Table - 3:8 - File Reader (Demographics.csv)   — ☐ ✕

File Edit Hilite Navigation View

Table "Demographics.csv" - Rows: 18484 Spec - Columns: 13 Properties Flow Variables

Row ID	I CustomerKey	S Marital...	S Gender	I Estimat...	I Sentim...	I WebAc...	I Number...
Row0	11000	M	M	90000	2	0	0
Row1	11001	S	M	60000	3	3	1
Row2	11002	M	M	60000	3	3	1
Row3	11003	S	F	70000	0	0	1
Row4	11004	S	F	80000	5	5	4
Row5	11005	S	M	70000	0	0	1
Row6	11006	S	F	70000	0	0	1
Row7	11007	M	M	60000	3	3	2
Row8	11008	S	F	60000	4	4	3
Row9	11009	S	M	70000	0	0	1
Row10	11010	S	F	70000	0	0	1
Row11	11011	M	M	60000	4	4	4
Row12	11012	M	F	100000	2	0	2

Figure 2.6 – A KNIME data table. Here, a cell is identified via its RowID value and column header

Each data column also has a data type, as you can see in *Figure 2.6* from the icons in the column headers. Basic data types are **Integer**, **Double**, **Boolean** (`true`/`false`), and **String**. However, more complex data types are also available, such as **Date&Time**, **Document**, **Image**, **Network**, and more. We will see some of these data types in the upcoming chapters.

Of course, a data column is not condemned to stay with that data type forever. If the condition exists, it can move to another data type. Some nodes are dedicated to conversions and can be found in the Node Repository under **Manipulation/Column/Convert & Replace**.

In the data that we have read, `CustomerKey` has been imported as a five-digit integer. However, it might be convenient to move from an integer type representation to a string type representation. For that, we use the **Number to String** node. The configuration window consists of an include/exclude framework to select those columns whose type needs changing. The opposite transformation is obtained with the **String to Number** node. The **Double to Int** node might also be useful for a transformation from double to integer.

> **Tip**
> The **String Manipulation** and **Math Formula** nodes, even though their primary task is data transformation, also present some conversion functionality.

We would like to draw your attention to the **Category To Number** node. This node comes in handy to discretize nominal classes and transform them into numbers, as neural networks only accept numbers as target classes.

Special data types, such as **Image** or **Date&Time**, offer their own conversion nodes. A very helpful node for that is the **String to Date&Time** node. **Date** or **Time** objects are often read as **String**, and this node converts them into the appropriate type object.

In the next section, we want to consolidate all this customer information, starting with the web activity before and after the migration. In these two datasets, the columns describing web activity have different names: First_WebActivity_ and First(WebActivity). Let's standardize them to the same name: First_WebActivity_.

This is what the **Column Rename** node does:

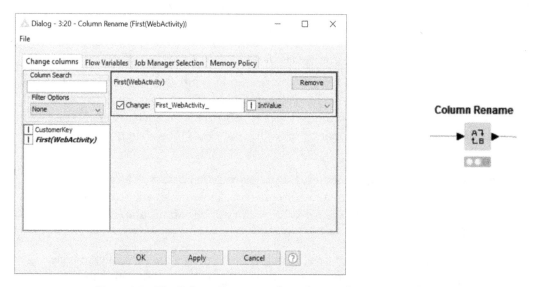

Figure 2.7 – The Column Rename node and its configuration window

The configuration window of the **Column Rename** node lists all the columns from the input data table on the left. Double-clicking on a column opens a frame on the right showing the current column name and requiring the new name and/or new type. All the nodes we have introduced in this section can be seen in the workflow in *Figure 2.13*.

Now, we are ready to concatenate the two web activity datasets and join all the other datasets by their CustomerKey values.

Transforming Data

We have read the data from files and databases. In this section, we will perform some operations to consolidate, filter, aggregate, and transform them. We will start with consolidation operations.

Joining and Concatenating

The web activity dataset from the old system comes from a CSV file and, after column renaming, consists of two data columns: `CustomerKey` and `First_WebActivity_`. `First_WebActivity_` ranks how active a customer is on the company's web site: 0 means **not active all** and 3 means **very active**.

The web activity dataset from the new web system comes from the SQLite database and consists of three columns: `CustomerKey`, `First_WebActivity_`, and `Count`. `Count` is just a progressive number associated with the data rows. It is not important for the upcoming analysis. We can decide later whether to remove it or keep it.

It would be nice to have both rankings for the web activity, from the old and the new system, together in one single data table. For this, we use the **Concatenate** node. Two input data tables are placed together in the same output data table. Data cells belonging to columns with the same name are placed in the same output column. Data columns existing in only one of the tables can be retained (union of columns) or removed (intersection of columns), as set in the node configuration window. The node configuration window also offers a few strategies to deal with rows with the same row IDs existing in both input tables.

We concatenated the two web activity data tables and kept the union of data columns in the output data table.

> **Important note**
> The Concatenate node icon shows three dots in its lower-left corner. Clicking these three dots gives you the chance to add more input ports and therefore to concatenate more input data tables.

Let's now move on to the sentiment analysis data. `SentimentAnalysis.table` produced a data table with `CustomerKey` and `SentimentAnalysis` columns. `SentimentAnalysis` includes the customer's sentiment toward the company and product, expressed as text. `SentimentRating.csv` produced a data table with two columns: `SentimentAnalysis` and `SentimentRating`. Both columns express the customer sentiment: one in text and one in ranking ordinals. This is a mapping data table, translating text into ranking sentiment and vice versa. Depending on the kind of analysis we will run, we might need the text expression or the ranking expression. So, to be on the safe side, let's join these two data tables together to have them all, `CustomerKey`, `SentimentAnalysis` (text), and `SentimentRating` (ordinals), in one data table only. This is obtained with the **Joiner** node.

The Joiner node joins data cells from two input data tables together into the same data row, according to a key value. In our case, the key values are provided by the `SentimentAnalysis` columns present in both input data tables. So, each customer (`CustomerKey`) will have the `SentimentAnalysis` text value and the corresponding `SentimentRating` value. The Joiner node offers four different join modes: **inner join** (intersection of key values in the two tables), **left outer join** (all key values from the left/top table), **right outer join** (all key values from the right/bottom table), and **full outer join** (all key values from both tables).

In *Figure 2.8*, you can find the two tabs of the configuration window of the Joiner node:

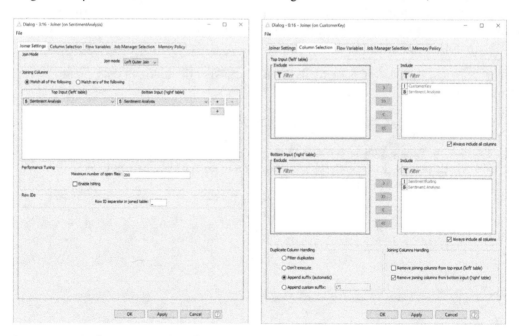

Figure 2.8 – Configuration window of the Joiner node: the Joiner Settings and Column Selection tabs

The configuration window of the Joiner node includes two tabs: **Joiner Settings** and **Column Selection**. The **Joiner Settings** tab exposes for selection the joiner mode and the data columns containing the key values for both input tables. The **Column Selection** tab sets the columns from both input tables to retain when building the final joint data rows. A few additional options are available to deal with columns with the same names in the two tables and to set what to do with the key columns after the joining is performed.

> **Important note**
>
> There can be more than one level of key columns for the join. Just select the + button in the **Joiner Settings** tab to add more key columns. If you have more than one level of key columns, you can decide whether a join is performed if all key values match (**Match all of the following**) or if just one key value matches (**Match any of the following**), as set in the top radio buttons (*Figure 2.8* on the left).

We joined the two sentiment tables using `SentimentAnalysis` as the key column in both tables and using a left outer join. The left outer join includes all key values from the left (upper) table (the customer table) and therefore makes sure that all sentiment values for all customers are retained in the output data table.

After joining `CustomerKey` with all the sentiment expressions, we will perform other similar join operations, multiple times, in cascade, using `CustomerKey` as the key column, to collect together the different pieces of data for the same customers in one single table (*Figure 2.13*).

If we inspect the output produced by the **File Reader** node on the `Demographics.csv` file, we notice two data columns that are also provided by other files: `WebActivity` and `SentimentRating`. They are old columns and should be substituted with the same columns from the `SentimentAnalysis.table` file and the web activity files. We could remove these two columns in the **Column Selection** tab of the **Joiner** node. Alternatively, we can just filter those two columns out with a dedicated node.

Let's see how to filter columns and rows out of a data table.

Column and Row Filtering

The **Column Filter** node is dedicated to filtering columns from the input data table. We can do that as follows:

- Manually select which columns to keep and which to exclude (**Manual Selection**).
- Use a wildcard or a Regex expression to match the names of the columns to exclude or to keep (**Wildcard/Regex Selection**).

- Define one or more data types for the columns to include or exclude (**Type Selection**).

All these options are available at the top of the configuration window of the **Column Filter** node. Selecting one of them changes the configuration window according to the required settings for that option. Here are the options.

- **Manual Selection**: Provides an include/exclude framework to move columns from one frame to the other to include or exclude input columns from the output data table (*Figure 2.9*).

- **Wildcard/Regex Selection**: This option provides a textbox to enter the expression to match the column names. Wildcard expressions use * for joker characters; for example, R* indicates all words starting with R, R*a indicates all words starting with R and ending with a, and so on. Regex refers to regular expressions.

- **Type Selection**: This option provides a multiple choice for the data types of the columns to include.

The configuration window of the Column Filter node is shown in *Figure 2.9*:

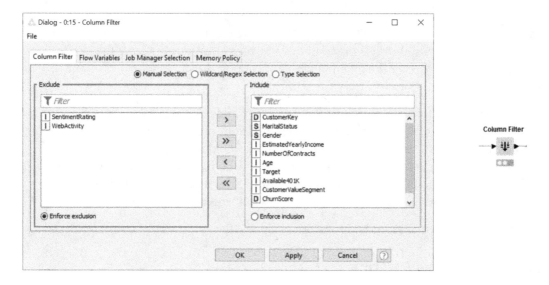

Figure 2.9 – The Column Filter node and its configuration window

So far, we have been filtering data by columns. The other flavor for data filtering is by rows. In this case, we want to remove or keep just some of the data rows in the table. For example, still working on the data from the `Demographics.csv` file, we might want to keep only the men in the dataset or remove all records with **CustomerKey 11177**. For this kind of filtering operation, there are many different nodes: **Row Filter**, **Row Filter (Labs)**, **Rule-based Row Filter**, **Reference Row Filter**, **Date&Time based Row Filter**, and more:

- The **Row Filter** node is very simple and very powerful: on the right, the filtering condition and on the left the filtering mode.

- **Filtering Condition** matches the content of cells in a data column with a condition. The input data column to match is selected at the top. The condition can consist of **pattern matching**, including wildcards and regex in the pattern expression; **range checking**, which is useful for numerical columns; and **missing value matching**.

  Filtering Mode on the left sets whether to include or exclude the matching rows, matching by attribute value, row number, or **RowID**:

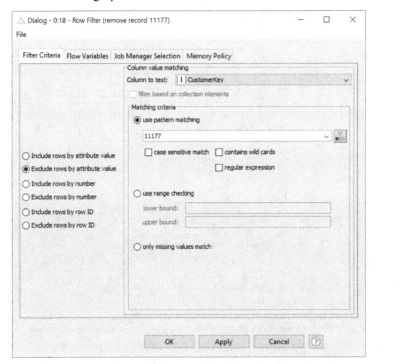

Figure 2.10 – The Row Filter node and its configuration window

Here, we filter out, using the **Exclude** option on the left, all data rows where the `CustomerKey` attribute has a value of `11177`.

- A similar result could have been obtained using a **Reference Row Filter** node. The Reference Row Filter node has two input ports. It matches the rows in the top table with the rows in the lower table according to the cell content in the set columns. Matching rows will be excluded or included according to the node configuration settings. In the workflow in *Figure 2.13*, we feed the value 11177 into the lower port of the **Reference Row Filter** node from a **Table Creator** node.

- The **Table Creator** node is an interesting node for temporary small data. It covers the role of an internal spreadsheet, which is where to store a few lines of data.

Another group of very important nodes is the ones performing aggregations.

Aggregations

Aggregations are a very important part of any data preparation. Whether for dashboard or machine learning algorithms, some aggregation operations are usually necessary. There are two commonly used nodes for aggregations: the **GroupBy** node and the **Pivoting** node.

In *Figure 2.11*, you can see the two tabs in the configuration window of the GroupBy node:

Figure 2.11 – The two tabs of the GroupBy node's configuration window:
Groups and Manual Aggregation

The **GroupBy** node isolates groups of data and on these groups calculates some measures, such as simple count, average, variance, percentages, and others. Identification of the groups happens in the tab named **Groups** of the configuration window; measure setting happens in one of the other tabs (*Figure 2.11*).

In the **Groups** tab, you select the data columns whose value combinations define the different groups of data. The node then creates one row for each group. For example, selecting the **Gender** column as the group column with distinct values of **male** and **female** means to identify those groups of data with **Gender** as **male** or **female**. Selecting the **Gender (male/female)** and **MaritalStatus (single/married)** columns as group columns means to identify the **single-female**, **single-male**, **married-female**, and **married-male** groups.

Then, we need to select the measures we want to provide for these groups. Here we can proceed by doing the following:

- Manually selecting the columns and the measures to apply one by one (**Manual Aggregation**)

- Selecting the columns based on a pattern, including wildcard or Regex expressions, and the measures to apply to each set of columns (**Pattern Based Aggregation**)

- Selecting the columns by type and the measures to apply to each set of columns (**Type Based Aggregation**)

Each measure setting mode has its own tab in the configuration window (*Figure 2.11*). In the **Manual Aggregation** tab, we set the simple **Count** measure on the CustomerKey column and the **Mean** measure on the Age column. For Gender as the group column, we then get the number and the average age of women and men in the input table.

> **Important note**
>
> The **GroupBy** node offers a large number of measures. We have seen **Count** and **Mean**. However, we could have also used percentage, median, variance, number of missing values, sum, mode, minimum, maximum, first, last, kurtosis, concatenation of (distinct) values, correlation, and more. It is worth taking some time to investigate all the measurement methods available within the **GroupBy** node.

Like the **GroupBy** node, we have the Pivoting node. The **Pivoting** node also identifies groups in the data and provides some aggregation measures on selected data columns for each group. The difference with the **GroupBy** node is in the shape of the result. Let's take the example of the Gender (**Group**) and MaritalStatus (**Pivot**) groups and the **Count** measure applied to the CustomerKey data column. The final result is a table with **male/female** as the row IDs, **married/single** as the column headers, and the count of occurrences of each combination as the cell content.

This means that the distinct values in the group columns generate rows and the distinct values in the pivoting columns generate columns.

The configuration window of the **Pivoting** node then has three tabs: **Groups** to select the group columns, **Pivots** to select the pivoting columns, and **Manual Aggregation** to manually select data columns and the measures to calculate on them. If more than one manual aggregation is used, the resulting pivoting table has one column for each combination of aggregation method and pivot value.

In addition, the node returns the total aggregation based on only the group columns on the second output port and the total aggregation based on only the pivoted columns at the third output port.

Let's move on now to a few more very flexible and very powerful nodes to perform data transformation.

Math Formula and String Manipulation nodes

KNIME Analytics Platform offers many nodes for data transformation. We cannot describe all of them here. So, while we leave the enjoyment of their discovery to you, we will describe two very powerful nodes here: the **String Manipulation** and **Math Formula** nodes.

The **String Manipulation** node applies transformations on string values in data cells. The transformations are listed in the **Function** panel in the node configuration window (*Figure 2.12*). There, you can see the function and its possible syntaxes. If you select a function in the list, in the panel on the right, named **Description**, a full description of the function task and syntax appears. The transformation, however, is implemented in the **Expression** editor at the bottom of the window.

First, you select (double-click) a transformation from the **Function** list, then you populate it with the appropriate arguments in the **Expression** editor. Arguments of a function can be constant strings, thus enclosed in " ", or values from other columns in the input data table. Values from columns are inserted automatically with the right syntax with a double-click on the column name in the **Column List** panel on the left.

Let's take an example:

1. In the data table resulting from the **GroupBy** node, we got two data rows: one for male (M) and one for female (F), containing the number of occurrences and the average age for each group (M/F). Let's change "M" to "Male" and "F" to Female".

2. Then, we would use the `replace(str, search, replace)` function, where `str` indicates the column to work on, `search` the string to search in the cell value, and `replace` the string to use as a replacement. Double-clicking on the **Gender** column in the **Column List** panel and completing the expression by hand, we end up with the following expression:

```
replace($Gender$, "M", "Male")
```

3. We get the following in a subsequent node:

```
replace($Gender$, "F", "Female")
```

The String Manipulation node and its configuration window are shown in *Figure 2.12*:

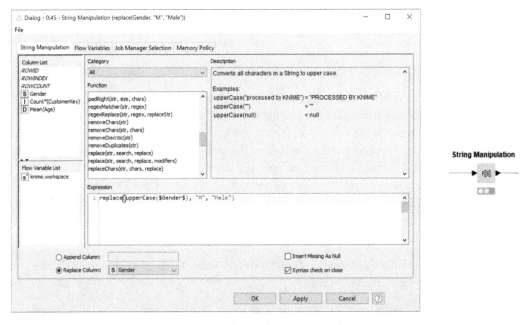

Figure 2.12 – The String Manipulation node and its configuration window

It is also possible to nest transformation functions. If, for example, we want to standardize all cells to make sure to include the "M" or "F" capital letters before applying the `replace()` transformation, we would nest the `uppercase(str)` function in it and end up with the following expression:

```
replace(upperCase($Gender$), "M", "Male")
```

We would get a similar expression for "F" and "Female".

4. Finally, we set to replace the original values in the Gender column with the new values, using the **Replace Column** option in the lower part of the configuration window.

It is also possible to apply the same transformation to more than one input data column, with the **String Manipulation (Multi Column)** node. This node essentially works like the **String Manipulation** node. It just applies the set expression to all selected data columns. The lower part of its configuration window is the same as for the **String Manipulation** node. In the upper part, though, you can select all columns on which to apply the expression.

> **Important note**
>
> In the **String Manipulation (Multi Column)** node, if we want to apply the same expression to all columns selected in the upper part of the configuration window, we need to use the $$CURRENTCOLUMN$$ general column name in the **Expression** editor. The very large number of string transformations in the **Function** list makes this node extremely powerful.

A node very similar to the String Manipulation node, even though working on a different task, is the **Math Formula** node. The Math Formula node implements a mathematical expression on the input data. Besides that, it works exactly the same as the String Manipulation node. In the configuration window, the available math functions are listed in the central **Function** panel. If a function from the list is selected, the description appears in the **Description** panel. The final expression is crafted in the **Expression** editor at the bottom. Insertion of column names in the **Expression** editor happens by double-clicking the column name in the **Column List** panel on the left. Nested mathematical functions are possible.

The **Math Formula (Multi Column)** node extends the **Math Formula** node to apply the same formula onto many selected columns.

Figure 2.13 shows the final workflow containing all the operations described in this chapter, which is also available on the KNIME Hub: https://hub.knime.com/kathrin/ spaces/Codeless%20Deep%20Learning%20with%20KNIME/latest/ Chapter%202/:

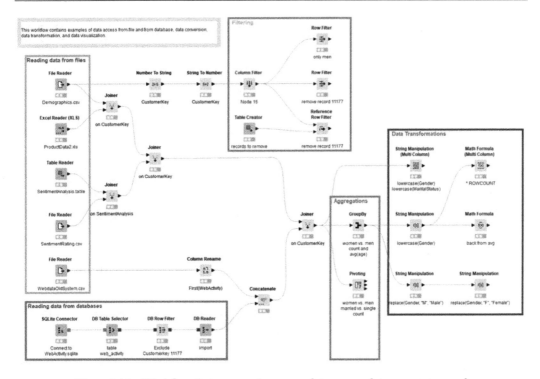

Figure 2.13 – Workflow that summarizes some data access, data conversion, and
data transformation nodes available in KNIME Analytics Platform

So far, we have seen static transformations on data. What about having a different
transformation for different conditions? Let's take the **Row Filter** node. Today, I might
want to filter out the female occurrences from the data table, while tomorrow the male
ones. How can I do that without having to change the configuration settings for all
involved nodes at every run? The time has come to introduce you to **Flow Variables**.

Parameterizing the Workflow

Let's consider a simple workflow: read the Demographics.csv file, filter all data rows
with Gender = M or F, and replace M or F with Male or Female, respectively. Once we
have decided whether to work on M or F, the workflow becomes quite simple and includes a
File Reader, **Row Filter**, and **String Manipulation** node with the replace() function:

1. Let's add one node that allows us to choose whether to work on M or F records: the
    String Configuration node. This node generates a flow variable. A flow variable is
    a parameter that travels with the data flow along the workflow branch and it can be
    used to overwrite settings in other nodes.

2. As far as we are concerned, for now, two settings are important in the configuration window of this node: the default value and the variable name. Let's use default value M for now, to work with Gender = M records, and let's name the flow variable gender_variable.

3. Executing the node creates a Flow Variable named gender_variable with value M:

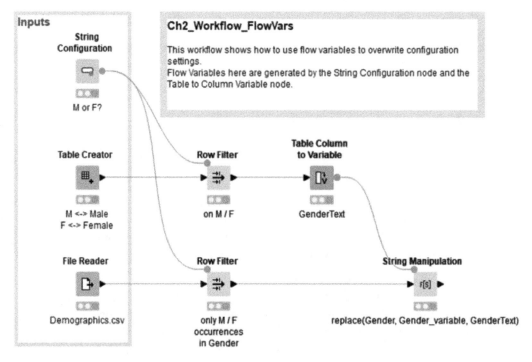

Figure 2.14 – This workflow shows how to use flow variables

4. Now, let's use the value of the **Flow Variable** to overwrite the filter setting in the **Row Filter** node. In the configuration window of the **Row Filter** node (*Figure 2.10*), on the right of the setting for **Use pattern matching** there is a button with a **V** on it. Through this button, we can overwrite the setting with the value contained in one of the available flow variables.

    Alternatively, if the configuration setting does not display this button, you can overwrite the setting via the **Flow Variables** tab at the top of the configuration window. In this tab, search for your setting, and in the corresponding empty space, select the Flow Variable to use. In our case, we overwrote the **Use pattern matching** setting with the Flow Variable gender_variable via the **V** button.

Did you notice the red connection between the **String Configuration** node and the **Row Filter** node? This is a **Flow Variable** connection. Flow variables are injected into nodes and branches via these connections.

> **Important note**
>
> All nodes have hidden red circle ports for the input and output of flow variables. Clicking on the flow variable port of a node and releasing on another node brings out the hidden flow variable port and connects the nodes. Alternatively, in the context menu of each node, the **Show Flow Variable Ports** option makes them visible.

5. After that, we create a small table with two rows, [M, Male] and [F, Female]. We select the row corresponding to the value in the gender_variable flow variable, and we aim to replace the M or F character with the text. For this last part, we need to replace the hardcoded strings in the **String Manipulation** node with the current text values. We already have the M or F character as a **Flow Variable**.

6. Now, we transform the Male/Female text into a new flow variable. We do this via the **Table Column To Variable** node. This node converts the values from a table column into flow variables with the row IDs as their variable name and the values in the selected column as the variable values.

    At this point, the **String Manipulation** node sees both **Flow Variables**: gender_variable, generated by the **String Configuration** node, and Row0, generated by the **Table Column to Variable** node. So, we can use the following syntax to perform the replacement operation alternatively with [M, Male] or [F, Female], depending on what has been selected in the **String Configuration** node:

    ```
    replace($Gender$, $${Sgender_variable}$$, $${SRow0}$$)
    ```

    Notice the difference in syntax in the expression when dealing with columns ($Gender$) and flow variables ($${Sgender_variable}$$). Also, flow variables can be inserted automatically and with the right syntax in the **Expression** editor, by double-clicking on the flow variable name in the **Flow Variable List** panel on the left of the String Manipulation node's configuration window (*Figure 2.12*).

The benefit of using flow variables is clear. When we decide to use F instead of M, we just change the setting in the **String Configuration** node instead of checking and changing the setting in every single node.

We have shown only a small fraction of the nodes dealing with flow variables. You can explore more of these nodes in the **Workflow Control/Variables** category in the Node Repository panel.

Summary

We do not have space in this book to describe more of the many nodes available in KNIME Analytics Platform. We will leave this exploratory task to you.

KNIME Analytics Platform includes more than 2,000 nodes and covers a large variety of functionalities. However, the factotum nodes that work in most situations are much fewer in number, such as, for example, File Reader, Row Filter, GroupBy, Join, Concatenation, Math Formula, String Manipulation, Rule Engine, and more. We have described most of them in this chapter to give you a solid basis to build more complex workflows for deep learning, which we will do in the next chapter.

Questions and Exercises

Check your level of understanding of the concepts presented in this chapter by answering the following questions:

1. How can I read a text file with lines of variable length?

    a) By using the CSV Reader node

    b) By using the File Reader node

    c) By using the File Reader node and the allow short lines enabled option

    d) By using the File Reader node and the Limit Rows enabled option

2. How can I filter records to the `Age > 42` column?

    a) By using the Column Filter node and selecting the `Age` column

    b) By using the Row Filter node and pattern matching `=42` with the **Include** option on the right

    c) By using the Row Filter node and range checking on, lower boundary *42*, with the **Include** option on the right

    d) By using the Row Filter node and range checking on, lower boundary *42*, with the **Exclude** option on the right

3. How can I find the average sentiment rating for single women?

    a) By using a GroupBy node with `Gender` and `MaritalStatus` as group columns and the mean operation on the `SentimentRating` column

    b) By using a GroupBy node with `Gender` as the group column and a count operation on the `CustomerKey` column

c) By using a GroupBy node with `CustomerKey` as the group column and a concatenate operation on the `SentimentAnalysis` column

d) By using a GroupBy node with `MaritalStatus` as the group column and a percent operation on the `SentimentRating` column

4. Why do we need flow variables?

a) To generate new values

b) To feed the necessary red connections

c) To populate the flow variables list in configuration windows

d) To parameterize the workflow

3
Getting Started with Neural Networks

Before we dive into the practical implementation of deep learning networks using KNIME Analytics Platform and its integration with the Keras library, we will briefly introduce a few theoretical concepts behind neural networks and deep learning. This is the only purely theoretical chapter in this book, and it is needed to understand the how and why of the following practical implementations.

Throughout this chapter, we will cover the following topics:

- Neural Networks and Deep Learning – Basic Concepts
- Designing your Network
- Training a Neural Network

We will start with the basic concepts of neural networks and deep learning: from the first artificial neuron as a simulation of the biological neuron to the training of a network of neurons, a fully connected feedforward neural network, using a backpropagation algorithm.

We will then discuss the design of a neural architecture as well as the training of the final neural network. Indeed, when designing a neural architecture, we need to appropriately select its topology, neural layers, and activation functions, and introduce some techniques to avoid overfitting.

Finally, before training, we need to know when to use which loss function and what the different parameters that have to be set for training are. This will be described in the last part of this chapter.

Neural Networks and Deep Learning – Basic Concepts

All you hear about at the moment is deep learning. Deep learning stems from the traditional discipline of neural networks, in the realm of machine learning.

The field of neural networks has gone through a number of stop-and-go phases. Since the early excitement for the first perceptron in the '60s and the subsequent lull when it became evident what the perceptron could not do; through the renewed enthusiasm for the backpropagation algorithm applied to multilayer feedforward neural networks and the subsequent lull when it became apparent that training recurrent networks required hardware capabilities that were not available at the time; right up to today's new deep learning paradigms, units, and architectures running on much more powerful, possibly GPU-equipped, hardware.

Let's start from the beginning and, in this section, go through the basic concepts behind neural networks and deep learning. While these basic notions might be familiar to you, especially if you have already attended a neural networks or deep learning course, we would still like to describe them here as a reference for descriptions of KNIME deep learning functionalities in the coming chapters, and for anyone who might be a neophyte to this field.

Artificial Neuron and Artificial Neural Networks

Artificial Neural Networks (ANNs) began with simulating the biological neuron, depicted on the left in *Figure 3.1* (Abbott, L.F. (1999) *Lapique's introduction of the integrate-and-fire model neuron (1907)*: https://web.archive.org/web/20070613230629/http:/neurotheory.columbia.edu/~larry/AbbottBrResBul99.pdf. *Brain Research Bulletin. 50 (5/6)*: 303–304). The biological neuron is a nerve cell consisting of a body (soma), a few input dendrites, and one output axon with one or more terminals. When activated, it generates a sharp electrical potential spike. The dendrites accept electrical input signals, usually from other neurons, through chemical synapses. The chemical reaction happening in the synapse enhances or reduces – in other words, it weighs – the input electrical signal before it reaches the body of the neuron. If the total electrical signal in the soma is high enough, the neuron produces an electrical spike along its axon. The axon terminals then bring out the spike to other neurons, again through chemical reactions in synapses:

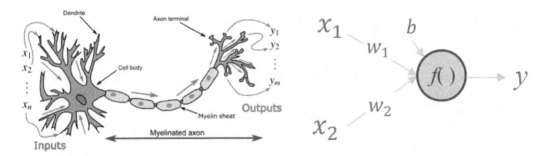

Figure 3.1 – On the left, a biological neuron with inputs xj at dendrites and output y at the axon terminal (image from Wikipedia). On the right, an artificial neuron (perceptron) with inputs xj connected to weights wj and producing output y

The simplest simulation tries to reproduce a biological neuron with just two inputs and one output, like on the right in *Figure 3.1*. The input signals at the dendrites are now called x_1 and x_2 and reach the soma of the artificial cell via two weights, w_1 and w_2 simulating the chemical reactions in the synapses. If the total input signal reaching the soma is higher than a given threshold b, simulating the "high enough" concept, an output signal y is generated. This simple artificial neuron is called a **perceptron**.

Two details to clarify here: the total input signal and the threshold function. There are many neural electrical input-output voltage models (Hodgkin, A. L.; Huxley, A. F. (1952), *A quantitative description of membrane current and its application to conduction and excitation in nerve*, https://www.ncbi.nlm.nih.gov/pmc/articles/ PMC1392413, *The Journal of Physiology. 117 (4)*: 500–544). The simplest way to represent the total input signal uses a weighted sum of all input signals, where the weights represent the role of the synapse reactions. The firing function of the neuron soma can be described via a step function $f()$. Thus, for our simplified simulation in *Figure 3.1*, the output y is calculated as follows:

$$y = f(x_1 w_1 + x_2 w_2 + b)$$

Here, $f()$ is a step function with threshold b:

$$f(net) = \begin{cases} 1 & if\ net \geq 0 \\ 0 & if\ net < 0 \end{cases} \text{ with } net = x_1 w_1 + x_2 w_2 + b.$$

Generalizing to a neuron with n input signals and with any other activation function $f()$, we get the following formula:

$$y = f\left(\sum_{j=0}^{n} x_j w_j\right) \text{ with } w_0 = b$$

Here, the threshold b has been transformed into a weight w_0 connected to an input signal x_0 that is constantly on – that is, constantly set to 1.

However, one single artificial neuron, just like one single biological neuron, does not have high computational capability. It can implement just a few simple functions, as we will see later in the next sub-section, *Understanding the need for hidden layers*. As in the biological world, networks of neurons have a much bigger computational potential than one single neuron alone. Networks of biological neurons, such as even simple brains, can learn and carry out very complex tasks. Similarly, networks of artificial neurons can learn and carry out very complex tasks. The key to the success of neural networks is this flexibility in forming more or less complex architectures and in training them to perform more or less complex tasks.

An example of a network of perceptrons is shown in *Figure 3.2*. This network has three layers of neurons: an input layer accepting the input signals x_j; a first hidden layer with two neurons connected to the outputs of the input layer; a second hidden layer with three neurons connected to the outputs of the first hidden layer; and finally an output layer with one neuron only, fed by the outputs of the hidden layer and producing the final output y of the network. Neurons are indicated by a circle including the Σ symbol for the weighted sum of the input signals and the f symbol for the activation function:

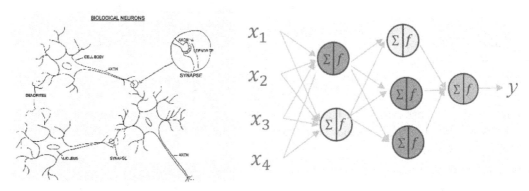

Figure 3.2 – On the left, a network of biological neurons (image from Wikipedia). On the right, a network of artificial neurons (multi-layer perceptron)

Notice that in this particular architecture, all connections move from the input to the output layer: this is a fully connected feedforward architecture. Of course, a **feedforward neural network** can have as many hidden layers as you want, and each neural layer can have as many artificial neurons as you want. A feedforward network of perceptrons is called a **Multi-Layer Perceptron (MLP)**.

Signal Propagation within a Feedforward Neural Network

A simple fully connected feedforward neural network can then be described as a function that transforms the input values x_j into the output value y, through a series of intermediate values o_k: the outputs of the hidden layers. For example, for the network in *Figure 3.3*, we have the following:

$$o_k^2 = f\left(\sum_{j=0}^{n} x_j \, w_{j,k}^2\right)$$

$$y = f\left(\sum_{k=0}^{m} o_k^2 \, w_{k,1}^3\right)$$

Here, n is the number of input values (and input units) x_j, m is the number of hidden neurons with output values o_k^2, y is the final output value (the only one in this architecture), and $f()$ is the neurons' activation functions. If we number the neural layers progressively from the input to the output, we will label layer 1 as the input layer, layer 2 as the hidden layer, and layer 3 as the output layer. This progressive numbering of the neural layers is also contained in the weight and hidden unit notations. o_k^l is the output value of the k neural unit in the l (hidden) layer, and $w_{j,k}^h$ is the weight connecting neural unit j in layer $h - 1$ with neural unit k in layer h.

> **Important note**
>
> Notice that, in this notation, l and h in o_k^l and in $w_{j,k}^h$ are NOT exponents. They just describe the network layer of the output unit for o_k^l and the destination layer for $w_{j,k}^h$.

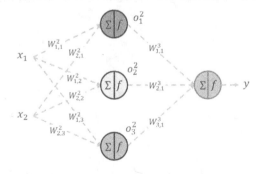

Figure 3.3 – Fully connected feedforward neural network with just one hidden layer and one output unit

There are many types of **activation functions** $f()$. We have seen the step function in the previous section, which however has a main flaw: it is neither continuous nor derivable. Some similar activation functions have been introduced over the years, which are easier to handle since they are continuous and derivable everywhere. Common examples are the **sigmoid** and the **hyperbolic tangent,** $tanh()$. Recently, a new activation function, named **Rectified Linear Unit** (**ReLU**), has been introduced, which seems to perform better with fully connected feedforward neural networks with many hidden layers. We will describe these activation functions in detail in the coming chapters.

> **Important note**
> Usually, neurons in the same layer have the same activation function $f()$.
> Different layers, though, can have different activation functions.

Another parameter of a network is its **topology,** or architecture. We have seen a fully connected feedforward network, where all connections move from the input toward the output and, under this constraint, all units are connected to all units in the next layer. However, this is of course not the only possible neural topology. Cross-connections within the same layer h, backward connections from layer h to layer $h - 1$, and autoconnections of a single neuron with itself are also possible.

Different connections and different architectures produce different data processing functions. For example, autoconnections introduce a time component, since the current output of neuron k at time t will be an additional input for the same neuron k at time $t + 1$; a feedforward neural network with as many outputs as inputs can implement an autoencoder and be used for compression or for outlier detection. We will see some of these different neural architectures and the tasks they can implement later in this book. For now, we just give you a little taste of possible neural topologies in *Figure 3.4*:

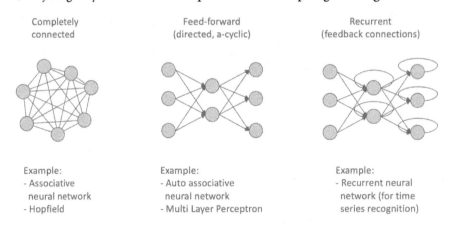

Completely connected	Feed-forward (directed, a-cyclic)	Recurrent (feedback connections)

Example:
- Associative neural network
- Hopfield

Example:
- Auto associative neural network
- Multi Layer Perceptron

Example:
- Recurrent neural network (for time series recognition)

Figure 3.4 – Some examples of neural network topologies

The first network from the left in *Figure 3.4* has its neurons all completely connected, so that the definition of the layer becomes unnecessary. This is a Hopfield network and is generally used as an associative memory.

The second network is a feedforward autoencoder: three layers, as many *n* input units as many *n* output units, and a hidden layer with *m* units, where usually $m < n$; this network architecture has been adopted for outlier detection or to implement a dimensionality reduction of the input space.

Finally, the third network presents units with autoconnections. As said before, autoconnections introduce a time component within the function implemented by the network and therefore are often adopted for time series analysis. This last network qualifies as a recurrent neural network.

Let's go back to fully connected feedforward neural networks. Now that we've seen how they are structured, let's try to understand why they are built this way.

Understanding the Need for Hidden Layers

The question now is: do we really need such complex neural architectures? What can the perceptron in *Figure 3.1* do and what can it not do? A perceptron, using a step function as the activation function, implements a line (a linear combination of the input signals) as a discriminant surface in a two-dimensional space, the parameters of the line being the weights and threshold of the perceptron.

Classic examples are the **OR** and **AND** problems, which can be solved by a line separating the "1" outputs from the "0" outputs. Therefore, a perceptron can implement a solution to both problems. However, it cannot implement a solution to the **XOR** problem. The XOR function outputs "1" when the two inputs are different (one is "0" and one is "1") and outputs "0" when the two inputs are the same (both are "0" or both are "1"). Indeed, the XOR operator is a nonlinearly separable problem and one line only is not sufficient to separate the "1" outputs from the "0" outputs (*Figure 3.5*):

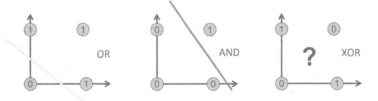

Figure 3.5 – A perceptron implements a linear discriminant surface, which is a line in a two-dimensional space. All linearly separable problems can be solved by a single perceptron. A perceptron cannot solve non-linearly separable problems

The only possibility to solve the XOR problem is to add one hidden layer with two units into the perceptron architecture, making it into an MLP (*Figure 3.6*). The two hidden units in green and red each implement one line to separate some "0"s and "1"s. The one unit in the output layer then builds a new line on top of the two previous lines and implements the final discriminant:

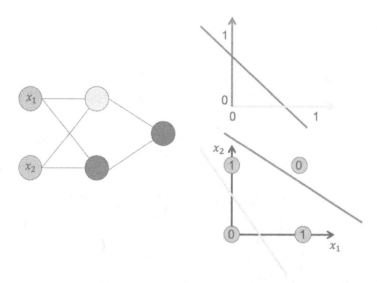

Figure 3.6 – One additional hidden layer with two units enables the MLP to solve the XOR problem

The example in *Figure 3.7* shows a three-layer network: one input layer receiving input values x_1 and x_2, one hidden layer with two units, and one output layer with one unit only.

The two hidden units implement two discrimination lines: $1 + \frac{1}{2}x_1 - x_2 = 0$ for the red unit and $2 - x_1 - x_2 = 0$ for the orange unit. The output line implements a discrimination line on top of these two as $o_{red} - o_{orange} - \frac{1}{2} = 0$, which is identified by the green area in the plane shown in *Figure 3.7*:

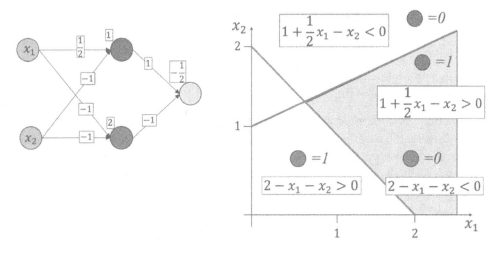

Figure 3.7 – The network on the left fires up only for the points in the green zone in the input space, as depicted on the right

As you see, adding just one hidden layer makes the neural network much more powerful in terms of possible functions to implement. However, there is more. The **Universal Approximation Theorem** states that a simple feedforward network with a single hidden layer and a sufficient number of neurons can approximate any continuous function on compact subsets of R^n, under mild assumptions on the activation function and assuming that the network has been sufficiently trained (Hornik K., Stinchcombe M., White H. (1989) *Multilayer feedforward networks are universal approximators*: http://www.sciencedirect.com/science/article/pii/0893608089900208 *Neural Networks, Vol. 2, Issue 5,* (*1989*) Pages 359-366). This theorem proves that neural networks have a kind of *universality* property. That is, any function can be approximated by a sufficiently large and sufficiently trained neural network. Sufficiently large refers to the number of neurons in a feedforward network. In addition, the cited paper refers to network architectures with just one single hidden layer with enough neurons.

Even very simple network architectures, thus, can be very powerful! Of course, this is all true under the assumption of a sufficiently large hidden layer (which might become too large for a reasonable training time) and a sufficient training time.

> *A feedforward network with a single layer is sufficient to represent any function, but the layer may be infeasibly large and may fail to learn and generalize correctly, (Goodfellow I., Bengio Y., Courville A. (2016). Deep Learning, MIT Press).*

We have seen that introducing one or more hidden layers to a feedforward neural network makes it extremely powerful. Let's see how to train it.

Training a Multilayer Perceptron

A neural network includes a few free parameters: the topology, the weights, and the parameters of the activation functions. Let's consider a fully connected feedforward network with a pre-defined activation function for all neurons, such as a sigmoid function, for example. Then, the only free parameters left are the weights.

Training a neural network means showing examples from the training set repeatedly and each time adjusting the parameter values, the weights, to fit a loss function, calculated on the desired input-output behavior. To find the weights that best fit the loss functions, the gradient descent algorithm or variants of **Stochastic Gradient Descent (SGD)** are used. The idea is to update the weights by taking steps in the direction of steepest descent on the error surface. The direction of steepest descent is equivalent to the negative of the gradient. To calculate the gradient efficiently, the backpropagation algorithm is used. Let's find out how it works.

The math behind backpropagation

A classic loss function for regression problems is the total squared error, defined as follows:

$$E = \sum_T \sum_j \frac{1}{2}(t_j - y_j)^2$$

Here, t_j and y_j are respectively the desired target and the real answer for output unit j, and the sum runs on all units of the output layer and on all examples in the training set T.

If we adopt the gradient descent strategy to reach a minimum in the loss function surface, at each training iteration, each weight of the network must be incremented in the opposite direction of the derivative of E in the weight space (Goodfellow I., Bengio Y., Courville A. (2016. *Deep Learning*, MIT Press):

$$\Delta w_{ij} = -\eta \frac{\partial E}{\partial w_{ij}}$$

This partial derivative of the error with respect to the weight is calculated using the chain rule:

$$\frac{\partial E}{\partial w_{ij}} = \frac{\partial E}{\partial o_j}\frac{\partial o_j}{\partial w_{ij}} = \frac{\partial E}{\partial o_j}\frac{\partial o_j}{\partial net_j}\frac{\partial net_j}{\partial w_{ij}}$$

Here, E is the loss function, o_j the output of neuron j, net_j its total input, and w_{ij} its input weight from neuron i in the previous layer:

For the weights connecting to units **in the output layer**, the derivatives will be as follows:

$$\frac{\partial E}{\partial o_j} = \frac{\partial E}{\partial y_j} = \sum_T \frac{\partial \left(\frac{1}{2}(t_j - y_j)^2\right)}{\partial y_j} = \sum_T -(t_j - y_j)$$

$$\frac{\partial o_j}{\partial net_j} = f'(net_j)$$

$$\frac{\partial net_j}{\partial w_{ij}} = \frac{\partial}{\partial w_{ij}} \sum_{k=1}^{n} w_{kj} \, o_k = o_i$$

So, finally:

$$\frac{\partial E}{\partial w_{ij}} = \sum_T (y_j - t_j) \, f'(net_j) \, o_i$$

Therefore, the weight change for weights connecting to output units is as follows:

$$\Delta w_{ij} = \sum_T -\eta (y_j - t_j) f'(net_j) o_i = \sum_T -\eta \, \delta_j^{out} \, o_i$$

Here, $\delta_j^{out} = (t_j - y_j) f'(net_j)$, o_i is the input i to the output node j, and η is the learning rate.

For the weights connecting to the **units in a hidden layer**, the calculation of the derivative, and therefore of the weight change, is a bit more complicated. While the last two derivatives remain the same also when referring to neurons in hidden layers, $\frac{\partial E}{\partial o_j}$ will need to be recalculated.

If we consider the loss function E as a function of all input sums to all neurons $l = 1, \dots, c$ in the next layer connected to neuron j, as $E(net_{l=1,\dots c})$, after a few math operations we reach a recursive expression:

$$\frac{\partial E(o_j)}{\partial o_j} = \sum_l \frac{\partial E}{\partial net_l} \frac{\partial net_l}{\partial o_j} = \sum_l \frac{\partial E}{\partial o_l} \frac{\partial o_l}{\partial net_l} w_{jl} = \sum_l \frac{\partial E}{\partial o_l} f'(net_l) w_{jl} = \sum_l \delta_l \, w_{jl}$$

Here, the following applies:

$$\delta_j = \frac{\partial E}{\partial o_l} \frac{\partial o_l}{\partial net_l} = \begin{cases} (o_j - t_j) f'(net_j) & for \ output \ units \\ \sum_l \delta_l \, w_{jl} \, f'(net_j) & for \ hidden \ units \end{cases}$$

The update formula for all weights, leading to output or hidden neurons, is this:

$$\Delta w_{ij} = \sum_T -\eta \, \delta_j \, o_i$$

This recursive formula tells us that δ_j^{hidden} for unit j in the hidden layer h can be calculated as the linear combination of all δ_l in layer $h + 1$, which will be δ_l^{out} if this is the output layer or δ_l^{hidden} if this is another hidden layer. This means that moving from the output layer backward toward the input layer, we can calculate all δ_j, starting from δ_j^{out} and then through all δ_j^{hidden}, as a combination of δ_j from the preceding layer, layer after layer. Together with δ_j, we can also calculate all weight updates Δw_{ij}.

The Idea Behind Backpropagation

So, the training of a feedforward neural network can be seen as a two-step process:

1. All training vectors are presented, one after the other, to the input layer of the network, and the signal is propagated throughout all network connections (and weights) till the output layer. After all of the training examples have passed through the network, the total squared error is calculated at the output layer as the sum of the single squared errors. This is the **forward pass**:

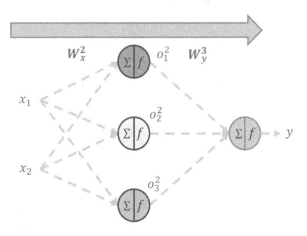

Figure 3.8 – In the forward pass of the backpropagation algorithm, all training examples are presented at the input layer and forward-propagated through the network till the output layer, to calculate the output values

2. All δ_j^{out} are calculated for all units in the output layer. Then, the δs are backpropagated from the output layer through all network connections (and weights) till the input layer and all δ_j^{hidden} in the hidden layers are also calculated. This is the **backward pass**:

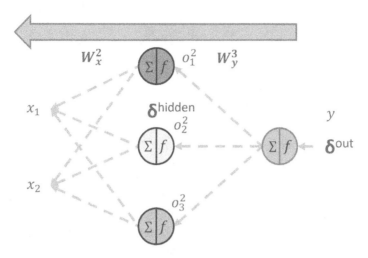

Figure 3.9 – In the backward pass of the backpropagation algorithm, all δs are calculated at the output layer and backpropagated through the network till the input layer. After all examples from the training set have passed through the network forth and back, all weights are updated

This algorithm is called **backpropagation**, as a reference to the δs backpropagating through the network during the second pass.

After all the training data has passed through the network forth and back, all weights are updated.

Also notice the first derivative of the unit activation function $f'(net_j)$ in δ_j. Of course, using a continuous derivable function $f()$ helps with the calculations. This is the reason why the $sigmoid()$ and $tanh()$ function have been so popular with neural architectures.

The gradient descent algorithm is not guaranteed to reach the global minimum of the error function, but it often ends up in a local minimum. If the local minimum does not ensure satisfactory performance of the network, the training process must be repeated starting from new initial conditions, meaning new initial values for the weights of the network.

Neural networks are very powerful in implementing input-output models and very flexible in terms of architecture and parameters. It is extremely easy to build huge neural networks, by adding more and more neurons and more and more hidden layers. Besides the longer training times, an additional risk is to run quickly into the **overfitting** of the training data. Overfitting is a drawback of too complex models, usually with too many free parameters to fit a simple task. The result of an over-dimensioned model for a simple task is that the model, at some point, will start using the extra parameters to memorize noise and errors in the training set, considerably worsening the model's performance. The power and flexibility of neural networks make them prone to overfitting, especially if we are dealing with small training sets.

> **Important note**
>
> Another big objection that has been leveled against neural networks since their introduction is their non-interpretability. The adjustment of the weights has no correspondence with any entity in the data domain. When dealing with neural networks, we need to accept that we are dealing with **black boxes** and we might not understand the decision process.

If interpretability is a requirement for our project, then maybe neural networks are not the tool for us. A few techniques have been proposed recently to extract knowledge on the decision process followed in black-box models, such as the **SHAPLEY** values or **Partial Dependency Plots** (Molnar C. *Interpretable Machine Learning*, `https://christophm.github.io/interpretable-ml-book/index.html`, GitHub). They are currently in their infancy and not immune from criticism. However, they constitute an interesting attempt to fix the interpretability problem of neural networks. These are beyond the scope of this book, so we will not be exploring them in any more detail.

With the basic theory covered, let's get into the design of a network.

Designing your Network

In the previous section, we learned that neural networks are characterized by a topology, weights, and activation functions. In particular, feedforward neural networks have an input and an output layer, plus a certain number of hidden layers in between. While the values for the network weights are automatically estimated via the training procedure, the network topology and the activation functions have to be predetermined during network design before training. Different network architectures and different activation functions implement different input-output tasks. Designing the appropriate neural architecture for a given task is still an active research field in the deep learning area (Goodfellow I., Bengio Y., Courville A. (2016). *Deep Learning*, MIT Press).

Other parameters are involved in the training algorithm of neural networks, such as the learning rate or the loss function. We have also seen that neural networks are prone to overfitting; this means that their flexibility makes it easy for them to run into the overfitting problem. Would it be possible to contain the weight growth, to change the loss function, or to self-limit the network structure during training as to avoid the overfitting problem?

This section gives you an overview of all those remaining parameters: the topology of the network, the parameters in the training algorithm, the possible activation functions, the loss functions, regularization terms, and more, always keeping an eye on containing the overfitting effect, making the training algorithm more efficient, and developing more powerful neural architectures.

Commonly Used Activation Functions

In summary, a single neural layer has a number of inputs $n \in \mathbb{N}$ and a number of outputs $m \in \mathbb{N}$. The calculation of the output value of a neuron i is performed in two steps:

1. Calculation of the weighted sum of the inputs plus a bias b:

$$z_i = b_i + \sum_{j=1}^{n} W_{ji}x_j = \sum_{j=0}^{n} W_{ji}x_j, \text{ for } i = 1, \dots, n \text{ and } x_0 = 1, W_{0i} = b_i$$

2. Application of an activation function $f_i(z_i, W)$ or $f_i(\mathbf{z}, W)$ to calculate the output $o_i \in \mathbb{R}$ based on the weight matrix W and either on $z_i \in \mathbb{R}$, or on $\mathbf{z} \in \mathbb{R}^m$:

$$f(z) = f\left(b_i + \sum_{j=1}^{n} W_{ji}x_j\right).$$

Note that $z_i \in \mathbb{R}$ is the weighted sum of the input values to the i th neuron and $\mathbf{z} \in \mathbb{R}^m$ is the vector of all weighted input sums.

A network can then also be seen as a chain of functions g_k, where each function implements a neural layer. Depending on the network architecture, each neural layer has different input values and uses a different activation function $f()$, and therefore implements a different function g_k, using the two calculation steps described previously.

The complexity of the total function implemented by the full network also depends on the number of layers involved; that is, it depends on the network depth.

A layer where all neurons are connected to all outputs of the previous layer is called a **dense layer**. Fully connected feedforward networks are just a chain of dense layers, where each layer has its own activation function. In feedforward neural networks, then, a function g_k is based on the number of the layer's neurons, the number of inputs, and the activation function. The key difference between layers is then the activation function. Let's look at the most commonly used activation functions in neural networks.

Sigmoid Function

The **sigmoid function** is an S-shaped function with values between 0 and 1. For the ith neuron in the layer, the function is defined as follows:

$$\sigma_i(z_i) = \frac{1}{1 + e^{-z_i}} = \frac{e^{z_i}}{e^{z_i} + 1}$$

It is plotted on the left in *Figure 3.10*.

For binary classification problems, this is the go-to function for the output neural layer, as the value range $(0,1)$ allows us to interpret the output as the probability of one of the two classes. In this case, the output neural layer consists of only one neuron, AKA unit size 1, with the sigmoidal activation function. Of course, the same function can also be used as an activation function for output and hidden layers with a bigger unit size:

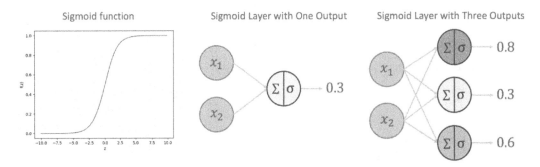

Figure 3.10 – The sigmoid function (on the left) can be used as the activation function of the single output neuron of a network implementing the solution to a binary classification problem (in the center). It can be used generically as an activation function for neurons placed in hidden or output layers in a network (on the right)

One of the biggest advantages of the sigmoid function is its derivability everywhere and its easy derivative expression. Indeed, when using the sigmoid activation function, the weight update rule for the backpropagation algorithm becomes very simple, since the first derivative of the activation function is simply $f'(z_j) = o_j (1 - o_j)$, where o_j is the output of neuron j.

On the other hand, one of the biggest disadvantages of using sigmoid as the neurons' activation function in more complex or deep neural architectures is the vanishing gradient problem. Indeed, when calculating the derivatives to update the network weights, the chain multiplication of output values (< 1) from sigmoid functions might produce very small values. In this case, too small gradients are produced at each training iteration, leading to slow convergence for the training algorithm.

Hyperbolic Tangent (Tanh)

A similar activation function is **hyperbolic tangent, tanh** for short. It is also an S-shaped function with the difference that the output values fall between -1 and 1, instead of between 0 and 1. For the i th neuron, the function is defined as follows:

$$f(z_i) = \frac{2}{1 + e^{-2z_i}} - 1$$

It is plotted on the left in *Figure 3.11*:

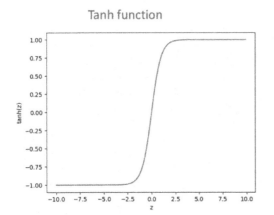
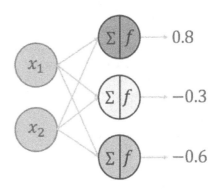

Figure 3.11 – The hyperbolic tangent function, tanh(), is also often used as an activation function for neural units. In this case, the neuron output value falls in (-1, +1)

Here also, one of the biggest advantages of the $tanh()$ function is its continuity and its derivability everywhere, which leads to simpler formulas for the updates of the weights in the training algorithm. $tanh()$ also has the advantage of being centered at 0, which can help to stabilize the training process.

Again, one of the biggest disadvantages of using tanh as an activation function in complex or deep neural architectures is the vanishing gradient problem.

Linear Function

A special activation function is the **linear activation function**, also known as the identity function:

$$f(z_i) = z_i$$

When would such a function be used? A neural layer with a linear activation function implements a linear regression model. Sometimes, a neural layer with a linear activation function is also introduced to keep the original network response, before it is transformed to get the required range or probability score. In this case, the last layer of the network is split into two layers: one with the linear activation function preserves the original output and the other one applies another activation function for the required output format.

In *Chapter 7, Implementing NLP Applications*, where we describe the *Generating Product Name* case study, this approach is used to introduce a new parameter called **temperature** after the linear activation function layer.

Rectified Linear Unit

We have seen that deep neural networks, using the sigmoid or tanh activation functions, often suffer from the problem of vanishing gradient.

An activation function that helps to overcome the problem of vanishing gradient is the **Rectified Linear Unit** function, **ReLU** for short. The ReLU function is like the linear function, at least from 0 on. Indeed, the ReLU function is 0 for negative values of z and is the identity function for positive values of z:

$$f(z_i) = \max \{0, z_i\}.$$

Figure 3.12 shows a plot of the ReLU function:

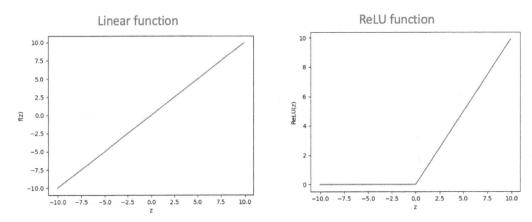

Figure 3.12 – The ReLU activation function

The ReLU activation function, while helping with the vanishing gradient problem, is not differentiable for $z = 0$. In practice, this is not a problem when training neural networks as usually one of the one-sided derivatives is used rather than reporting that the derivative is not defined.

Softmax Function

All activation functions introduced until now are functions that have a single value as output. This means only the weighted sum z_i is used to calculate the output value of the i th neuron, independently from weighted sums z_j, with $j \neq i$ being used to calculate the outputs of the other neurons in the same layer. The **softmax function**, on the other hand, works on the whole output vector o and not just on one single value o_i.

In general, the softmax function transforms a vector $u \in \mathbb{R}^n$ of size $n \in \mathbb{N}$ into a vector $v \in [0,1]^n$, which is a vector v of the same size n with values between 0 and 1, with the constraint that all values v_i sum to 1:

$$\sum_{i=1}^{n} v_i = 1$$

This additional constraint allows us to interpret the components of vector v as probabilities of different classes. Therefore, the softmax activation function is often the function of choice for the last neural layer in a multiclass classification problem. The ith element of the output vector is calculated as follows:

$$\sigma(z_i) = \frac{e^{z_i}}{\sum_{j=1}^{n} e^{z_j}}$$

Figure 3.13 shows an example network that uses the softmax function in the last layer, where all output values sum up to 1:

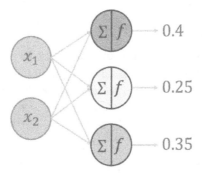

Softmax Layer with Three Outputs

Figure 3.13 – A simple neural layer with the softmax activation function

> **Important note**
>
> The softmax function is also used by the logistic regression algorithm for multiclass classification problems.

Other supported activation functions

Many more activation functions have been introduced over the years, since the sigmoid.

Variants of ReLU are **Leaky Rectified Linear Unit** and **Parametric Rectified Linear Unit** (**PReLU**). LeakyReLU offers an almost zero line ($0.1\, z_i$) for negative values of the function argument rather than just zero as in the pure ReLU. PReLU makes this line with parametric slope ($\alpha\, z_i$) rather than fixed slope as in the LeakyReLU. Parameter α becomes part of the parameters that the network must train.

Here are the definitions of LeakyReLU and PreLU:

- LeakyReLU: $f(z_i) = \max\{0.1\, z_i, z_i\}$
- PReLU: $f(z_i) = \max\{\alpha\, z_i, z_i\}$

Other variants of ReLU, introduced to remedy dead ReLUs, are **Exponential Linear Unit** (**ELU**) and **Scaled Exponential Linear Unit** (**SELU**). Similar to LeakyReLU, ELU has a small slope for negative values. Instead of a straight line, it uses a log curve. Scaled ELU adds one more parameter β to ELU for the network to train:

- ELU:
$$f(z_i) = \begin{cases} z_i & if\ z_i \geq 0 \\ \alpha\,(e^{z_i} - 1) & if\ z_i < 0 \end{cases}$$

- SELU:
$$f(z_i) = \beta \begin{cases} z_i & if\ z_i \geq 0 \\ \alpha\,(e^{z_i} - 1) & if\ z_i < 0 \end{cases}$$

An approximation of the sigmoid activation function is the **hard sigmoid activation function**. It is faster to calculate than sigmoid. Despite being an approximation of the sigmoid activation function, it still provides reasonable results on classification tasks. However, since it's just an approximation, it performs worse on regression tasks:

- Hard-Sigmoid:
$$f(z_i) = \begin{cases} 1 & if\ z_i \geq +2.5 \\ z_i & if -2.5 < z_i < +2.5 \\ 0 & if\ z_i \leq -2.5 \end{cases}$$

The **SoftPlus** activation function is also quite popular. This is a smoothed version of the ReLU activation function:

- SoftPlus: $f(z_i) = \ln(1 + e^{z_i})$

Let's look at *Figure 3.14*:

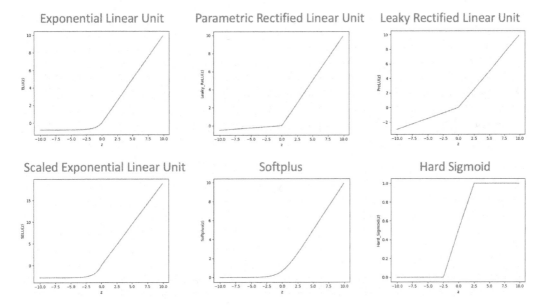

Figure 3.14 – Plots of some additional popular activation functions, mainly variants of ReLU and sigmoid functions

The images in *Figure 3.14* show the plots of the aforementioned activation functions.

Regularization Techniques to Avoid Overfitting

No matter what kind of algorithm you use, the goal is always a model that not only performs well on the training data but also generalizes to new data.

Large neural networks, trained on too small datasets, often incur the problem of fitting the training data too well and missing the capability to generalize to new data. This problem is known as overfitting. *Figure 3.15* shows a regression input-output function implemented by a neural network on the training data (full crosses) and on the test data (empty crosses). On the left, we see a regression function that does not even manage to fit the training data properly, much less the test data. This is probably due to an insufficient architecture size or short training time (**underfitting**). In the center, we find a regression curve decently fitting both training and test data. On the right, we have a regression curve fitting the training data perfectly and failing in the fit on the test data; this is the **overfitting** problem:

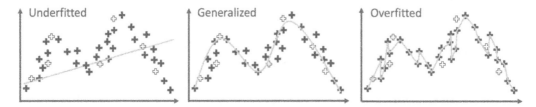

Figure 3.15 – From left to right, the regression curve implemented by a network underfitting, fitting just fine, and overfitting the training data

How can we know in advance the right size of the neural architecture and the right number of epochs for the training algorithm? A few tricks can be adopted to address the problem of overfitting without worrying too much about the exact size of the network and the number of epochs: norm regularization, dropout, and early stopping.

Norm Regularization

One sign of overfitting is the high values of the weights. Thus, the idea behind norm regularization is to penalize weights with high values by adding a penalty term $\Omega(W)$ to the objective function, AKA the loss function:

$$E\big(y, \hat{y}(W, x)\big)$$

Here, $y \in \mathbb{R}^N$ are the true values and $\hat{y}(W, x) \in \mathbb{R}^N$ are the predicted values. A new loss function $\tilde{E}(y, \hat{y}(W, x), \lambda)$ is obtained with the addition of this penalty term:

$$\tilde{E}\big(y, \hat{y}(W, x), \lambda\big) = E\big(y, \hat{y}(W, x)\big) + \lambda\Omega(W)$$

The training algorithm, thus, while minimizing this new loss function, will reach a weight configuration with smaller values. This is a well-known **regularization** approach you might already know from the linear or logistic regression algorithms.

The parameter $\lambda \in \mathbb{R}_+$ is used to control the penalty effect. $\lambda = 0$ is equivalent to no regularization. Higher values of λ implement a stronger regularization effect and lead to smaller weights.

There are two commonly used penalty norm functions: the **L1 norm** and the **L2 norm**. The L1 norm is the sum of the absolute values of the weights and the L2 norm is the sum of the squares of the weights:

$$L_1(W) = \sum_{i=1}^{n} |W_i| \qquad\qquad L_2(W) = \sum_{i=1}^{n} W_i^2$$

$L1$ and $L2$ are both common methods to avoid overfitting with one big difference. $L2$ regularization generally leads to smaller weights but lacks the ability to reduce the weights all the way to zero. On the other hand, $L1$ regularization allows for a few larger weights while reducing all other weights to zero. When designing a loss function, it is also possible to use a mixture of both $L1$ and $L2$ regularization.

In addition, you can also apply regularization terms to weights of selected layers. Three different norm regularizations have been designed to act on single layers: **kernel regularization**, **bias regularization**, and **activity regularization**.

Kernel regularization penalizes the weights, but not the biases; bias regularization penalizes the biases only; and activity regularization leads to smaller output values for the selected layer.

Dropout

Another common approach in machine learning to avoid overfitting is to introduce the dropout technique, which is another regularization technique.

The idea is, at each training iteration, to ignore (drop) randomly some of the neurons in either the input layer or a hidden layer with all its input and output connections. At each iteration, different neurons are dropped. Therefore, the number of neurons in the architecture, and which of them are trained, effectively changes from iteration to iteration. The randomization introduced in this way helps to control the overfitting effect.

Dropout makes sure that individual neurons and layers do not rely on single neurons in the preceding layers, thus becoming more robust and less prone to overfitting:

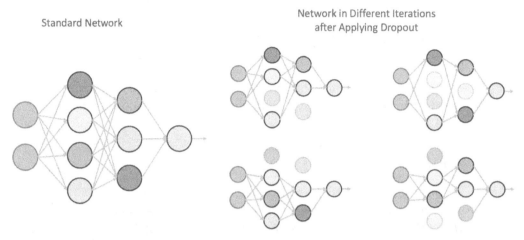

Figure 3.16 – The dropout technique selects some neurons in each layer and drops them from being updated in the current training iteration. The full network on the left is trained only partially in the four training iterations described on the right.

Dropout is applied to each layer of the network separately. This often translates into a temporary layer, the dropout layer, being inserted after the layer we want to randomize. The dropout layer controls how many neurons of the previous layer are dropped at each training iteration.

To control how many neurons in a layer are dropped, a new parameter is introduced: the **drop rate**. The drop rate defines the fraction of neurons in the layer that should be dropped from training at each iteration.

Tip

Here are two quick tips for dropout:

First, dropout leads to layers with fewer neurons and therefore reduces the layer capacity. It is recommended to start with a high number of neurons per layer.

Second, dropout is only applied to the input or hidden layers, not to the output layer since we want the response of the model to always be the same at each iteration.

Early Stopping

Another option to avoid overfitting is to stop the training process before the network starts overfitting, which is known as **early stopping**. To detect the point where the algorithm starts to fit the training data better than the test data, an additional validation set with new data is used. During training, the network performances are monitored on both the training set and the validation set. At the beginning of the training phase, the network performance on both the training and validation sets improves. At some point, though, the performance of the network on the training set keeps improving while on the validation set it starts deteriorating. Once the performance starts to get worse on the validation set, the training is stopped.

Other Commonly used Layers

So far, we have introduced two different kinds of layers: dense layers to design fully connected neural networks with different activation functions and the dropout layer for regularization. With these layers, you can design, for example, an autoencoder, as we will do in *Chapter 5, Autoencoder for Fraud Detection*. But actually, there are many more layers available for all kinds of different tasks.

Convolutional Layers

One area where neural networks are extremely powerful is image analysis, for example, image classification. Feedforward neural networks are also frequently used in this area. Often, though, the sequence of dense layers is not used alone, but in combination with another series of convolutional layers. **Convolutional layers** are placed after the input of the neural network, to extract features and then create a better representation of the image to pass to the next dense layers – the feedforward architecture – for the classification. These networks are called **Convolutional Neural Networks**, **CNNs** for short.

Chapter 9, Convolutional Neural Networks for Image Classification, explains in detail how convolutional layers work. It will also introduce some other related neural layers that are suitable to analyze data with spatial relationships, such as the flatten layer and the max pooling layer.

Recurrent Neural Networks

A family of neural networks that doesn't belong to feedforward networks is that of **Recurrent Neural Networks**, **RNNs** for short. RNNs are obtained by introducing auto- or backward connections (recurrent connections) into feedforward neural networks. This allows the network to take context into account, since it remembers inputs from the past, and therefore it can capture the dynamic of a signal. These networks are really powerful when it comes to sequential data, such as times series data or text.

Different layers for RNNs have been introduced in the past, for example, **Long Short-Term Memory (LSTM)** layers or **Gated Recurrent Unit (GRU)** layers. *Chapter 6, Recurrent Neural Networks for Demand Prediction*, covers RNNs in detail as well as the architecture of LSTM units.

Training a Neural Network

After network architecture and activation functions, the last design step before you can start training a neural network is the choice of loss function.

We will start with an overview of possible loss functions for regression, binary classification, and multiclass classification problems. Then, we will introduce some optimizers and additional training parameters for the training algorithms.

Loss Functions

In order to train a feedforward neural network, an appropriate error function, often called a **loss function**, and a matching last layer have to be selected. Let's start with an overview of commonly used loss functions for regression problems.

Loss Functions for Regression Problems

In the case of a regression problem, where the goal is to predict one single numerical value, the output layer should have one unit only and use the linear activation function. Possible loss functions to train this kind of network must refer to numerical error metrics:

- **Mean Squared Error (MSE) Loss**: The mean squared error is the default error metric for regression problems. For $N \in \mathbb{N}$ training samples, it is calculated as follows:

$$MSE(\boldsymbol{y}, \hat{\boldsymbol{y}}) = \frac{1}{N} \sum_{i=1}^{N} (y_i - \hat{y}_i)^2$$

  Here, $\boldsymbol{y} \in \mathbb{R}^N$ are the true values and $\hat{\boldsymbol{y}} \in \mathbb{R}^N$ are the predicted values. The MSE gives more importance to large error values and it is always positive. A perfect predictor would have an MSE of 0.

- **Mean Squared Logarithmic Error (MSLE) Loss**: The MSLE is a loss function that penalizes large errors less than the MSE. It is calculated by applying the logarithm on the predicted and the true values, before using the MSE. For $N \in \mathbb{N}$ training samples, it is calculated as follows:

$$MSLE(\boldsymbol{y}, \hat{\boldsymbol{y}}) = \frac{1}{N} \sum_{i=1}^{N} (\log{(y_i + 1)} - \log{(\hat{y}_i + 1)})^2$$

MSLE applies to numbers greater or equal to 0, such as prices. 1 is added to both y and $\hat{y}$ to avoid having $log(0)$.

This loss function is recommended if the range of the target values is large and larger errors shouldn't be penalized significantly more than smaller errors. The MSLE is always positive and a perfect model has a loss of 0.

- **Mean Absolute Error (MAE) Loss**: The MAE loss function is a more robust loss function with regards to outliers. This means it punishes large errors even less than the previous two loss functions, MSE and MSLE. For $N \in \mathbb{N}$ training samples, it is calculated as follows:

$$MAE(\mathbf{y}, \hat{\mathbf{y}}) = \frac{1}{N} \sum_{i=1}^{N} |y_i - \hat{y}_i|.$$

In summary, we can say that we can choose between three different loss functions for regression problems: MSE, MSLE, and MAE. Let's continue with loss functions for binary and multiclass classification problems.

Loss Functions for Binary Classification Problems

The common approach for binary classification is to encode the two classes with $y = 0$ and $y = 1$ and to train a network to predict the probability for class $y = 1$. Here the output layer consists of just one unit with the sigmoid activation function. For this approach, the recommended default loss function is **binary cross entropy**.

On a training set of $N \in \mathbb{N}$ samples, the binary cross-entropy can be calculated as follows:

$$CE = -\frac{1}{N} \sum_{i=1}^{N} y_i \, \log\big(p(y_i)\big) + (1 - y_i) \, \log\big(1 - p(y_i)\big)$$

Here, y_i is the class label, the true value ($y_i = 0$ / 1) for the ith sample in the training set, and $p(y_i)$ is the probability predicted by the network for that class. Since this a binary classification problem, the second part of the loss function calculates exactly the same value for the other class. $p(y_i)$ is the predicted value $\hat{y}_i$ in the previously shown loss functions.

Other possible loss functions for binary classification problems are **Hinge** and **Squared Hinge**. In this case, the two classes have to be encoded as -1 and 1 and therefore the unit in the output layer must use the tanh activation function.

Loss Functions for Multiclass Classification Problems

In multiclass classification problems, usually, each class is represented by an integer value (class = 1, 2, 3, …) and a one-hot encoding is used to represent the different classes. The output layer should have as neural units as many classes all with softmax activation function, so as to predict a score that can be interpreted as the probability of each class.

The default loss function for multiclass classification problems is **categorical cross-entropy**. On a training set of $N \in \mathbb{N}$ samples, the categorical cross-entropy can be calculated as an extension to C classes of the binary cross-entropy:

$$CE = -\frac{1}{N} \sum_{i=1}^{N} \sum_{k=1}^{C} y_{i,k} \, \log\left(p(y_{i,k})\right)$$

Here, $y_{i,k}$ is the class label k, the true value ($y_k = 0 \, / \, 1$) for the ith sample in the training set, and $p(y_{i,k})$ is the corresponding probability predicted by the network for class k. Again, $p(y_{i,k})$ is the predicted value $\widehat{y_{i,k}}$ by output neuron k for training sample i.

For multiclass classification problems with too many different classes, such as language modeling where each word in the dictionary is one class, **sparse categorical cross-entropy** is used.

Another commonly used loss function here is the **Kullback-Leibler divergence**.

In addition to the commonly used loss functions, as introduced previously, it is also possible to define custom loss functions to best fit the use case at hand.

Parameters and Optimization of the Training Algorithm

Now that our network is designed, using the correct activation function in the output layer as well as an appropriate loss function, we can start training the network. Modern training algorithms are generally based on the SGD strategy, using backpropagation to update the values of the network weights. Over the last few years, different variants of SGD algorithms (optimizers) have been produced, optimized to train networks on datasets with different properties. For example, **Adagrad** and its extension **Adadelta** work well on sparse data. **Adam** involves a moving average of the gradient and of the squared gradient for the weight updates. The Keras documentation page gives an overview of all the available training algorithms: `https://keras.io/optimizers/`.

> **Important note**
>
> Backpropagation is typically referred to as the algorithm that calculates the gradients of the weights. The algorithm to train a neural network is usually some variant of SGD and it makes use of backpropagation to update the network weights.

A big role in the training algorithm is played by the **learning rate** η. The learning rate defines the size of the step taken along the direction of the gradient descent on the error surface during the learning phase. A too-small η produces tiny steps and therefore takes a long time to reach the minimum of the loss function, especially if the loss function happens to have flat slopes. A too-large η produces large steps that might overshoot and miss the minimum of the loss function, especially if the loss function is narrow and with steep slopes. The choice of the right value of learning rate η is critical. A possible solution could be to use an adaptive learning rate, starting large and progressively decreasing with the number of training iterations.

In *Figure 3.17*, there are examples for moving on the loss function with a too-small, too-large, and adaptive learning rate:

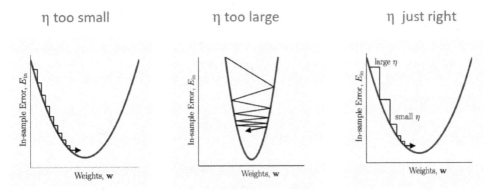

Figure 3.17 – The progressive decrease of the error with a too-small learning rate **η** (on the left), a too-large learning rate **η** (in the center), and an adaptive learning rate **η** in a one-dimensional weight space

All loss functions are defined as a sum over all training samples. This leads to algorithms that update the weights after all training samples have passed through the network. This training strategy is called **batch training**. It is the correct way to proceed; however, it is also computationally expensive and often slow.

The alternative is to use the **online training** strategy, where weights are updated after the pass of each training sample. This strategy is less computationally expensive, but it is just an approximation of the original backpropagation algorithm. It is also prone to running into oscillations. In this case, it is good practice to use smaller values for the learning rate.

Virtually all modern deep learning frameworks make use of a mixture of batch and online training, where they use small batches of training examples to perform a single update step.

The **Momentum** term is added to the weight delta Δw_{ij} to increase the weight update as long as they have the same sign as the previous delta. Momentum speeds up the training on long flat error surfaces and can help the network pass a local minimum. The weight update then would include an extra term:

$$\Delta w_{ij}(n) = \sum_T -\eta \, \delta_j \, o_i + \alpha \, \Delta w_{ij}(n-1)$$

Here, n is the current training iteration and α is the momentum term.

Additional Training Parameters

Two other important setting options for the training process are the training batch size and the number of epochs.

- **Training batch size**: The training **batch size** defines the number of samples used in one training iteration. If the training batch size is set to the full number of samples in the training set, the training will run in the so-called batch mode, which is computationally expensive and slow. In general, it is recommended to train a model in mini-batch mode, where only part of the data is used for each iteration. It is recommended to shuffle the data before each epoch, to have different batches in different epochs.

- **Number of epochs**: The number of epochs defines the number of cycles that run over the full training dataset.

To summarize, the algorithm goes through the whole training set m times, where m is the number of epochs. Each epoch consists of a number of iterations and, for each iteration, a subset of the training set (a batch) is used. At the end of each iteration, weights are updated following the online training strategy.

Summary

We have reached the end of this chapter, where we have learned the basic theoretical concepts behind neural networks and deep learning networks. All of this will be helpful to understand the steps for the practical implementation of deep learning networks described in the coming chapters.

We started with the artificial neuron and moved on to describe how to assemble and train a network of neurons, a fully connected feedforward neural network, via a variant of the gradient descent algorithm, using the backpropagation algorithm to calculate the gradient.

We concluded the chapter with a few hints on how to design and train a neural network. First, we described some commonly used network topologies, neural layers, and activation functions to design the appropriate neural architecture.

We then moved to analyze the effects of some parameters involved in the training algorithm. We introduced a few more parameters and techniques to optimize the training algorithm against a selected loss function.

In the next chapter, you will learn how you can perform all the steps we introduced in this chapter using KNIME Analytics Platform.

Questions and Exercises

Test how well you have understood the concepts in this chapter by answering the following questions:

1. A feedforward neural network is an architecture where:

   a. Each neuron from the previous layer is connected to each neuron in the next layer.

   b. There are auto and backward connections.

   c. There is just one unit in the output layer.

   d. There are as many input units as there are output units.

2. Why do we need hidden layers in a feedforward neural network?

   a. For more computational power

   b. To speed up calculations

   c. To implement more complex functions

   d. For symmetry

3. The backpropagation algorithm updates the network weights proportionally to:

   a. The output errors backpropagated through the network

   b. The input values forward propagated through the network

   c. The batch size

   d. The deltas calculated at the output layer and backpropagated through the network

4. Which loss function is commonly used for a multiclass classification problem?

    a. MAE

    b. RMSE

    c. Categorical cross-entropy

    d. Binary cross-entropy

5. What kind of networks are suited for image analysis?

    a. RNNs

    b. CNNs

    c. Fully connected feedforward networks

    d. Autoencoders

6. How is the last layer of a network commonly configured when solving a binary classification problem?

    a. Two units with the sigmoid activation function

    b. One unit with the linear activation function

    c. Two units with the ReLU activation function

    d. One unit with the sigmoid activation function

7. When are RNNs used?

    a. On data with many missing values

    b. On image data

    c. On sequential data

    d. On sparse datasets

4
Building and Training a Feedforward Neural Network

In *Chapter 3*, *Getting Started with Neural Networks*, you learned the basic theory behind neural networks and deep learning. This chapter sets that knowledge into practice. We will implement two very simple classification examples: a multiclass classification using the **iris flower** dataset, and a binary classification using the adult dataset, also known as the **census income** dataset.

These two datasets are quite small and the corresponding classification solutions are also quite simple. A fully connected feedforward network will be sufficient in both examples. However, we decided to show them here as toy examples to describe all of the required steps to build, train, and apply a fully connected feedforward classification network with **KNIME Analytics Platform** and **KNIME Keras Integration**.

These steps include commonly used preprocessing techniques, the design of the neural architecture, the setting of the activation functions, the training and application of the network, and lastly, the evaluation of the results.

Thus, this chapter covers the following main topics:

- Preparing the Data
- Building a Feedforward Neural Architecture
- Training the Network
- Testing and Applying the Network

Preparing the Data

In *Chapter 3*, *Getting Started with Neural Networks*, we introduced the backpropagation algorithm, which is used by gradient descent algorithms to train a neural network. These algorithms work on numbers and can't handle nominal/categorical input features or class values. Therefore, nominal input features or nominal output values must be encoded into numerical values if we want the network to make use of them. In this section, we will show several numerical encoding techniques and the corresponding nodes in KNIME Analytics Platform to carry them out.

Besides that, we will also go through many other classic data preprocessing steps to feed machine learning algorithms: creating training, validation, and test sets from the original dataset; normalization; and missing value imputation.

Along the way, we will also show you how to import data, how to perform a few additional data operations, and some commonly used tricks within KNIME Analytics Platform. The workflows described in this chapter are available on the KNIME Hub: https://hub. knime.com/kathrin/spaces/Codeless%20Deep%20Learning%20with%20 KNIME/latest/Chapter%204/.

Datasets and Classification Examples

Before we dive into the different preprocessing steps, let's have a quick look at the two selected datasets and the associated classification examples:

- Classification of three iris flowers based on the Iris dataset
- Classification of income (binary class) based on the data from the adult dataset

Our first dataset gives us an example of a multiclass classification problem.

The Iris dataset consists of examples of flowers from three species of iris plants: Iris-setosa, Iris-virginica, and Iris-versicolor. Each flower is described through four measures: sepal length (cm), sepal width (cm), petal length (cm), and petal width (cm). This is a small dataset with 50 examples for each species, with 150 samples in total. *Figure 4.1* shows an overview of the dataset.

The goal is to train a neural network with one hidden layer (eight units and the ReLU activation function) to distinguish the three species from each other based on the four input features.

Part of the Iris dataset is displayed in the following tables:

Figure 4.1 – Overview of the Iris dataset, used here to implement a multiclass classification

The second example dataset provides us with a binary classification problem.

The adult dataset consists of 32,561 samples of people living in the US. Each record describes a person through 14 demographics features, including their current annual income (> 50K/<= 50K). *Figure 4.2* shows an overview of the features in the dataset: numerical features, such as age and hours worked per week, and nominal features, such as work class and marital status.

The goal is to train a neural network to predict whether a person earns more or less than 50K per year, using all the other attributes as input features. The network we want to use should have two hidden layers, each one with eight units and the ReLU activation function.

Some of the census income dataset displayed in tables looks as follows:

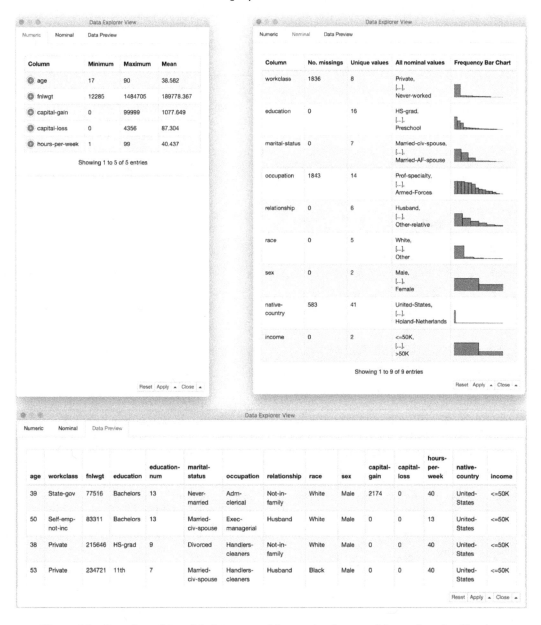

Figure 4.2 – Overview of the adult dataset, used here to implement a binary class classification

> **Tip**
>
> To get an overview of the dataset, you can use the **Data Explorer** node. This node displays some statistical measures of the input data within an interactive view. In *Figure 4.1* and *Figure 4.2*, you can see the view of the node for the two example datasets.

To summarize the Iris dataset, it consists of four numerical features, plus the iris nominal class; the adult dataset consists of 14 mixed features, numerical and nominal. The first step in the data preparation would, therefore, be to transform all nominal features into numerical ones. Let's move on, then, to the encoding techniques.

Encoding of Nominal Features

Nominal features, sometimes also called categorical features, can assume only string-type values. For example, the only possible values for a feature describing hair color can be a string type, such as black, brown, blond, and red; a feature describing gender traditionally assumes only two string-type values, female and male; and the possible values for an education feature can be strings, such as Doctorate, Masters, Bachelors, or Some-college. This last example is taken from the column named education in the adult dataset. These values should be transformed into numbers before being fed to a neural network.

There are two common ways to encode nominal features:

- **Integer encoding**
- **One-hot encoding**

Integer encoding assigns an integer value to each possible nominal value of a feature. For example, "black" can be 1, "brown" can be 2, "blond" can be 3, and "red" can be 4. We have chosen the numbers 1, 2, 3, and 4 but it could have been any other set of numbers. This approach introduces an artificial relationship between the different values – for example, that "black" is closer to "brown" than to "red". This can reflect a true relationship across values in ordinal or hierarchical features, such as education, where "Doctorate" is closer to "Masters" than to "Some-college". However, in other cases, such as the previously mentioned hair color one, it introduces a new additional relationship that does not reflect reality and can bias the model during learning. Generally speaking, using the integer encoding approach on nominal unordered features can lead to worse-performing models.

One-hot vector encoding overcomes this problem by representing each feature with a vector, where the distance across all the vectors is always the same. The vector consists of the same quantity of binary components as possible values in the original feature. Each component is then associated with one of the values and is set to 1 for that value; the other components remain set to 0. In the hair color example, `"black"` becomes [1,0,0,0], `"brown"` becomes [0,1,0,0], `"blond"` becomes [0,0,1,0], and `"red"` becomes [0,0,0,1].

> **Important note**
>
> A one-hot vector is a vector with a single 1 and all other values being 0. It can be used to encode different classes without adding any artificial distance between them.

Let's see now how to implement these encodings with KNIME nodes.

Integer Encoding in KNIME Analytics Platform

To perform integer encoding, you can use the **Category to Number** node. This node has one data input port (represented by a black triangle in the following diagram) and two output ports:

- A data output port (black triangle) with the integer-encoded data
- A PMML model output port (blue square) with the mapping rules

Figure 4.3 shows you the node, as well as its configuration window:

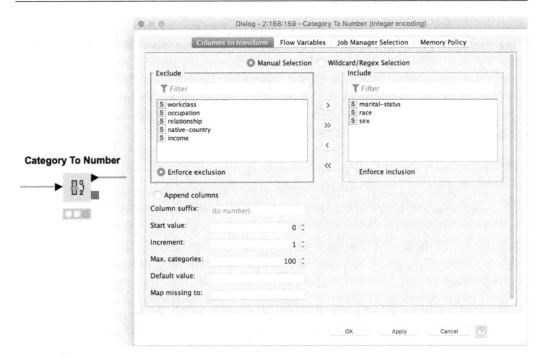

Figure 4.3 – The Category to Number node performs an integer encoding on the selected columns

In the upper part of the configuration window, you can select the string-type input columns to apply the integer encoding to. The columns in the **Include** framework will be transformed, while the columns in the **Exclude** framework will be left unchanged. You can move columns from one framework to the other using the buttons between them.

By default, values in the original columns are replaced with the integer-encoded values. However, the **Append columns** checkbox creates additional columns for the integer-encoded values so as not to overwrite the original columns. If you activate this checkbox, you can also define a custom suffix for the new columns' headers.

In the lower part of the configuration window, you can define the encoding rule: the start value, the increment, the maximum allowed number of categories, and an integer value for all missing values.

The default integer value is transferred to the output PMML transformation model. **PMML** stands for **Predictive Model Markup Language** and is a way to describe and exchange predictive models between different applications. The PMML model at the blue square output port contains the mapping function built in this node and to be applied to other datasets. When applying this integer encoding PMML model, the default value is assigned to all input values not represented by the current mapping (if any). If no default value is present, a missing value will be used instead.

> **Tip**
> To apply the same integer encoding mapping stored in the PMML output port to another dataset, you can use the **Category to Number (Apply)** node.

The **Category to Number** node defines the mapping automatically. This means you cannot manually define which nominal value should be represented by which integer value. If you wish to do so, you have other options in KNIME Analytics Platform, and we will introduce two of them: the **Cell Replacer** node and the **Rule Engine** node.

The **Cell Replacer** node replaces cell values in a column according to a dictionary table. It has two inputs:

- The top input for the table with the target column whose values are to be replaced
- The lower input for the dictionary table

Figure 4.4 shows the configuration window of the Cell Replacer node:

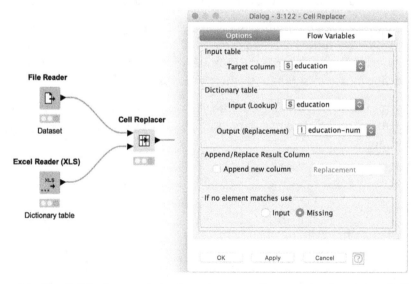

Figure 4.4 – The Cell Replacer node implements an encoding mapping based on a dictionary

In the upper part of the configuration window, you can select the target column from the input table at the top input port; this means the column whose values you want to replace based on the dictionary values.

In the **Dictionary table** part of the configuration window, you can select, from the data table at the lower input port, the column with the lookup values – that is, the **Input (Lookup)** column – and the column containing the replacement values – that is, the **Output (Replacement)** column.

Any occurrence in the target column (first input) that matches the lookup value is replaced with the corresponding replacement value. The result is stored in the output column, which is either added to the table or replaces the original target column.

Missing values are treated as ordinary values; that is, they are valid values both as lookup and replacement values. If there are duplicates in the lookup column in the dictionary table, the last occurrence (lowest row) defines the replacement pair.

For the integer encoding example, you need a dictionary table to map the nominal values and the integer values. For example, each education level should be mapped to a corresponding integer value. You can then feed the original dataset into the top input port and this map/dictionary table into the lowest input port.

> **Tip**
> The **Table Creator** node can be helpful to manually create the lookup table.

If you don't have a dictionary table and you don't want to create one, you can use the **Rule Engine** node.

The Rule Engine node transforms the values in the input columns according to a set of manually defined rules, which are defined in its configuration window.

Figure 4.5 shows you the configuration window of the Rule Engine node:

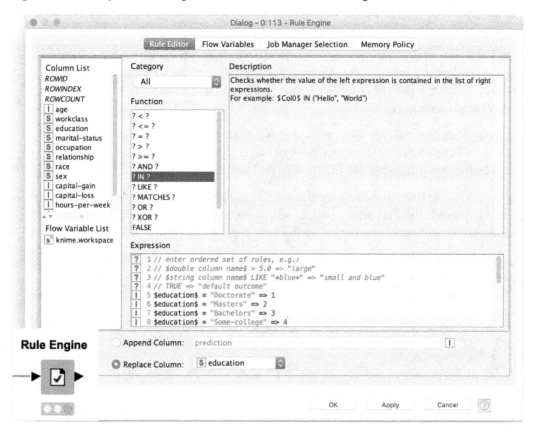

Figure 4.5 – The Rule Engine node implements an integer encoding from user-defined rules

In the **Expression** part of the configuration window, you can define the set of rules to apply. Each rule consists of an antecedent (condition) and a consequence, joined by =>, in the form of "antecedent => consequence". The results are either inserted into a new column or replace the values in a selected column. For each data row in the input table, the rule-matching process moves from the top rule to the lowest: the first matching rule determines the outcome, and then the rule process stops. The last default condition, collecting all the remaining data rows, is expressed as "TRUE => consequence".

The outcome of a rule may be a string (in between " or / symbols), a number, a Boolean constant, or a reference to another column. If no rule matches, the outcome is a missing value. References to other columns are represented by the column name in between $. You can insert a column reference by hand or by double-clicking on a column in **Column List** on the left side of the configuration window.

Besides the **Expression** panel, you find the **Function**, **Column List**, and **Flow Variable List** panels. The **Function** panel lists all functions, the **Column List** panel lists all input columns, and **Flow Variable List** contains all the available flow variables. Double-clicking on any of them adds them to the **Expression** window with the right syntax. Also, selecting any of the functions shows a description as well as an example.

To summarize, there are many ways to implement integer encoding in KNIME Analytics Platform. We introduced three options:

- The **Category to Number** node offers an automatic, easy approach if you do not want to define the mapping by hand.

- The **Cell Replacer** node is really useful if you have a lookup table at hand.

- The **Rule Engine** node is useful if you want to manually define the mapping between the nominal values and the integer values via a set of rules.

Next, let's look at one-hot encoding in KNIME Analytics Platform.

One-Hot-Encoding in KNIME Analytics Platform

To perform one-hot encoding on nominal features, there is the **One to Many** node. This node takes the list of nominal values available in a column, builds a vector with as many components, and produces the one-hot encoding of each value: one value to become many binary cells, hence the name.

In the configuration window, you can select the string-type columns on which to perform the one-hot encoding. For each column, as many new columns will be created as there are different values. The header of each new column will be the original value in the nominal column and its cells take a value of either 0 or 1, depending on the presence or absence of the header value in the original column.

Figure 4.6 shows the configuration window of the node:

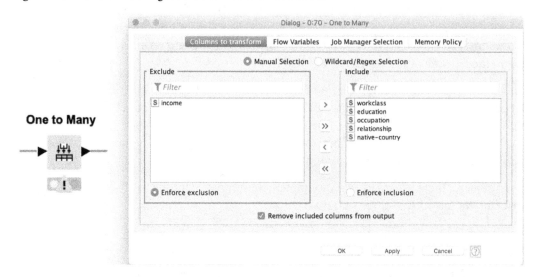

Figure 4.6 – The One to Many node implements the one-hot encoding for nominal features

Creating one-hot encoded vectors leads to very large and very sparse data tables with many zeros. This can weigh on the workflow performance during execution. The Keras Learner node does accept large and sparse one-hot-encoded data tables. However, it also offers a very nice optional feature that avoids this whole step of explicitly creating the data table with the one-hot-encoded vectors. It can create the one-hot-encoded vectors internally from an integer-encoded version of the original column. In this way, the one-hot encoding representation of the data remains hidden within the **Keras Network Learner** node and is never passed from node to node. In this case, the value of each integer-encoded cell must be presented to the Keras Network Learner node as a collection type cell. To create a collection type cell, you can use the **Create Collection Column** node. In the *Training the Network* section of this chapter, you will see how to configure the Keras Network Learner node properly to make use of this feature.

Figure 4.7 shows the configuration window of the **Create Collection Column** node. In the **Exclude-Include** frame, you select one or more columns to aggregate in a collection-type column. In the lower part of the configuration window, you can decide whether to remove the original columns and define the new collection type column's name:

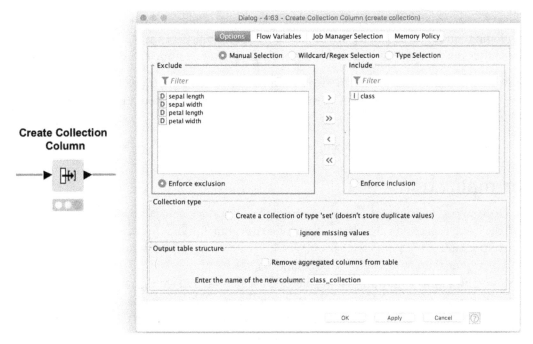

Figure 4.7 – The Create Collection Column node aggregates the values from multiple columns as a collection into one single column

Notice that for this two-step one-hot encoding – first integer encoding, then one-hot encoding – you need to create the integer encoding column with one of the nodes listed in the previous section, and then apply the **Create Collection Column** node to just one column: the integer-encoded column that we have just created.

Encoding of Categorical Target Variables

In the last chapter, we talked about different activation functions and loss functions that can be used to build network architectures and train networks to solve classification problems. Of course, the activation function in the output layer and the loss function must match. Not only that, but the class encoding must also match the chosen activation and loss function. This means that not only must nominal input features be encoded, but class values too. The same encoding techniques and nodes, as described in this section, can be used for class encoding as well.

A common approach to binary classification is to encode the two classes with $y = 0$ and $y = 1$ and then to train the network to predict the probability for the $y = 1$ class. In this case, either the Category to Number node or the Rule Engine node can work.

In the case of a multiclass problem, there are also two options to encode the class column: the **One to Many** node on its own or the Category to Number followed by the Create Collection Column node.

Another recommended preprocessing step for neural networks is normalization.

Normalization

Most neural networks are trained using some variant of stochastic gradient descent with the backpropagation algorithm to calculate the gradient. Input features with non-comparable ranges can create problems during learning, as the input features with the largest range can overpower the calculation of the weight update, possibly even overshooting a local minimum. This can create oscillations and slow down the convergence of the learning process. To speed up the learning phase, it is recommended to normalize the data in advance; for example, by using the z-score normalization so that the values in each column are Gaussian-distributed with a mean of 0.0 and a standard deviation of 1.0.

In *Figure 4.8*, you can see the **Normalizer** node and its configuration window, as well as the **Normalizer (Apply)** node:

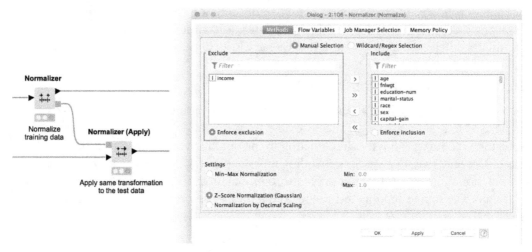

Figure 4.8 – The Normalizer node creates a normalization function for the selected input columns. The Normalizer (Apply) node applies the same normalization function to another dataset

The Normalizer node creates a normalization function on the selected input columns and normalizes them. The Normalizer (Apply) node takes an external predefined normalization function and applies it to the input data. A classic case for the application of this pair of nodes is on training and test sets. The Normalizer node normalizes the training data and the Normalizer (Apply) node applies the same normalization transformation to the test data.

The Normalizer node has one data input port and two output ports:

- One data output port with the normalized input data
- One model output port containing the normalization parameters, which can be used on another dataset in a Normalizer (Apply) node

In the configuration window of the Normalizer node, you can select the numerical columns to normalize and the normalization method.

The configuration window of the Normalizer (Apply) node is minimal since all of the necessary parameters are contained in the input normalization model.

> **Tip**
> With a Partitioning node, you can create the training and test sets *before* normalizing the data.

Other Helpful Preprocessing Nodes

Missing values can be a problem when training a neural network, as the backpropagation algorithm can't handle them. The placeholder value to represent missing values in a KNIME data table is a red question mark.

A powerful node to impute missing values is the **Missing Value** node. This node allows you to select between many imputation methods, such as mean value, fixed value, and most frequent value, to name just a few.

Figure 4.9 shows the two tabs of the configuration window of the node. In the first tab, the **Default** tab, you can select an imputation method to apply to all columns of the same type in the dataset; all columns besides those set in the second tab of the configuration, the **Column Settings** tab. In this second tab, you can define the imputation method for each individual column:

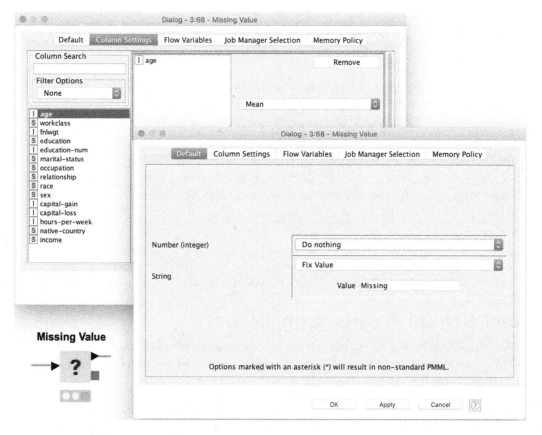

Figure 4.9 – The Missing Value node selects among many imputation methods for missing values

Most neural networks are trained in a supervised way. Therefore, another necessary step is the creation of a training set and a test set, and optionally a validation set. To create different disjoint subsets, you can use the **Partitioning** node.

In the configuration window of the Partitioning node in *Figure 4.10*, you can set the size for the first partition, by either an absolute or a relative percentage number. Below that, you can set the sampling technique to create this first subset, by random extraction following the data distribution according to the categories in a selected column (stratified sampling), linearly every *n* data rows, or just sequentially starting from the top. The top output port produces the resulting partition; the lower output port produces all other remaining data rows:

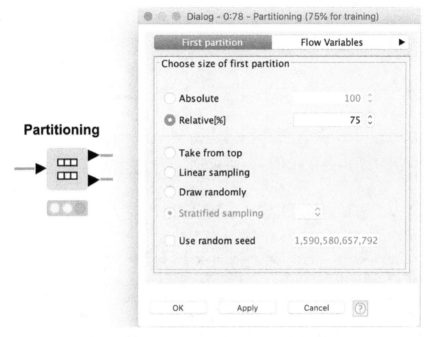

Figure 4.10 – The Partitioning node creates two disjoint subsets

For classification problems, the **Stratified sampling** option is recommended. It ensures that the distribution of the categories in the selected column is (approximately) retained in the two partitions. For time-series analysis, the **Take from top** option is preferable, if your data is sorted ascending by date. Samples further back in time will be in one partition and more recent samples in the other.

To create an additional validation set, a sequence of two Partitioning nodes is needed.

We have talked about encoding for categorical features, normalization for numerical features, missing value imputation, and partitioning of the dataset. It is likely that those are not the only nodes you might need to prepare your data for the neural network.

Let's see how the data preparation works in practice, by implementing the data preparation part on the two example datasets we have described previously.

Data Preparation on the Iris Dataset

In *Figure 4.11*, you can see the part of the workflow dedicated to accessing and preparing the data for the upcoming neural network.

The workflow starts with reading the Iris dataset using the **Table Reader** node.

> **Tip**
> You can find the dataset in the data folder for this chapter.

As the dataset has only numerical input features (petal and sepal measures), there is no need for encoding:

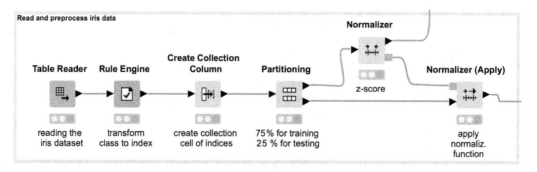

Figure 4.11 – This workflow snippet shows the preprocessing for the data in the iris dataset example

However, the target variable contains three different categories: the names of each flower species. The categories in this nominal column need to be converted into numbers via some encoding technique. To avoid the introduction of non-existent relationships, we opted for one-hot encoding. To implement the one-hot encoding, we chose the combination of integer encoding via nodes and one-hot encoding within the Keras Learner node. We will talk about the one-hot encoding internal to the Keras Learner node in the *Training the Network* section. Here, we will focus on the creation of an integer encoding of the flower classes inside a collection type column:

1. In order to transform the species names into an index, we use the **Rule Engine** node, with the following rules:

```
$class$ = "Iris-setosa" => 0
$class$ = "Iris-virginica" => 1
TRUE => 2
```

In addition, we decided to replace the values in the class column.

2. Afterward, we pass the results from the Rule Engine node through a **Create Collection Column** node, to format the encoded class values as collection type cells. This means we include the class column, and we exclude all other columns in the configuration window.

3. Next, the training and test sets are created with a **Partitioning** node, using 75% of the data for training and the remaining 25% for testing.

4. Lastly, the data is normalized using the z-score normalization.

The Iris dataset is quite small and quite well defined. Only a few nodes, the minimum required, were sufficient to implement the data preparation part.

Let's see now what happens on a more complex (but still small) dataset, such as the adult dataset.

Data Preparation on the Adult Dataset

The workflow in *Figure 4.12* is part of the example on income prediction that reads and preprocesses the adult dataset:

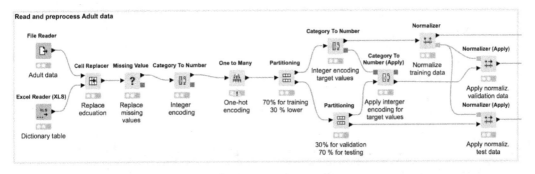

Figure 4.12 – This workflow snippet shows the preprocessing for the data in the adult dataset example

Like for the Iris dataset, you can find the two datasets used in the workflow in the data folder for this chapter: the adult dataset and a dictionary Excel sheet. In the adult dataset, education levels are spelled out as text. The dictionary Excel file provides a map between the education levels and the corresponding standard integer codes. We could use these integer codes as the numerical encoding of the education input feature.

Next, the **Cell Replacer** node replaces all educational levels with the corresponding codes. We get one encoding practically without effort.

Some of the nominal columns have missing values. Inside the **Missing Value** node, they get imputed with a fixed value: `"Missing"`.

Next, we proceed with the encoding of all other nominal features, besides education. For the following features, an integer encoding is used, implemented by the **Category to Number** node: marital status, race, and sex. We can afford to use the integer encoding here, because the features are either binary or with just a few categories.

For the remaining nominal features – work class, occupation, relationship, and native-country – one-hot encoding is used, implemented by the **One to Many** node. Remember that this node creates one new column for each value in each of the selected columns. So, after this transformation, the dataset has 82, instead of the original 14, features.

Next, the training, validation, and test sets are created with a sequence of two **Partitioning** nodes, always using a stratified sampling based on the `Income` class column.

Lastly, the `Income` column gets integer encoded on all subsets and all their data is normalized.

> **Tip**
> To hide complexity and to tidy up your workflows, you can create **metanodes**. Metanodes are depicted as gray nodes and contain sub-workflows of nodes. To create a metanode, select the nodes you want to hide, right-click, and select **Create Metanode**.

Our data is ready. Let's now build the neural network.

Building a Feedforward Neural Architecture

To build a neural network architecture using the KNIME Keras integration, you can use a chain of Keras layer nodes. The available nodes to construct layers are grouped by categories in the **Keras->Layers** folder in the **Node Repository**, such as **Advanced Activations**, **Convolution**, **Core**, **Embedding**, and **Recurrent**, to name just a few.

Each layer displayed in the **Keras->Layers** folder has a specialty. For example, layers in **Advanced Activations** create layers with units with specific activation functions; layers in **Convolution** create layers for convolutional neural networks; **Core** contains all classic layers, such as the **Input** layer to collect the input values and the **Dense** layer for a fully connected feedforward neural network; and so on.

We will explore many of these layers along the way in this book. However, in this current chapter, we will limit ourselves to the basic layers needed in a fully connected feedforward neural network.

The first layer in any network is the layer that receives the input values. Let's start from the Keras Input Layer node.

The Keras Input Layer Node

Building a neural network always starts with defining the input layer of the network. The **Keras Input Layer** node can help you with this task. Indeed, this node builds the required inputs for the network to accept the input values.

On the left of *Figure 4.13*, you can see the Keras Input Layer node and on the right its configuration window. As you can see, the node does not have an input port, just one output port of a different shape and color (red square) from the nodes encountered so far: this is the **Keras Network Port**:

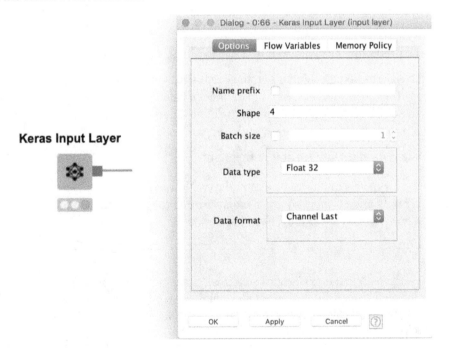

Figure 4.13 – The Keras Input Layer node defines the input layer of your neural network

> **Tip**
> The color and shape of a port indicate which ports can be connected with each other. Most of the time, only ports of the same color and shape can be connected, but there are exceptions. For example, you can connect a gray square, which is a Python DL port, with a Keras port, a red square.

Each layer node has a configuration window, with the setting options required for this specific layer. Compared to other layer nodes, this node has a simple configuration window with only a few setting options.

The most important setting is **Shape**. **Shape** allows you to define the input shape of your network, meaning how many neurons your input layer has. Remember, the number of neurons in the input layer has to match the number of your preprocessed input columns.

The Iris dataset has four features that we will use as inputs: sepal length, sepal width, petal length, and petal width. Therefore, the input shape here is 4.

In addition, in the configuration window of the Keras Input Layer node, you can set the following:

- A **Name prefix** for the layer, so it is easier to identify it later on (optional).
- A **Batch size** (optional). Remember, the batch size is one of the setting options for the training. The recommended way is to define the batch size in the learner and executor node. In addition, you have the option to define it here. If a batch size is defined, then the batch size option in the learner and executor nodes are not available.
- The **Data type** and **Data format** of the input.

Your network now has its first layer, the input layer. Now, you can continue to build your network by creating and connecting the next layer node to the output of the Keras Input Layer node – for example, a **Keras Dense Layer** node.

> **Tip**
> To create a node and immediately connect it to an existing node, select the existing node in the workflow editor and double-click the new node in the Node Repository. This will create the new node and connect it automatically to the selected existing node.

The Keras Dense Layer Node

The **Keras Dense Layer** node implements a classic layer in a feedforward fully connected network. The parameters to set here are the number of neural units and the activation function.

Figure 4.14 shows the configuration window of this node. The setting options are split into two tabs: **Options** and **Advanced**.

The **Options** tab contains the most important settings, such as the number of neurons, also known as units, and the activation function.

In addition, the **Input tensor** setting defines the part of the input tensor coming from the previous node. In a feedforward network, the input tensor is the output tensor from the previous layer. However, some layer nodes – such as, for example, the **Keras LSTM Layer** node – create not just one hidden output tensor, but multiple. In such cases, you must select one among the different input tensors, or hidden states, produced by the previous layer node. Keras Input Layer, like Keras Dense Layer, produces only one output vector and this is what we select as input tensor to our Keras Dense Layer node.

In the upper part of the **Advanced** tab, you can select how to randomly initialize the weights and biases of the network; this means the starting values for all weights and biases before the first iteration of the learning process.

The lower part of the **Advanced** tab allows you to add norm regularization for the weights in this layer. Norm regularization is a technique to avoid overfitting, which we introduced in *Chapter 3, Getting Started with Neural Networks*. In the configuration window, you can select whether to apply it to the kernel weight matrix, the bias vector, and/or the layer activation. After activating the corresponding checkbox, you can select between using the L1 norm as a penalty term, the L2 norm as a penalty term, or both. Lastly, you can set the value for the regularization parameter, $\lambda \in \mathbb{R}$, for the penalty terms and constraints on the weight and bias values.

By using the **Keras Input Layer** node and multiple Keras Dense Layer nodes, you can build a feedforward network for many different tasks, such as, for example, to classify iris flowers:

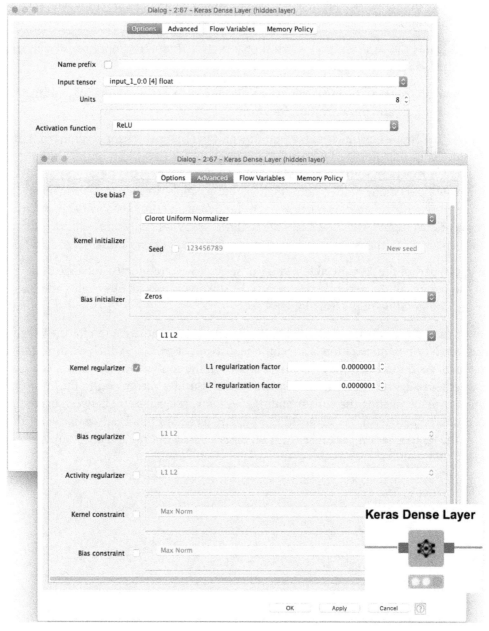

Figure 4.14 – The Keras Dense Layer node allows you to add a fully connected layer to your neural network, including a selection of commonly used activation functions

Configuration of the other layer nodes is similar to what was described here for the dense and input layers, and you will learn more about them in the next chapters.

Since both basic examples used in this chapter refer to feedforward networks, we now have all of the necessary pieces to build both feedforward neural networks.

Building a Neural Network for Iris Flower Classification

For the multiclass classification problem using the Iris dataset, the goal was to build a fully connected feedforward neural network with three layers:

- One input layer with four units, one for each input feature
- One hidden layer with eight units and the ReLU activation function
- One output layer with three units, one for each output class, meaning one for each iris species, with the softmax activation function

We opted for the ReLU activation function in the hidden layer for its better performance when used in hidden layers, and for the softmax activation function in the output layer for its probabilistic interpretability. The output unit with the highest output from the softmax function is the unit with the highest class probability.

Figure 4.15 shows the neural network architecture used for the iris classification problem:

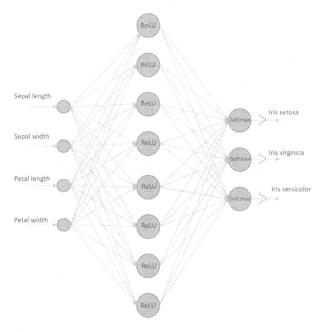

Figure 4.15 – A diagram of the feedforward network used for the iris flower example

Figure 4.16 shows the workflow snippet with the three layer nodes building the network and their configuration windows, including the number of units and activation functions:

Figure 4.16 – This workflow snippet builds the neural network in Figure 4.15 for the Iris dataset example. The configuration windows below them show you the nodes' configurations

The input layer has four input units, Shape = 4, for the four numerical input features. The first Keras Dense Layer node, which is the hidden layer, has eight units and uses the ReLU activation function. In the output layer, the softmax activation function is used with three units, one unit for each class.

> **Tip**
>
> In the last layer, the name prefix **Output** has been used. This makes it easier to identify the layer in the **Executor** node and has the advantage that the layer name doesn't change if more Keras Dense Layer nodes are added as hidden layers.

Building a Neural Network for Income Prediction

The second proposed example was a binary classification problem: predicting income (greater or lower than 50K per year) in the adult dataset. Here, we adopted a neural network with two hidden layers, with four layers in total:

- One input layer with 81 units, as many as input features
- One hidden layer with six units and the ReLU activation function
- One more hidden layer with six units and the ReLU activation function
- One output layer with one unit and the sigmoid activation function

The output layer uses a classic implementation for the binary classification problem: one single unit with the sigmoid activation function. The sigmoid function, spanning a range of 0 and 1, can easily implement class attribution using 0 for one class and 1 for the other. Thus, for a binary classification problem, where the two classes are encoded as 0 and 1, one sigmoid function alone can produce the probability for the class encoded as 1.

Figure 4.17 shows you the workflow snippet that builds this fully connected feedforward neural network:

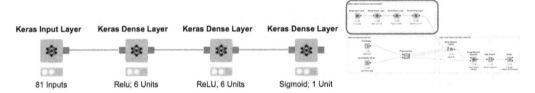

Figure 4.17 – This workflow snippet builds the fully connected feedforward neural network used as a solution for the adult dataset example

After preprocessing, the adult dataset ends up having 82 columns, 81 input features, and the target column. Therefore, the input layer has Shape = 81. Next, the two hidden layers are built using two Keras Dense Layer nodes with Units = 6 and the ReLU activation function. The output layer consists of a Keras Dense Layer node, again with Units = 1 and the sigmoid activation function.

In this section, you've learned how to build a feedforward neural network using the KNIME Keras integration nodes. The next step is to set the other required parameters for the network training, such as, for example, the loss function, and then to train the network.

Training the Network

We have the data ready and we have the network. The goal of this section is to show you how to train the network with the data in the training set. This requires the selection of the loss function, the setting of the training parameters, the specification of the training set and the validation set, and the tracking of the training progress.

The key node for network training and for all these training settings is the **Keras Network Learner** node. This is a really powerful, really flexible node, with many possible settings, distributed over four tabs: **Input Data**, **Target Data**, **Options**, and **Advanced Options**.

The Keras Network Learner node has three input ports:

- **Top port**: The neural network you want to train
- **Middle port**: The training set
- **Lowest port**: The optional validation set

It has one output port, exporting the trained network.

In addition, the node has the **Learning Monitor** view, which you can use to monitor the network training progress.

Let's find out first how to select the loss function before we continue with the training parameters.

Selecting the Loss Function

In *Chapter 3, Getting Started with Neural Networks*, we introduced many loss functions, each one suitable for a specific task, as the last design choice for your network. For example, mean squared error is commonly used in regression problems or categorical cross-entropy in multiclass classification problems. In the lower part of the **Target Data** tab, you can either select between different standard prepackaged loss functions or define your own custom loss function using Python (see *Figure 4.18*):

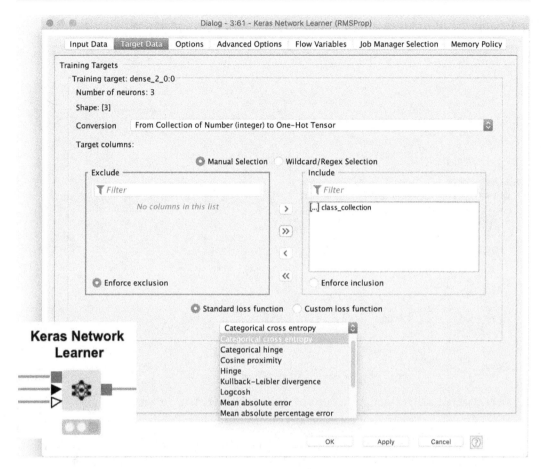

Figure 4.18 – In the Target Data tab of the Keras Network Learner node, you can select the target columns and the loss function

Now that the network structure is defined and you have selected the correct loss function, the next step is to define which columns of the input dataset are the inputs for your network and which column contains the target values.

Defining the Input and Output Data

Defining the input and output columns is something you can do in the **Input Data** and **Target Data** tabs. Let's focus first on the input data.

The input data is the data that your network expects as input, which means the columns that fit the input size of the network. In the **Input Data** tab, the number of input neurons for the selected network and the consequent shape are reported at the very top:

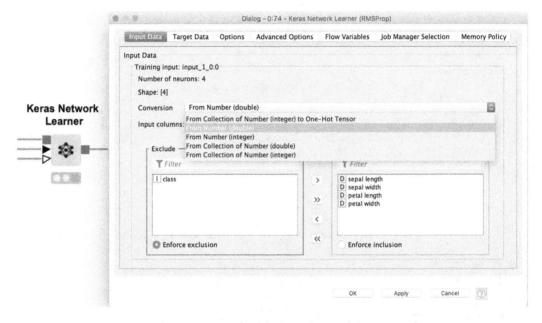

Figure 4.19 – In the Input Data tab of the Keras Network Learner node, you can select the input column(s) and the correct conversion

Next, you must select the conversion type; this means the transformation for the selected input columns into a format that is accepted by the network input specification. The possible conversion types are as follows:

- **From Collection of Number (integer) to One-Hot Tensor**
- **From Number (double)**
- **From Number (integer)**
- **From Collection of Number (double)**
- **From Collection of Number (integer)**
- **From Image**

Conversion type 1, **From Collection of Numbers (integer) to One-Hot Tensor**, is a really helpful transformation when the network requires one-hot vectors. Instead of creating a matrix with all the one-hot vectors, which takes up space and resources, you can input a sequence of integer-encoded values and then transform them, one by one, into one-hot vectors. During execution, the node creates the one-hot vectors and inputs them into the network. The whole process is hidden from the end user and no additional large, sparse data tables are created.

The other conversion types just take the input columns in the specified format (double, integer, or image) and present them to the network.

After selecting the conversion type, you can select the input columns to the network through an include-exclude frame. Notice that the frame has been pre-loaded with all the input columns matching the selected conversion type.

Let's now select the target column. The target data must match the specifications from the output layer. This means that, if your output layer has 20 units, your target data must be 20-dimensional vectors; or, if your output layer has only one unit, your target data must also consist of one single value for each training sample or data row.

In the **Target Data** tab, at the very top, the number of neurons in the output layer of the network and the resulting shape is reported. Like in the **Input Data** tab, here you can select from many conversion options to translate from the input dataset into the network specifications. The menu, with all the available conversion types to select from, has been preloaded with the conversion types that fit the specifications of the output layer of the network.

For multiclass classification problems, the conversion type from a collection of numbers (integer) to one-hot tensor is really helpful. Instead of creating the one-hot vectors in advance, you need only to encode the position of the class (1) in the input collection cell.

Let's move on to the training parameters.

Setting the Training Parameters

Now that the network and the loss function have been defined, the next step is to set the training parameters. For example, which optimizer do you want to use? How many epochs do you want to train for? There are many parameters to be defined.

All the training parameters can be found in the **Options** and **Advanced Options** tabs. In *Figure 4.20*, you can see the **Options** tab of the **Keras Network Learner** node:

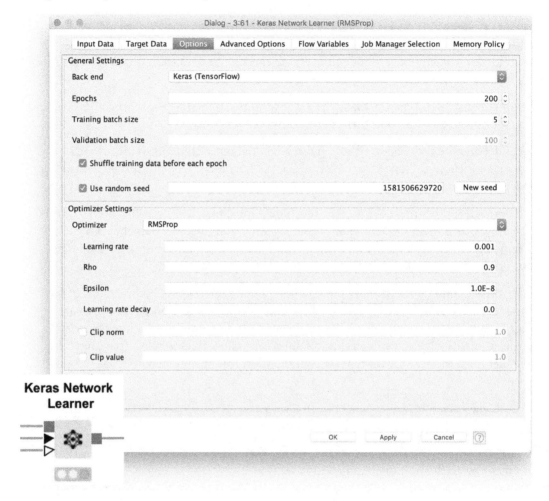

Figure 4.20 – In the Options tab of the Keras Network Learner node, you can set all the training parameters

In the upper part of the **Options** tab, in the configuration window, you can define the number of epochs and the batch size. This determines the number of data rows from the training and validation sets to feed the network in batches within each training iteration.

> **Important note**
> If you defined a batch size in the Keras Input Layer node, the batch size settings are deactivated.

Under that, there are two checkboxes. One shuffles the training data randomly before each epoch, and one sets a random seed. Shuffling the training data often improves the learning process. Indeed, updating the network with the same batches in the same order in each epoch can have a detrimental effect on the convergence speed of the training. If the shuffling checkbox is selected, the random seed checkbox becomes active and the displayed number is used to generate the random sequence for the shuffling operation. The usage of a random seed produces a repeatable random shuffling procedure and therefore allows us to repeat the results of a specific training run. Clicking the **New seed** button generates a new random seed and a new random shuffling procedure. Disabling the checkbox for the random seed creates a new seed for each node execution.

In the lower part of the **Options** tab, you can select the **Optimizer algorithm,** and its parameters to use during training. The optimizer algorithm is the training algorithm. For example, you can select the **RMSProp** optimizer and then the corresponding **Learning rate** and **Learning rate decay** values. When the node is selected, the **Description** panel on the right is populated with details about the node. A list of optimizers is provided, as well as links to the original Keras library explaining all the parameters required in this frame.

At the very bottom of the **Options** tab, you can constrain the size of the gradient values. If **Clip norm** is checked, the gradients whose L2 norm exceeds the given norm will be clipped to that norm. If **Clip value** is checked, the gradients whose absolute value exceeds the given value will be clipped to that value (or the negated value, respectively).

The **Advanced Options** tab contains a few additional settings for special termination and learning rate reduction cases. The last option allows you to specify which GPU to use on systems with multiple GPUs.

Tracking the Training Progress

After setting all the training parameters, you can start training your network by executing the node. While executing the node, you can check the learning progress in the **Learning Monitor** view. You can open the **Learning Monitor** view by right-clicking on the Keras Network Learner node and selecting **View: Learning Monitor**; see *Figure 4.21*.

By default, the **Learning Monitor** view shows the evolution of the accuracy curve, in red, on the training set after each weight update, which means after a data batch has passed through the network. The accuracy values are reported on the y axis and the progressive number of the batch on the x axis.

Clicking on **Loss** above the line plot shows the loss curve on the training set instead of the accuracy.

More information about the training progress is available in the **Keras Log Output** view. This can be selected in the top part of the Keras Learning node's view, in the last tab after **Accuracy** and **Loss**:

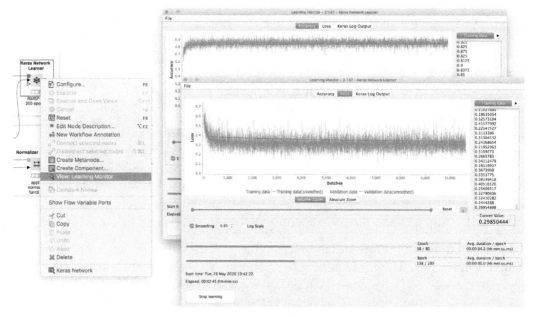

Figure 4.21 – The Learning Monitor view shows the progress of the learning process

> **Tip**
> The **Learning Monitor** view of the Keras Network Learner node allows you to track the learning of your model. You can open it by right-clicking on the executing node and selecting **View: Learning Monitor**.

If you are using a validation set, a blue line appears in the accuracy/loss plot. The blue line shows the corresponding progress of the training procedure on the validation set.

Under the plot, you have the option to zoom in on the x axis – the batch axis – to see the progress after each batch in more detail.

The **Smoothing** checkbox introduces the moving average curve of the original accuracy or loss curve. The **Log Scale** checkbox changes the curve representation to a logarithmic scale for a more detailed evaluation of the training run.

Finally, at the bottom of the view, you can see the **Stop learning** button. This is an option for on-demand early stopping of the training process. If training is stopped before it is finished, the network is saved in the current status.

Training Settings for Iris Flower Classification

For the iris flower classification example based on the Iris dataset, we used the following settings in the Network Learner node.

In the first tab, the **Input Data** tab, the four numerical inputs are selected as the input features. During the data preparation part, we applied no nominal feature encoding on the input features. So, we just feed them as they are into the input layer of the network, by using the **From Number (double)** conversion type.

In the second tab, the **Target Data** tab, the target column is selected. If you remember, during the data preparation part, we integer encoded the class into a collection cell to proceed later with the one-hot encoding conversion. So, we selected the `class_ collection` input column, containing the integer-encoded class as a collection, and we applied the **From Collection of Number (integer) to One-Hot Tensor** conversion. Therefore, during the execution, the Keras Network Learner node creates the one-hot encoding version of the three classes in a three-dimensional vector, as it is also required to match the network output. In the lower part of this second tab, select the **Categorical cross entropy** loss function.

In the third tab, named **Options**, the training parameters are defined. The network is trained using 50 epochs, a training batch size of 5, and the **RMSProp** optimizer.

The settings in the **Advanced Options** tab are left inactive, by default.

Training Settings for Income Prediction

For a multiclass classification problem, such as the income prediction example based on the adult dataset, the settings are a bit different. We used the following settings.

In the first tab, **Input Data**, the **From Number (double)** conversion is selected and the 81 input feature columns are included. Only the target column, `Income`, is in the `Exclude` part. Here, in the data preparation phase, some of the input features were already numerical and have not been encoded, some have been integer encoded, and some have been one-hot encoded via KNIME native nodes. So, all input features are ready to be fed as they are into the network. Notice that, since we decided to mix integer encoding, one-hot encoding, and original features, the only possible encoding applicable to all those different features is a simple **From Number** type of transformation.

Also, in the second tab, **Target Data**, the **From Number (double)** conversion is selected, as the target is just a numerical value: 0 or 1. This also fits the one output from the sigmoid function in the output layer of the network. In the include-exclude frame, only the target column, Income, is included. Next, the **Binary cross entropy** loss function is selected, to fit a binary classification problem such as this one.

In the third tab, **Options**, we set the network to be trained for 80 epochs with a training batch size of 80 data rows. In this example, we also use a validation set, to be able to already see, during training, the network progress on data not included in the training set. For the processing of the validation set, a batch size of 40 data rows is set. Lastly, we select **Adam** as the optimizer for this training process.

Again, the settings in the last tab, **Advanced Options**, are disabled by default.

Testing and Applying the Network

Now that the neural network has been trained, the last step is to apply the network to the test set and evaluate its performance.

Executing the Network

To execute a trained network, you can use the **Keras Network Executor** node, as in *Figure 4.22*. The node has two input ports: a Keras network port for the trained network and a data input port for the test set or new data.

In the first tab of the configuration window, named **Options**, you can select, in the upper part, the backend engine, the batch size for the input data, and whether to also keep the original input columns in the output data table.

Under that, you can specify the input columns and the required conversion. Like in the Keras Network Learner node, the input specifications from the neural network are printed at the top. Remember that, since you are using the same network and the same format for the data, the settings for the input features must be the same as the ones in the Keras Network Learner node.

In the last part of this tab, you can add the settings for the output(s). First, you need to specify where to take the output from; this should be the output layer from the input network. To add one output layer, click on the **add output** button. In the new window, you see a menu containing all layers from the input network. If you configured prefixes in the layer nodes, you could see them in the drop-down menu, making it easier for you to recognize the layer of interest. Select the output layer:

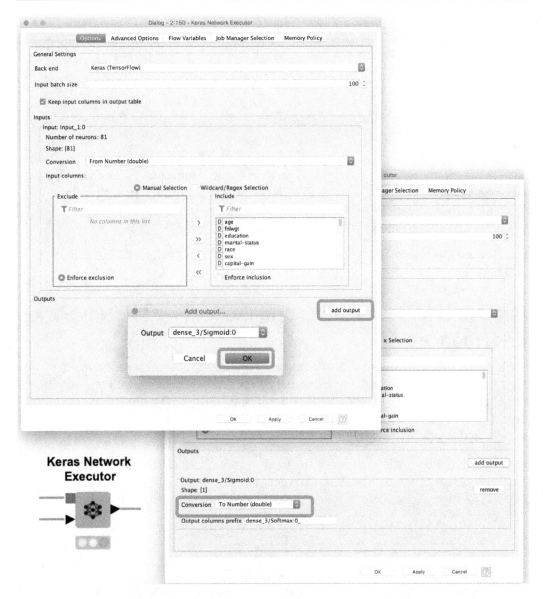

Figure 4.22 – The Keras Network Executor node runs the network on new data. In the configuration window, you can select the outputs by clicking on the add output button

In all use cases included in this book, the last layer of the network is used as the output layer. This layer is easily recognizable, as it is the only one without the **(hidden)** suffix in the drop-down list.

> **Tip**
> You can also output the output of a hidden layer, for example, for debugging purposes.

Finally, select the appropriate conversion type, to get the output values in the shape you prefer – for example, in one cell as a list (**To List of Number (double)**) or with a new column for each output unit (**To Number (double)**). In this last case, you can define a prefix to append to the names of the output columns.

The **Advanced Options** part contains settings to let the network run on GPU-enabled machines.

Extracting the Predictions and Evaluating the Network Performance

Depending on the use case, the network outputs might need some postprocessing to extract the predictions. For example, in a binary classification problem, with one output unit and a sigmoid activation function, the output value is the probability for the class encoded as 1. In this case, to produce the actual class assignment, you could apply a threshold to the probability inside a Rule Engine node.

The last step is the evaluation of the model. To evaluate a classification model, you can use either the **Scorer** node or the **ROC Curve** node. The output of the Scorer node gives you common performance metrics, such as the accuracy, Cohen's kappa, or the confusion matrix.

> **Tip**
> Another really nice node to evaluate the performance for the binary classification problem is the **Binary Classification Inspector** node. The node is part of the KNIME Machine Learning Interpretability Extension: `https://hub.knime.com/knime/extensions/org.knime.features.mli/latest`.

For the evaluation of regression solutions, the **Numeric Scorer** node calculates some error measures, such as mean squared error, root mean squared error, mean absolute error, mean absolute percentage error, mean signed difference, and R-squared.

Testing the Network Trained to Classify Iris Flowers

In *Figure 4.23*, you can see the part of the workflow that applies the trained network, extracts the predictions, and evaluates the network trained to classify iris flowers:

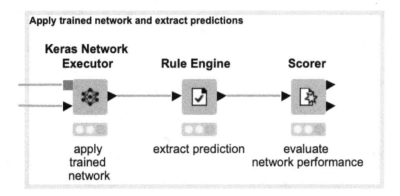

Figure 4.23 – This workflow snippet applies the trained network and extracts
and evaluates the predictions for the iris flower example

In the configuration window of the **Keras Network Executor** node, the four input features are selected as input columns. In the lower part of the **Options** tab, the output layer has been selected by clicking on the **add output** button. As we didn't use any prefixes in the configuration window of the layer nodes, the last layer here is just called "`dense_2/Softmax:0_`", as a **Conversion** type of **To Number (double)** is selected. As the Iris dataset has three different possible class values, the node adds three new columns with the three probabilities for the three classes. Another conversion option is **To List of Number (double)**. This conversion option would lead to only one new column, with all the class probabilities in one cell packaged as a list.

Next, the predictions are extracted with the Rule Engine node. The probabilities for the different classes are in the `$Output_1/Softmax:0_0`for class 0, and `Output_1/Softmax:0_1` columns for class 1, and `Output_1/Softmax:0_2` for class 2. Here, the class with the highest probability is selected as the predicted outcome.

The first rule checks whether the class encoded as 0 has the highest probability by comparing it to the probability for the other two classes. The second rule does the same for the class encoded as 1, and the third rule for the class encoded as 2. The last rule defines a default value.

These rules are applied with the following code:

```
$Output_1/Softmax:0_0$ > $Output_1/Softmax:0_1$ AND $Output_1/
Softmax:0_0$ > $Output_1/Softmax:0_2$ => 0
$Output_1/Softmax:0_1$ > $Output_1/Softmax:0_0$ AND $Output_1/
Softmax:0_1$ >$Output_1/Softmax:0_2$ => 1
$Output_1/Softmax:0_2$ > $Output_1/Softmax:0_0$ AND $Output_1/
Softmax:0_2$ >$Output_1/Softmax:0_1$ => 2
TRUE => 3
```

Lastly, the Scorer node is used to evaluate network performance.

Testing the Network Trained for Income Prediction

The same node combination with different settings can be used to apply the trained network, extract the predictions, and evaluate the model for the income prediction example on the adult dataset.

In the configuration window of the Keras Network Executor node, in the **Options** tab, the 81 input features are included, and the dense_3 output layer is added as the output. In this case, the output of the network is the probability for the class encoded as 1, ">50K".

Finally, the Rule Engine node checks whether the output probability is higher or lower than the 0.5 threshold using the following code:

```
$dense_3/Softmax:0_0$ < 0.5=> "<=50K"
TRUE => ">50K"
```

Lastly, the network performance is evaluated with the Scorer node.

With this, we have gone through the whole process, from data access and data preparation to defining, training, applying, and evaluating a neural network using KNIME Analytics Platform.

Summary

We have reached the end of this chapter, where you have learned how to perform the different steps involved in training a neural network in KNIME Analytics Platform.

We started with common preprocessing steps, including different encodings, normalization, and missing value handling. Next, you learned how to define a neural network architecture by using different Keras layer nodes without writing code. We then moved on to the training of the neural network and you learned how to define the loss function, as well as how you can monitor the learning progress, apply the network to new data, and extract the predictions.

Each section closed with small example sessions, preparing you to perform all these steps on your own.

In the next chapter, you will see how these steps can be applied to the first use case of the book: fraud detection using an autoencoder.

Questions and Exercises

Check your level of understanding of the concepts presented in this chapter by answering the following questions:

1. How can you set the loss function to train your neural network?

    a) By using the Keras Loss Function node

    b) By using the Keras Output Layer node

    c) In the configuration window of the Keras Network Learner node

    d) In the configuration window of the Keras Network Executor node

2. How can you one-hot encode your features?

    a) By using the One Hot Encoding node

    b) By using the One to Many node

    c) By creating an integer encoding using the Category to Number node and afterward, the Integer to One Hot Encoding node

    d) By creating an integer encoding, transforming it into a collection cell, and selecting the right conversion

3. How can you define the number of neurons for the input of your network?

a) By using a Keras Input Layer node.

b) By using a Keras Dense Layer node without any input network.

c) The input dimension is set automatically based on the selected features in the Keras Network Learner node.

d) By using a Keras Start Layer node.

4. How can you monitor the training of your neural network on a validation set?

a) Feed a validation set into the optional input port of the Keras Network Learner node and open the training monitor view. The performance of the validation set is shown in red.

b) Click on the **apply on validation set** button in the training monitor view.

c) Feed a validation set into the optional input port of the Keras Network Learner node and open the training monitor view. The performance of the validation set is shown in blue.

d) Feed a validation set into the optional input port of the Keras Network Learner node and open the validation set tab of the training monitor view. Build a workflow to read the Iris dataset and to train a neural network with one hidden layer (eight units and the ReLU activation function) to distinguish the three species from each other based on the four input features.

Section 2: Deep Learning Networks

Here, we move on to more advanced concepts in neural networks (deep learning) and how to implement them within KNIME Analytics Platform, based on some case studies.

This section comprises the following chapters:

- *Chapter 5, Autoencoder for Fraud Detection*
- *Chapter 6, Recurrent Neural Networks for Demand Prediction*
- *Chapter 7, Implementing NLP Applications*
- *Chapter 8, Neural Machine Translation*
- *Chapter 9, Convolutional Neural Networks for Image Classification*

5
Autoencoder for Fraud Detection

At this point in the book, you should already know the basic math and concepts behind neural networks and some deep learning paradigms, as well as the most useful KNIME nodes for data preparation, how to build a neural network, how to train it and test it, and finally, how to evaluate it. We have built together, in *Chapter 4, Building and Training a Feedforward Neural Network*, two examples of fully connected feedforward neural networks: one to solve a multiclass classification problem on the Iris dataset and one to solve a binary classification problem on the Adult dataset.

Those were two simple examples using quite small datasets, in which all the classes were adequately represented, with just a few hidden layers in the network and a straightforward encoding of the output classes. However, they served their purpose: to teach you how to assemble, train, and apply a neural network in KNIME Analytics Platform.

Now, the time has come to explore more realistic examples and apply more complex neural architectures and more advanced deep learning paradigms in order to solve more complicated problems based sometimes on ill-conditioned datasets. In the following chapters, you will look at some of these more realistic case studies, requiring some more creative solutions than just a fully connected feedforward network for classification.

We will start with a binary classification problem with a dataset that has data from only one of the two classes. Here, the classic classification approach cannot work, since one of the two classes is missing from the training set. There are many problems of this kind, such as anomaly detection to predict mechanical failures or fraud detection to distinguish legitimate from fraudulent credit card transactions.

This chapter investigates an alternative neural approach to design a solution for this extreme situation in fraud detection: the **autoencoder** architecture.

We will cover the following topics:

- Introducing Autoencoders
- Why is Fraud Detection so hard?
- Building and Training the Autoencoder
- Optimizing the Autoencoder Strategy
- Deploying the Fraud Detector

Introducing Autoencoders

In previous chapters, we have seen that neural networks are very powerful algorithms. The power of each network lies in its architecture, activation functions, and regularization terms, plus a few other features. Among the varieties of neural architectures, there is a very versatile one, especially useful for three tasks: detecting unknown events, detecting unexpected events, and reducing the dimensionality of the input space. This neural network is the **autoencoder**.

Architecture of the Autoencoder

The autoencoder (or **autoassociator**) is a multilayer feedforward neural network, trained to reproduce the input vector onto the output layer. Like many neural networks, it is trained using the gradient descent algorithm, or one of its modern variations, against a loss function, such as the **Mean Squared Error** (**MSE**). It can have as many hidden layers as desired. Regularization terms and other general parameters that are useful for avoiding overfitting or for improving the learning process can be applied here as well.

The only constraint on the architecture is that the number of input units must be the same as the number of output units, as the goal is to train the autoencoder to reproduce the input vector onto the output layer.

The simplest autoencoder has only three layers: one input layer, one hidden layer, and one output layer. More complex structured autoencoders might include additional hidden layers:

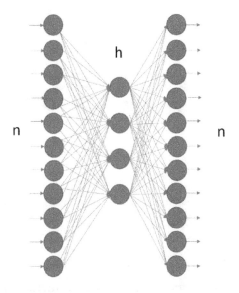

Figure 5.1 – A simple autoencoder

Autoencoders can be used for many different tasks. Let's first see how an autoencoder can be used for dimensionality reduction.

Reducing the Input Dimensionality with an Autoencoder

Let's consider an autoencoder with a very simple architecture: one input layer with n units; one output layer, also with n units; and one hidden layer with h units. If $h < n$, the autoencoder produces a compression of the input vector onto the hidden layer, reducing its dimensionality from n to h.

In this case, the first part of the network, moving the data from a vector with size $[1 \; x \; n]$ to a vector with size $[1 \; x \; h]$, plays the role of the encoder. The second part of the network, reconstructing the input vector from a $[1 \; x \; h]$ space back into a $[1 \; x \; n]$ space, is the decoder. The compression rate is then n/h. The larger the value of n and the smaller the value of h, the higher the compression rate:

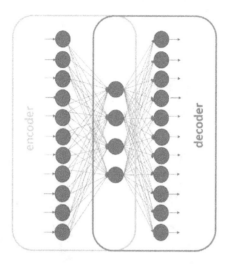

Figure 5.2 – Encoder and decoder subnetworks in a three-layer autoencoder

When using the autoencoder for **dimensionality reduction**, the full network is first trained to reproduce the input vector onto the output layer. Then, before deployment, it is split into two parts: the **encoder** (input layer and hidden layer) and the **decoder** (hidden layer and output layer). The two subnetworks are stored separately.

> **Tip**
>
> If you are interested in the output of the bottleneck layer, you can configure the **Keras Network Executor** node to output the middle layer. Alternatively, you can split the network within the **DL Python Network Editor** node by writing a few lines of Python code.

During the deployment phase, in order to compress an input record, we just pass it through the encoder and save the output of the hidden layer as the compressed record. Then, in order to reconstruct the original vector, we pass the compressed record through the decoder and save the output values of the output layer as the reconstructed vector.

If a more complex structure is used for the autoencoder – for example, with more than one hidden layer – one of the hidden layers must work as the compressor output, producing the compressed record and separating the encoder from the decoder subnetwork.

Now, the question when we talk about data compression is how faithfully can the original record be reconstructed? How much information is lost by using the output of the hidden layer instead of the original data vector? Of course, this all depends on how well the autoencoder performs and how large our error tolerance is.

During testing, when we apply the network to new data, we denormalize the output values and we calculate the chosen error metric – for example, the **Root Mean Square Error** (**RMSE**) – between the original input data and the reconstructed data on the whole test set. This error value gives us a measure of the quality of the reconstructed data. Of course, the higher the compression rate, the higher the reconstruction error. The problem thus becomes to train the network to achieve acceptable performance, as per our error tolerance.

Let's move on to the next application field of autoencoders: anomaly detection.

Detecting Anomalies Using an Autoencoder

In most classification/prediction problems, we have a set of examples covering all event classes and based on this dataset, we train a model to classify events. However, sometimes, the event class we want to predict is so rare and unexpected that no (or almost no) examples are available at all. In this case, we do not talk about classification or prediction but about **anomaly detection**.

An anomaly can be any rare, unexpected, unknown event: a cardiac arrhythmia, a mechanical breakdown, a fraudulent transaction, or other rare, unexpected, unknown events. In this case, since no examples of anomalies are available in the training set, we need to use neural networks in a more creative way than for conventional, standard classification. The autoencoder structure lends itself to such creative usage, as required for the solution of an anomaly detection problem (see, for example, A.G. Gebresilassie, *Neural Networks for Anomaly (Outliers) Detection*, `https://blog.goodaudience.com/` `neural-networks-for-anomaly-outliers-detection-a454e3fdaae8`).

Since no anomaly examples are available, the autoencoder is trained only on non-anomaly examples. Let's call these examples of the "normal" class. On a training set full of "normal" data, the autoencoder network is trained to reproduce the input feature vector onto the output layer.

The idea is that, when required to reproduce a vector of the "normal" class, the autoencoder is likely to perform a decent job because that is what it was trained to do. However, when required to reproduce an anomaly on the output layer, it will hopefully fail because it won't have seen this kind of vector throughout the whole training phase. Therefore, if we calculate the distance – any distance – between the original vector and the reproduced vector, we see a small distance for input vectors of the "normal" class and a much larger distance for input vectors representing an anomaly.

Thus, by setting a threshold, K, we should be able to detect anomalies with the following rule:

IF $\varepsilon_k < K$ THEN $\boldsymbol{x}_k$ -> "normal"

IF $\varepsilon_k \geq K$ THEN $\boldsymbol{x}_k$ -> "anomaly"

Here, ε_k is the reconstruction error for the input vector, $\boldsymbol{x}_k$, and K is the set threshold.

This sort of solution has already been implemented successfully for fraud detection, as described in a blog post, *Credit Card Fraud Detection using Autoencoders in Keras --TensorFlow for Hackers (Part VII)*, by Venelin Valkov (`https://medium.com/@ curiousily/credit-card-fraud-detection-using-autoencoders-in- keras-tensorflow-for-hackers-part-vii-20e0c85301bd`). In this chapter, we will use the same idea to build a similar solution using a different autoencoder structure.

Let's find out how the idea of an autoencoder can be used to detect fraudulent transactions.

Why is Detecting Fraud so Hard?

Fraud detection is a set of activities undertaken to prevent money or property from being obtained through false pretenses. Fraud detection is applied in many industries, such as banking or insurance. In banking, fraud may include forging checks or using stolen credit cards. For this example, we will focus on fraud in credit card transactions.

This kind of fraud, in credit card transactions, is a huge problem for credit card issuers as well as for the final payers. The European Central Bank reported that in 2016, the total number of card fraud cases using cards issued in the **Single Euro Payments Area (SEPA)** amounted to 17.3 million, and the total number of card transactions using cards issued in SEPA amounted to 74.9 billion (`https://www.ecb.europa.eu/pub/cardfraud/ html/ecb.cardfraudreport201809.en.html#toc1`).

However, the amount of fraud is not the only problem. From a data science perspective, fraud detection is also a very hard task to solve, because of the small amount of data available on fraudulent transactions. That is, often we have tons of data on legitimate credit card transactions and just a handful on fraudulent transactions. A classic approach (training, then applying a model) is not possible in this case since the examples for one of the two classes are missing.

Fraud detection, however, can also be seen as anomaly detection. Anomaly detection is any event that is unexpected within a dataset. A fraudulent transaction is indeed an unexpected event and therefore we can consider it an anomaly in a dataset of legitimate *normal* credit card transactions.

There are a few different approaches to fraud detection.

One option is the discriminative approach. Based on a training set with both classes, legitimate and fraudulent transactions, we build a model that distinguishes between data from the two classes. This could be a simple threshold-based rule or a supervised machine learning model. This is the classic approach based on a training set including enough examples from both classes.

Alternatively, you can treat a fraud detection problem as outlier detection. In this case, you can use a clustering algorithm that leaves space for outliers (noise), such as **DBSCAN**; or you can use the **isolation forest technique**, which isolates outliers with just a few cuts with respect to legitimate data. Fraudulent transactions, though, must belong to the original dataset, to be isolated as outliers.

Another approach, called the **generative approach**, involves using only legitimate transactions during the training phase. This allows us to reproduce the input vector onto the output layer. Once the model for the autoencoder has been trained, we use it during deployment to reproduce the input transaction. We then calculate the distance (or error) between the input values and the output values. If that distance falls below a given threshold, the transaction is likely to be legitimate; otherwise, it is flagged as a fraud candidate.

In this example, we will use the credit card dataset by Kaggle. This dataset contains credit card transactions from European cardholders in September 2013. Fraudulent transactions have been labeled with 1, while legitimate transactions are labeled with 0. The dataset contains 284,807 transactions, but only 492 (0.2%) of them are fraudulent. Due to privacy reasons, principal components are used instead of the original transaction features. Thus, each credit card transaction is represented by 30 features: 28 principal components extracted from the original credit card data, the transaction time, and the transaction amount.

Let's proceed with the building, training, and testing of the autoencoder.

Building and Training the Autoencoder

Let's go into detail about the particular application we will build to tackle fraud detection with a neural autoencoder. Like all data science projects, it includes two separate applications: one to train and optimize the whole strategy on dedicated datasets, and one to set it in action to analyze real-world credit card transactions. The first application is implemented with the **training workflow**; the second application is implemented with the **deployment workflow**.

> **Tip**
> Often, training and deployment are separate applications since they work on different data and have different goals.

The training workflow uses a lab dataset to produce an acceptable model to implement the task, sometimes requiring a few different trials. The deployment workflow does not change the model or the strategy anymore; it just applies it to real-world transactions to get fraud alarms.

In this section, we will focus on the training phase, including the following steps:

- **Data Access**: Here, we read the lab data from the file, including all 28 principal components, the transaction amount, and the corresponding time.

- **Data Preparation**: The data comes already clean and transformed via **Principal Component Analysis (PCA)**. What remains doing in this phase is to create all the data subsets required for the training, optimization, and testing of the neural autoencoder and the whole strategy.

- **Building the Neural Network**: An autoencoder is a feedforward neural network with as many inputs as outputs. Let's then decide the number of hidden layers, the number of hidden neurons, and the activation functions in each layer, and then build it accordingly.

- **Training the Neural Autoencoder**: In this part, the autoencoder is trained on a training set of just legitimate transactions with one of the training algorithms (the optimizers), according to the selected training parameters, such as, at least, the loss function, the number of epochs, and the batch size.

- **Rule for Fraud Alarms**: After the network has been trained and it is able to reproduce legitimate transactions on the output layer, we need to complete the strategy by calculating the distance between the input and output layers and by setting a threshold-based rule to trigger fraud alarms.

- **Testing the whole Strategy**: The last step is to test the whole strategy performance. How many legitimate transactions are correctly recognized? How many fraud alarms are correctly triggered and how many are false alarms?

Data Access and Data Preparation

The credit card dataset from Kaggle comes already clean and transformed. We now need to create all the data subsets. Specifically, we need a training and a validation set for the training of the autoencoder. They must consist of only legitimate transactions. The training set is used to train the network and the validation set is used to monitor the performance of the autoencoder on unseen data during training.

Then, we need an additional data subset, the threshold optimization set, to optimize the threshold, K, in the rule-based fraud alarm generator. This last subset should include all fraudulent transactions, in addition to a number of legitimate transactions, as follows:

- 2/3 of all legitimate transactions are dedicated to the autoencoder.
- 90% of those legitimate transactions form the **training set**.
- 10% form the **validation set**.
- 1/3 (96K) of all legitimate transactions and all 492 fraudulent transactions form the **threshold optimization set**, used to optimize the value of threshold K.

This all translates into one **Row Splitter** node to separate legitimate transactions from fraudulent transactions, one **Concatenate** node to add back the fraudulent transactions into the threshold optimization set, and a number of **Partitioning** nodes. All data extraction in the Partitioning nodes is performed at random:

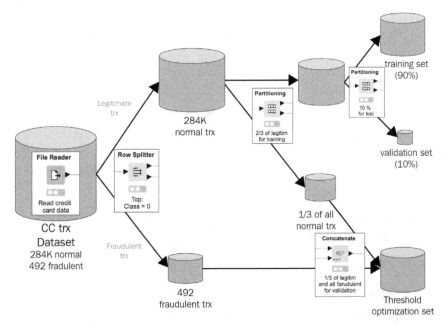

Figure 5.3 – The datasets used in the fraud detection process

> **Important note**
>
> The training set, validation set, and threshold optimization set must be completely separated. No records can be shared across any of the subsets. This is to ensure a meaningful performance measure during evaluation and an independent optimization procedure.

Next, all data in each subset must be normalized to fall in $[0,1]$. Normalization is defined on the training set and applied to the other two subsets. The normalization parameters are also saved for the deployment workflow using the **Model Writer** node:

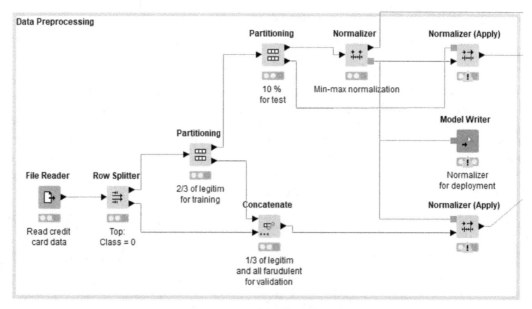

Figure 5.4 – The workflow implementing data preparation for fraud detection

The workflow in *Figure 5.4* shows how the creation of the different datasets and the normalization can be performed in KNIME Analytics Platform.

Building the Autoencoder

For this case study, we built an autoencoder with five hidden layers, with 30-40-20-8-20-40-30 units, and sigmoid as the activation function.

The neural network was built using the following (see *Figure 5.5*):

- The **Keras Input Layer** node with Shape = 30

- Five **Keras Dense Layer** nodes to implement the hidden layers, using sigmoid as the activation function and 40, 20, 8, 20, and 40 units, respectively

- The **Keras Dense Layer** node for the output layer, with 30 units and sigmoid as the activation function:

Figure 5.5 – Structure of the neural autoencoder trained to reproduce credit card transactions from the input layer onto the output layer

Now that we've built the autoencoder, let's train and test it using the data.

Training and Testing the Autoencoder

To train and validate the network, we use the **Keras Network Learner** node, with the training set and the validation set at the input ports, and the following settings (*Figure 5.6*):

- The number of epochs is set to 50, the batch size for the training and validation set is set to 300, and the **Adam** (an optimized version of backpropagation) training algorithm is used, in the **Options** tab.

- The loss function is set to be the MSE in the **Target** tab.

- The target and input features are the same in the **Input** tab and in the **Target** tab and are accepted as simple **Double** numbers.

In the **Loss** tab of the **Learning Monitor** view of the Keras Network Learner node, you can see two curves now: one is the mean loss (or error) per training sample in a batch (in red) and the other one is the mean loss per sample on the validation data (in blue).

At the end of the training phase, the final mean loss value fell in around [0.0012, 0016] for batches from the training set and in [0.0013, 0.0018] for batches from the validation set. The calculated loss is the mean reconstruction error for one batch, calculated by the following formula:

$$E = \frac{1}{N}\frac{1}{n}\sum_{k=1}^{N}\sum_{i=1}^{n}(y_{ik} - \hat{y}_{ik})^2$$

Here, N is the batch size, n is the number of units on the output layer, y_{ik} is the output value of neuron i in the output layer for training sample k, and $\hat{y}_{ik}$ is the corresponding target answer.

After training, the network is applied to the optimization set, using the **Keras Network Executor** node, and it is saved for deployment as a Keras file using the **Keras Network Writer** node.

Figure 5.6 shows the configuration for the **Options** tab in the Keras Network Executor node: all 30 input features are passed as **Double** numbers and the input columns are kept so that the reconstruction error can be calculated later on. The last layer is selected as the output and the values are exported as simple **Double** numbers:

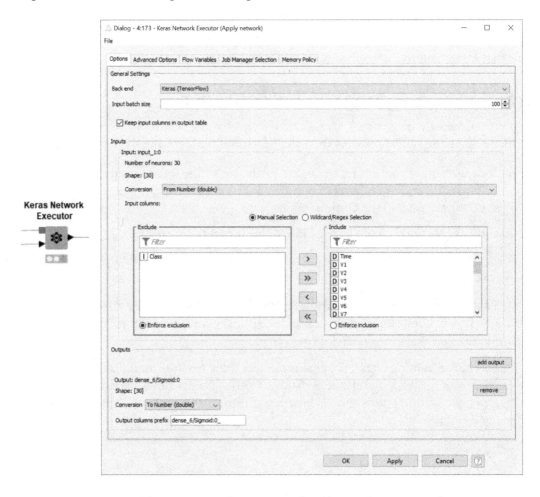

Figure 5.6 – The Keras Network Executor node and its configuration window

The next step is to calculate the distance between the original feature vector and the reproduced feature vector, and to apply a threshold, K, to discover fraud candidates.

Detecting Fraudulent Transactions

When the model training is finished, the autoencoder has learned how to reproduce feature vectors representing legitimate transactions onto the output layer. How can we now spot suspicious transactions? If we have a new transaction, x_k, how can we tell whether it is a suspicious or a legitimate one?

First, we run this new transaction, x_k, through the autoencoder via the Keras Network Executor node. The reproduction of the original transaction is generated at the output layer. Now, a reconstruction error, ε_k, is calculated, as the distance between the original transaction vector and the reproduced one. A transaction is then considered a fraud candidate according to the following rule:

IF $\varepsilon_k < K$ THEN x_k ->   "legitimate trx"

IF $\varepsilon_k \geq K$ THEN x_k -> "fraud candidate trx"

Here, ε_k is the reconstruction error value for transaction x_k and K is a threshold. The MSE was also adopted for the reconstruction error:

$$\varepsilon_k = \frac{1}{n} \sum_{i=1}^{n} (y_{ik} - x_{ik})^2$$

Here, x_{ik} is the ith feature of transaction x_k, and y_{ik} is the corresponding value on the output layer of the network.

ε_k is calculated via a **Math Formula** node, and the previous rule is implemented via a **Rule Engine** node, assuming, for now, threshold K to be 0.02. 1 is the fraud candidate class and 0 is the legitimate transaction class. A **Scorer (Javascript)** node finally calculates some performance metrics for the whole approach: 83.64% accuracy, with 83.60% specificity and 99.95% sensitivity on class 1. Specificity is the ratio between the number of true legitimate transactions and all transactions that did not raise any alarm. Sensitivity, on the opposite side, measures the ratio of fraud alarms that actually hit a fraudulent transaction.

Specificity produces a measure of the frauds we might have missed, while sensitivity produces a measure of the frauds we hit:

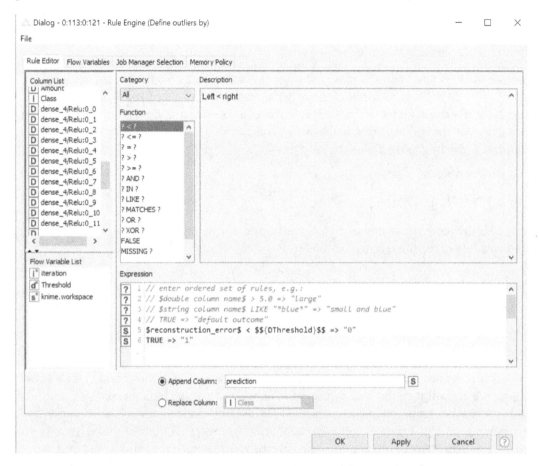

Figure 5.7 – The rule implemented in the Rule Engine node, comparing reconstruction error with threshold

Now that our model is trained and tested, it needs to be optimized.

Optimizing the Autoencoder Strategy

What is the best value to use for threshold K? In the last section, we adopted $K = 0.02$ based on our experience. However, is this the best value for K? Threshold K, in this case, is not automatically optimized via the training procedure. It is just a static parameter external to the training algorithm. In KNIME Analytics Platform, it is also possible to optimize static parameters outside of the **Learner** nodes.

Optimizing Threshold *K*

Threshold *K* is defined on a separate subset of data, called the **optimization set**. There are two options here:

- If an optimization set with labeled fraudulent transactions is available, the value of threshold *K* is optimized against any accuracy measure for fraud detection.

- If no labeled fraudulent transactions are available in the dataset, the value of threshold *K* is defined as a high percentile of the reconstruction errors on the optimization set.

During the data preparation phase, we generated three data subsets: the training set and validation set for the Keras Network Learner node to train and validate the autoencoder, and one last subset, which we called the threshold optimization set. This final subset includes 1/3 of all the legitimate transactions and the handful of fraudulent transactions. We can use this subset to optimize the value of threshold *K* against the accuracy of the whole fraud detection strategy.

To optimize a parameter means to find the value within a range that maximizes or minimizes a given measure. Based on our experience, we assume the value of *K* to be a positive number (> 0) and to lie below 0.02. So, to optimize the value of threshold *K* means to find the value in [0.001, 0.02] that maximizes the accuracy of the whole application.

The accuracy of the application is calculated via a Scorer (JavaScript) node, considering the results of the Rule Engine node as the predictions and comparing them with the original class (0 = legitimate transaction, 1 = fraudulent transaction) in the optimization set.

The spanning of the value interval and the identification of the threshold value for the maximum accuracy is performed by an **optimization loop**. Every loop in KNIME Analytics Platform is implemented via two nodes: a loop start node and a loop end node. In the optimization loop, these two nodes are the **Parameter Optimization Loop Start** node and the **Parameter Optimization Loop End** node.

The **Parameter Optimization Loop Start** node spans parameter values in a given interval with a given step size. Interval [0.001, 0.02] and step size 0.001 have been chosen here based on the range of the reconstruction error feature, as shown in the **Lower Bound** and **Upper Bound** cells in the **Spec** tab of the data table at the output port of the Math Formula node, named **MSE input-output distance**, after the Keras Network Executor node.

The **Parameter Optimization Loop End** node collects all results as flow variables, detects the best (maximum or minimum) value for the target measure, and exports it together with the parameter that generated it. In our case, the target measure is the accuracy, measured on the predictions from the Rule Engine node, which must be maximized against values for threshold *K*.

All nodes in between the loop start and the loop end make the body of the loop – that is, the part that gets repeated as many times as needed until the input interval of parameter values has all been covered. In the loop body, we add the additional constraint that the optimal accuracy should be found only for those parameters where the specificity and sensitivity are close in value. This is the goal of the metanode named `Coefficient 0/1`. Here, if the specificity and sensitivity are more than 10% apart, the coefficient is set to `0`, otherwise to `1`. This coefficient then multiplies the overall accuracy coming from the Scorer (JavaScript) node. In this way, the maximum accuracy is detected only for those cases where the specificity and sensitivity are close to each other:

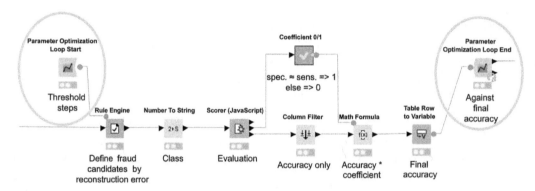

After extracting the optimal threshold, we transform it into a flow variable and pass it to the final rule implementation.

Wrapping up into a Component

Now, this whole threshold optimization part seems to be a logical self-contained block. To keep our workflow clean and proper, we could wrap this block inside a metanode. Even better, we could make sure that the wrapping is close and tight via a stronger type of metanode: the **component**.

> **Tip**
>
> A metanode just collects and packages nodes. A component, on the other hand, collects and packages nodes together and, in addition, inherits the views of contained Widget and JavaScript nodes and the configuration windows of contained Configuration nodes. Even further, a component does not allow external flow variables to enter or internal flow variables to exit unless specifically defined.

A component is created in a similar way to a metanode. Just select the nodes to group together, right-click, and select **Create Component...**. When a component is created, its context (right-click) menu offers a number of commands to open, expand, modify via setup, and share it. To inspect the content of a component, just *Ctrl* + double-click the component. Once inside, you can see two nodes: **Component Input** and **Component Output**. In the configuration window of these two nodes, you can set the flow variables to import inside and export outside of the component, respectively.

In the component we created, we set up the **Component Output** node to export the flow variable containing the value for the optimal threshold. This flow variable needs to exit the component to be used in the final rule for fraud detection. The final rule is implemented in a new Rule Engine node and the final predictions are evaluated against the original classes in a new Scorer (JavaScript) node.

The final workflow to train and test the neural autoencoder using credit card transaction data and to implement the fraud detection rule with the optimal threshold is shown in *Figure 5.9*. The workflow, named `01_Autoencoder_for_Fraud_Detection_Training`, is downloadable from the KNIME Hub: `https://hub.knime.com/kathrin/spaces/Codeless%20Deep%20Learning%20with%20KNIME/latest/Chapter%205/`:

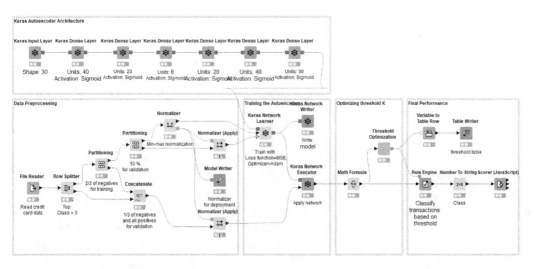

Figure 5.9 – The workflow to train and test the autoencoder and to find the optimal threshold, K

Now that we have found the best threshold, let's have a look at the performance of the autoencoder.

Performance Metrics

In this section, we report the performance measures of this approach on the threshold optimization set after applying the fraud detection rule. The optimal threshold value was found to be $K = 0.003$ for an accuracy of 93.52%.

In *Figure 5.10*, you can see the **confusion matrix**, the class statistics based on it, and the general performance measures, all of them describing how well the fraud detector is performing on the optimization set:

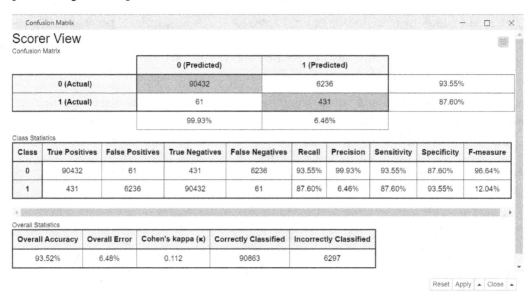

Figure 5.10 – Performance metrics of the final fraud detector with optimized threshold K

Let's consider class 1 (fraud) as the positive class. The high number of false positives (6,236) shows the weakness of this approach: it is prone to generating false positives. In other words, it tends to label perfectly legitimate transactions as fraud candidates. Now, there are case studies where false positives are not a huge problem, and this is one of those. In the case of a false positive, the price to pay is to send a message to the credit card owner about the current transaction. If the message turns out to be useless, the damage is not much compared to the possible risk. Of course, this tolerance does not apply to all case studies. A false positive in medical diagnosis carries a much heavier responsibility than a wrong fraud alarm in a credit card transaction.

> **Important note**
>
> The whole process could also be forced to lean more toward fraud candidates or legitimate transactions, by introducing an expertise-based bias in the definition of threshold K.

In general, the autoencoder captures 87% of the fraudulent transactions and 93% of the legitimate transactions in the validation set, for an overall accuracy of 85% and a Cohen's kappa of 0.112. Considering the high imbalance between the number of normal and fraudulent transactions in the validation set (96,668 versus 492), the results are still promising.

Notice that this false positive-prone approach is a desperate solution for a case study where no, or almost no, examples from one of the classes exist. A supervised classifier on a training set with labeled examples would probably reach better performances. But this is the data we have to deal with!

We have now trained the autoencoder and found the best threshold for our rule system. We will see, in the next section, how to deploy it in the real world on real data.

Deploying the Fraud Detector

At this point, we have an autoencoder network and a rule with acceptable performance for fraud detection. In this section, we will implement the **deployment** workflow.

The deployment workflow (*Figure 5.11*), like all deployment workflows, takes in new transaction data, passes it through the autoencoder, calculates the distance, applies the fraud detection rule, and finally, flags the input transaction as fraud or legitimate.

This workflow, named `02_Autoencoder_for_Fraud_Detection_Deployment`, is downloadable from the KNIME Hub: `https://hub.knime.com/kathrin/spaces/Codeless%20Deep%20Learning%20with%20KNIME/latest/Chapter%205/`:

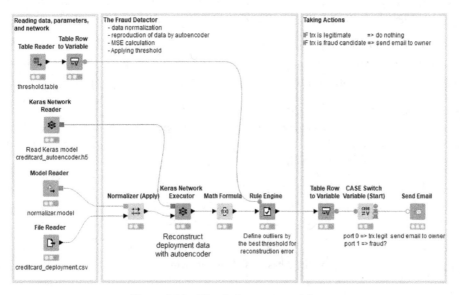

Figure 5.11 – The deployment workflow

Let's have a look at the different parts of the workflow in detail.

Reading Network, New Transactions, and Normalization Parameters

In this workflow, first the autoencoder model is read from the previously saved Keras file, using the **Keras Network Reader** node.

At the same time, data from some new credit card transactions are read from the file using the **File Reader** node. This particular file contains two new transactions.

The transactions are normalized with the same parameters built on the training data and previously saved in the file named `normalizer model`. These normalization parameters are read from the file using the **Model Reader** node.

The last file to read contains the value of the optimized threshold, K.

Applying the Fraud Detector

Transaction data is fed into the autoencoder network and reproduced on the output layer with the Keras Network Executor node.

Afterward, the MSEs between the original features and the reconstructed features for each transaction are calculated using the **Math Formula** node.

The Rule Engine node applies the threshold, K, as defined during the optimization phase, to detect possible fraud candidates.

The following table shows the reconstruction errors for the two transactions and the consequent class assignment. The application (autoencoder and distance rule) defines the first transaction as legitimate and the second transaction as a fraud candidate:

CC Trx #	Reconstruction Error	Prediction
Trx 1	0.0026	$0.0026 < 0.003 \Rightarrow 0$ (legit)
Trx 2	0.0110	$0.0110 \geq 0.003 \Rightarrow 1$ (fraud)

Figure 5.12 – Reconstruction errors and fraud class assignment for credit card transactions in the dataset used for deployment

Taking Actions

In the last part of the workflow, we need to take action:

- IF transaction is legitimate (class 0) => do nothing
- IF transaction is fraud candidate (class 1) => send message to owner to confirm

IF-THEN conditions involving actions are implemented in KNIME Analytics Platform via switch blocks. Similar to loops, switch blocks have a start node and an end node. The end node in switch blocks is optional, however. The switch start node activates only one of the output ports, enabling de facto only one possible further path for the data flow. The switch end node collects the results from the different branches. The most versatile switch block is the **CASE switch** in all its declinations: for data, flow variables, or models.

The active port, and then the active branch, is controlled via the configuration window of the **Switch CASE Start** node. This configuration setting is usually controlled via a flow variable, whose values enable one or the other output each time.

In our case, we have two branches. The upper branch is connected to port 0, activated by class 0, and performs nothing. The second branch is connected to port 1, activated by class 1, and sends an email to the owner of the credit card.

We conclude here the section on the implementation of the autoencoder-based strategy for fraud detection.

Summary

In this chapter, we discussed approaches for building a fraud detector for credit card transactions in the desperate case when no, or almost no, examples of the fraud class are available. This solution trains a neural autoencoder to reproduce legitimate transactions from the input onto the output layer. Some postprocessing is necessary to set an alarm for the fraud candidate based on the reconstruction error.

In describing this solution, we have introduced the concept of training and deployment applications, components, optimization loops, and switch blocks.

In the next chapter, we will discuss a special family of neural networks, so-called recurrent neural networks, and how they can be used to train neural networks for sequential data.

Questions and Exercises

Check your level of understanding of the concepts presented in this chapter by answering the following questions:

1. What is the goal of an autoencoder during training?

    a) To reproduce the input to the output

    b) To learn an automatic encoding

    c) To encode the training data

    d) To train a network that can distinguish between two classes

2. What are common use cases for autoencoders?

    a) Time series prediction

    b) Anomaly detection

    c) Multiclass classification problems

    d) Regression problems

3. How can an autoencoder be used for dimensionality reduction?

    a) By training a network with an output layer with less number than input layers

    b) By training an autoencoder and extracting only the encoder

    c) By building an autoencoder and extracting only the decoder

    d) By building a network with more hidden neurons than the input and output layers

6
Recurrent Neural Networks for Demand Prediction

We have gathered some experience, by now, with fully connected feedforward neural networks in two variants: implementing a classification task by assigning an input sample to a class in a set of predefined classes or trying to reproduce the shape of an input vector via an autoencoder architecture. In both cases, the output response depends only on the values of the current input vector. At time t, the output response, $y(t)$, depends on, and only on, the input vector, $x(t)$, at time t. The network has no memory of what came before $x(t)$ and produces $y(t)$ only based on input $x(t)$.

With **Recurrent Neural Networks** (**RNNs**), we introduce the time component t. We are going to discover networks where the output response, $y(t)$, at time t depends on the current input sample, $x(t)$, as well as on previous input samples, $x(t-1)$, $x(t-2)$, ... $x(t-n)$, where the memory of the network of the past n samples depends on the network architecture.

We will first introduce the general concept of RNNs, and then the specific concept of **Long Short-Term Memory (LSTM)** in the realm of a classic time series analysis task: **demand prediction**. Then, we will show how to feed the network with not only static vectors, $x(t)$, but also sequences of vectors, such as $x(t)$, $x(t-1)$, $x(t-2)$, ... $x(t-n)$, spanning n samples of the past input signal. These sequences of input vectors (tensors) built on the training set are used to train and evaluate a practical implementation of an LSTM-based RNN.

In summary, this chapter will cover the following topics:

- Introducing RNNs
- The Demand Prediction Problem
- Data Preparation – Creating the Past
- Building, Training, and Deploying an LSTM-Based RNN

Introducing RNNs

Let's start with an overview of RNNs.

RNNs are a family of neural networks that cannot be constrained in the feedforward architecture.

> **Important note**
> RNNs are obtained by introducing auto or backward connections – that is, recurrent connections – into feedforward neural networks.

When introducing a recurrent connection, we introduce the concept of time. This allows RNNs to take context into account; that is, to remember inputs from the past by capturing the dynamic of the signal.

Introducing recurrent connections changes the nature of the neural network from static to dynamic and is therefore suitable for analyzing time series. Indeed, RNNs are often used to create solutions to problems involving time-ordered sequences, such as time series analysis, language modeling, free text generation, automatic machine translation, speech recognition, image captioning, and other similar problems investigating the time evolution of a given signal.

Recurrent Neural Networks

As stated in the previous section, the introduction of an auto or backward connection into a feedforward network transforms it into an RNN. For example, let's consider the simple feedforward network depicted in *Figure 6.1*, looking at its detailed representation on the left and its compact representation on the right:

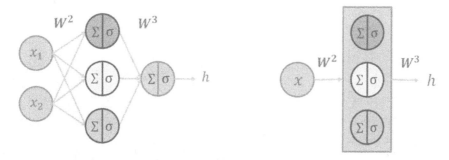

Figure 6.1 – A simple fully connected feedforward network on the left and its more compact matrix-based representation on the right

The compact representation of the network in *Figure 6.1* includes one multi-dimensional input, x, one possibly multi-dimensional output, h, one hidden layer represented by the box containing the neuron icons, and the two weight matrixes from the input to the hidden layer, W^2, and from the hidden to the output layer, W^3.

Let's now introduce to this network a recurrent connection, feeding the output vector, h, back into the input layer in addition to the original input vector, x (*Figure 6.2*). This simple change to the network architecture changes the network behavior. Before, the function implemented by the network was just $h(t) = f(x(t))$, where t is the current time when the input sample, x, is presented to the network. Now, the function implemented by the recurrent network assumes the shape $h(t) = f(x(t), h(t-1))$; that is, the current output depends on the current input, as well as on the output produced in the previous step for the previous input sample. We have introduced the concept of time:

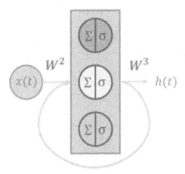

Figure 6.2 – Adding a recurrent connection to the feedforward network

Thanks to these recurrent connections, the output of RNNs also contains a bit of the history of the input signal. We then say that they have memory. How far in the past the memory span goes depends on the recurrent architecture and the paradigms contained in it. For this reason, RNNs are more suitable than feedforward networks for analyzing sequential data, because they can also process information from the past. Past input information is metabolized via the output feedback into the input layer through the recurrent connection.

The problem now becomes how to train a network where the output depends on the previous output(s) as well. As you can imagine, a number of algorithms have been proposed over the years. The simplest one, and therefore the most commonly adopted, is **Back Propagation Through Time (BPTT)** (Goodfellow I, Bengio Y., Courville A., *Deep Learning*, MIT Press, (2016)).

BPTT is based on the concept of *unrolling* the network over time. To understand the concept of *unrolling*, let's take a few glimpses at the network at different times, t, during training:

- At time t, we have the original feedforward network, with weight matrixes W^2 and W^3, input $x(t)$ and $h(t-1)$, and output $h(t)$.

- At time $t+1$, we again have the original feedforward network, with weight matrixes W^2 and W^3, but this time with input $x(t+1)$ and $h(t)$ and output $h(t+1)$.

- At time $t+2$, again, we have the original feedforward network, with weight matrixes W^2 and W^3, but this time with input $x(t+2)$ and $h(t+1)$ and output $h(t+2)$.

- This continues for the n samples in the input sequence.

Practically, we can copy the same original feedforward network with static weight matrixes W^2 and W^3 n times, which is as many n samples as in the input sequence (*Figure 6.3*). Each copy of the original network at time t will have the current input vector, $x(t)$, and the previous output vector, $h(t-1)$, as input. More generically, at each time t, the network copy will produce an output, $y(t)$, and a related state, $s(t)$. The state, $s(t)$, is the network memory and feeds the next copy of the static network, while $h(t)$ is the dedicated output of each network copy. In some recurrent architectures, $h(t)$ and $s(t)$ are identical.

Let's summarize. We have a recurrent network with the following features:

- Fed by input tensor $x(t)$, of $[n, m]$ size, consisting of a sequence of n m-dimensional vectors

- Producing an output tensor, $h(t)$, of $[l, k]$ size, consisting of a sequence of l k-dimensional vectors

- Producing a state tensor, $s(t)$, related to output tensor $h(t)$, used as the network memory

> **Important note**
>
> This recurrent network can also be just a sub-network that is a hidden unit in a bigger neural architecture. In this case, it is fed by the outputs of previous layers, and its output forms the input to the next layers in the bigger network. Then, $h(t)$ is not the output of the whole network, but just the output of this recurrent unit – that is, an intermediate hidden state of the full network.

In *Figure 6.3*, we propose the unrollment over four time steps of the simple recurrent network in *Figure 6.2*:

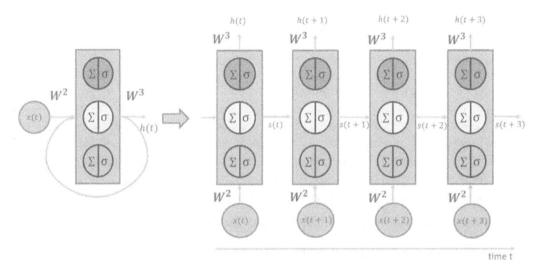

Figure 6.3 – Unrolling a recurrent network though time

At this point, we have transformed the recurrent sub-network into a sequence of n copies of the original feedforward network – that is, into a much larger static feedforward network. As large as it might be, we do already know how to train fully connected feedforward networks with the backpropagation algorithm. So, the backpropagation algorithm has been adapted to include the unrolling process and to train the resulting feedforward network. This is the basic BPTT algorithm. Many variations of the BPTT algorithm have also been proposed over the years.

We will now dive into the details of the simplest recurrent network, the one made of just one layer of recurrent units.

Recurrent Neural Units

The simplest recurrent neural unit consists of a network with just one single hidden layer, with activation function $tanh()$, with an auto connection. Using the same unrolling-over-time process, we can represent this unit as n copies of a feedforward network with one hidden layer of just one unit (*Figure 6.4*):

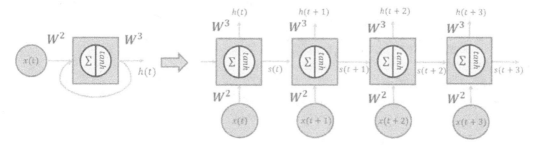

Figure 6.4 – The simplest recurrent neural unit

In this case, the output, $h(t)$, is also the state of the network, which is fed back into the input – that is, into the input of the next copy of the unrolled network at time $t + 1$.

This simple recurrent unit already shows some memory, in the sense that the current output also depends on previously presented samples at the input layer. However, its architecture is a bit too simple to show a considerable memory span. Of course, it depends on the task to solve how long of a memory span is needed. A classic example is sentence completion.

To complete a sentence, you need to know the topic of the sentence, and to know the topic, you need to know the previous words in the sentence. For example, analyzing the sentence *Cars drive on the* …, we realize that the topic is *cars* and then the only logical answer would be *road*. To complete this sentence, we need a memory of just four words. Let's now take a more complex sentence, such as *I love the beach. My favorite sound is the crashing of the* …. Here, many answers are possible, including *cars*, *glass*, or *waves*. To understand which is the logical answer, we need to go back in the sentence to the word *beach*, which is nine words backward. The memory span needed to analyze this sentence is more than double the memory span needed to analyze the previous sentence. This short example shows that sometimes a longer memory span is needed to give the correct answer.

The simple recurrent neural unit provides some memory, but often not enough to solve most required tasks. We need something more powerful that can crawl backward farther in the past than just what the simple recurrent unit can do. This is exactly why LSTM units were introduced.

Long Short-Term Memory

LSTM was introduced for the first time in 1997 (Hochreiter, Sepp and Schmidhuber, Jürgen (1997), *Long Short-term Memory. Neural computation, 9.* 1735-80. 10.1162/ neco.1997.9.8.1735, `https://www.researchgate.net/` `publication/13853244_Long_Short-term_Memory`). It is a more complex type of recurrent unit, using an additional hidden vector, the cell state or memory state, $s(t)$, and the concept of gates.

Figure 6.5 shows the structure of an unrolled LSTM unit (C. Olah, *Understanding LSTM Networks*, 2015, `https://colah.github.io/posts/2015-08-` `Understanding-LSTMs/`):

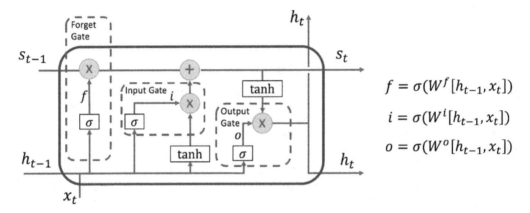

$$f = \sigma(W^f[h_{t-1}, x_t])$$

$$i = \sigma(W^i[h_{t-1}, x_t])$$

$$o = \sigma(W^o[h_{t-1}, x_t])$$

Figure 6.5 – LSTM layer

As you can see, the different copies of the unit are connected by two hidden vectors. The one on the top is the cell state vector, $s(t)$, used to make information travel through the different unit copies. The second one on the bottom is the output vector of the unit.

Next, we have the gates, three in total. Gates can open or close (or partially open/close) and, in this way, they make decisions on what to store or delete from a hidden vector. A gate consists of a sigmoid function and a pointwise multiplication. Indeed, the sigmoid function takes values in [0,1]. Specifically, $\sigma = 0$ removes the input (forgets it), while $\sigma = 1$ lets the input pass unaltered (remembers it). In between $\sigma = 0$ and $\sigma = 1$, a variety of nuances of remembering and forgetting are possible.

The weights of these sigmoid layers, which implement the gates, are adjusted via the learning process. That is, the gates learn when to allow data to enter, leave, or be deleted through the iterative process of making guesses, backpropagating error, and adjusting weights via gradient descent. The training algorithm for LSTM layers is again an adaptation of the backpropagation algorithm.

An LSTM layer contains three gates: a forget gate, an input gate, and an output gate (*Figure 6.5*). Let's have a closer look at these gates.

The Forget Gate

The first gate from the left, the **forget gate**, filters the components from the cell state vector. Based on the values in the current input vector, $x(t)$ and in the output vector of the previous unit, $h(t-1)$, the gate produces a forget or remember decision, as follows:

$$f(t) = \sigma\big(W^f[h(t-1), x(t)]\big)$$

Here, W^f is the weight matrix of the forget gate.

The vector of decision $f(t)$ is then pointwise multiplied by the hidden cell state vector, $s(t-1)$, to decide what to remember ($\sigma = 1$) and what to forget ($\sigma = 0$) from the previous state.

The question now is why do we want to forget? If LSTM units have been introduced to obtain a longer memory, why should we need to forget something? Take, for example, analyzing a document in a text corpus; you might need to forget all knowledge about the previous document since the two documents are probably unrelated. Therefore, with each new document, the memory should be reset to 0.

Even within the same text, if you move to the next sentence and the subject of the text changes, and with the new subject a new gender appears, then you might want to forget the gender of the previous subject, to be ready to incorporate the new one and to adjust the corresponding part of speech accordingly.

The Input Gate

The goal of the input gate is more straightforward: it keeps the input information that is new and useful. Here, again, a sigmoid gate lets input components pass completely ($\sigma = 1$), blocks them completely ($\sigma = 0$), or something in between depending on their importance to the final, current, and future outputs.

This decision is implemented again as follows:

$$i(t) = \sigma\big(W^i[h(t-1), x(t)]\big)$$

This is done with a new set of weights, W^i, of course.

The input gate doesn't operate on the previous cell state, $s(t-1)$, directly. Instead, a new cell state candidate, $\tilde{s}(t)$, is created, based on the values in the current input vector, $x(t)$, and in the output vector of the previous unit, $h(t-1)$, using a tanh layer.

This looks as follows:

$\tilde{s}(t) = tanh(W^s[h(t-1), x(t)])$

Again, this is with another set of weights, W^s.

The input gate now decides which information of the cell candidate state vector, $\tilde{s}(t)$, should be added to the cell state vector, $s(t)$. Therefore, the candidate state, $\tilde{s}(t)$, is multiplied pointwise by the output of the sigmoid layer of the input gate, $i(t)$, and then added to the filtered cell state vector, $f(t) * s(t-1)$. The final state, $s(t)$, then results in the following:

$$s(t) = f(t) * s(t-1) + i(t) * \tilde{s}(t)$$

What have we done here? We have added new content to the previous cell state vector, $s(t)$. Let's suppose we want to look at a new sentence in the text where $x(t)$ is a subject with a different gender. In the forget gate, we forgot about the gender previously stored in the cell state vector. Now, we need to fill in the void and push the new gender into memory – that is, into the new cell state vector.

The Output Gate

Finally, the output gate! We have the new cell state, $s(t)$, to pass to the next copy of the unit; we just need to output something for this current time, t.

Again, like all other gates, the output gate applies a sigmoid function to all components of the input vector, $x(t)$, and of the previous output vector, $h(t-1)$, in order to decide what to block and what to pass from the newly created state vector, $s(t)$, into the final output vector, $h(t)$. All decisions, $o(t)$, are then pointwise multiplied by the newly created state vector, $s(t)$, previously normalized through a $tanh()$ function to fall in $[-1, 1]$:

$o(t) = \sigma(W^o[h(t-1), x(t)])$

$h(t) = o(t) * tanh(s(t))$

This is with a new set of weights, W^o, for this output gate.

In this case, the output vector, $h(t)$, and the state vector, $s(t)$, produced by the LSTM recurrent unit are different, $h(t)$ being a filtered version of $s(t)$.

Why do we need a different output from the unit cell state? Well, sometimes the output needs to be something different from the memory. For example, while the cell state is supposed to carry the memory of the gender to the next unit copy, the output might be required to produce the number, plural or singular, of the subject rather than its gender.

LSTM layers are a very powerful recurrent architecture, capable of keeping the memory of a large number of previous inputs. These layers thus fit – and are often used to solve – problems involving ordered sequences of data. If the ordered sequences of data are sorted based on time, then we talk about time series. Indeed, LSTM-based RNNs have been applied often and successfully to time series analysis problems. A classic task to solve in time series analysis is demand prediction. In the next section, we will explore an application of LSTM-based neural networks to solve a demand prediction problem.

The Demand Prediction Problem

Let's continue then by exploring a demand prediction problem and how it can be treated as a time series analysis problem.

Demand prediction is a task related to the need to make estimates about the future. We all agree that knowing what lies ahead in the future makes life much easier. This is true for life events as well as, for example, the prices of washing machines and refrigerators, or demand for electrical energy in an entire city. Knowing how many bottles of olive oil customers will want tomorrow or next week allows for better restocking plans in retail stores. Knowing of a likely increase in the demand for gas or diesel allows a trucking company to better plan its finances. There are countless examples where this kind of knowledge of the future can be of help.

Demand Prediction

Demand prediction, or demand forecasting, is a big branch of data science. Its goal is to make estimations about future demand using historical data and possibly other external information. Demand prediction can refer to any kind of numbers: visitors to a restaurant, generated kW/h, school new registrations, beer bottles, diaper packages, home appliances, fashion clothing and accessories, and so on. Demand forecasting may be used in production planning, inventory management, and at times in assessing future capacity requirements, or in making decisions on whether to enter a new market.

Demand prediction techniques are usually based on time series analysis. Previous values of demand for a given product, goods, or service are stored and sorted over time to form a time series. When past values in the time series are used to predict future values in the same time series, we are talking about autoregressive analysis techniques. When past values from other external time series are also used to predict future values in the time series, then we are talking about multi-regression analysis techniques.

Time series analysis is a field of data science with a lot of tradition, as it already offers a wide range of classical techniques. Traditional forecasting techniques stem from statistics and their top techniques are found in the **Autoregressive Integrated Moving Average (ARIMA)** model and its variations. These techniques require the assumption of a number of statistical hypotheses, are hard to verify, and are often not realistic. On the other hand, they are satisfied with a relatively small amount of past data.

Recently, with the growing popularity of **machine learning** algorithms, a few data-based regression techniques have also been applied to demand prediction problems. The advantages of these machine learning techniques consist of the absence of required statistical hypotheses and less overhead in data transformation. The disadvantages consist of the need for a larger amount of data. Also, notice that in the case of time series where all required statistical hypotheses are verified, traditional methods tend to perform better.

Let's try to predict the next m values in the time series based on the past n values. When using a machine learning model for time series analysis, such as, for example, linear regression or a regression tree, we need to supply the vector of the past n samples as input to train the model to predict the next m values. While this strategy is commonly implemented and yields satisfactory results, it is still a static approach to time series analysis – **static** in the sense that each output response depends only on the corresponding input vector. The order of presentation of input samples to the model does not influence the response. There is no concept of an input sequence, but just of an input vector.

Tip

KNIME Analytics Platform offers a few nodes and standard components to deal with time series analysis. The key node here is the **Lag Column** node to build a vector of past samples. In addition to the Lag Column node, a number of components dedicated to time series analysis are available in the EXAMPLES/00_Components/Time Series folder in the **KNIME Explorer** panel. These components use the KNIME GUI to run the statsmodels Python module in the background. Because of that, they require the installation of the KNIME Python integration (https://www.knime.com/blog/setting-up-the-knime-python-extension-revisited-for-python-30-and-20).

In *Figure 6.6*, you can see the list of available components for time series analysis tasks within KNIME Analytics Platform:

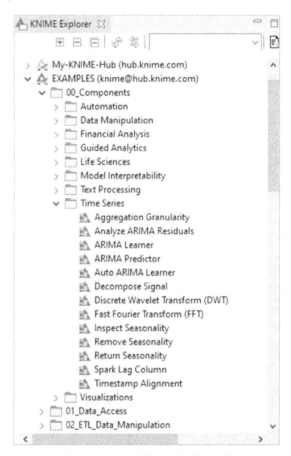

Figure 6.6 – The EXAMPLES/00_Components/Time Series folder contains components dedicated to time series analysis

All things considered, these machine learning-based strategies, using regression models, do not fully exploit the sequential structure of the data, where the fact that $x(t)$ comes after $x(t-1)$ carries some additional information. This is where RNNs, and particularly LSTMs, might offer an edge on the other machine learning algorithms, thanks to their internal **memory**.

Let's now introduce the case study for this chapter: predicting energy demand in **kilowatts (kW)** needed by the hour.

Predicting Energy Demand

As an example of demand prediction, we want to tackle the problem of electrical energy prediction – that is, of predicting the number of kW needed in the next hour by an average household consumer.

One of the hardest problems in the energy industry is matching supply and demand. On the one hand, over-production of energy can be a waste of resources; on the other hand, under-production can leave people without the basic commodities of modern life. The prediction of electrical energy demand at each point in time is therefore a very important topic in data science.

For this reason, a couple of years ago energy companies started to monitor the electricity consumption of each household, store, or other entity, by means of smart meters. A pilot project was launched in 2009 by the Irish **Commission for Energy Regulation** (**CER**).

The Smart Metering Electricity **Customer Behaviour Trials** (**CBTs**) took place between 2009 and 2010 with over 5,000 Irish homes and businesses participating. The purpose of the trials was to assess the impact on consumers' electricity consumption, in order to inform the cost-benefit analysis for a national rollout. Electric Ireland residential and business customers and Bord Gáis Energy business customers who participated in the trials had an electricity smart meter installed in their homes or on their premises and agreed to take part in the research to help establish how smart metering can help shape energy usage behaviors across a variety of demographics, lifestyles, and home sizes.

The original dataset contains over 5,000 time series, each one measuring the electricity usage for each installed smart meter for a bit over a year. All original time series have been aligned and standardized to report energy measures by the hour.

The final goal is to predict energy demand across all users. At this point, we have a dilemma: should we train one model for each time series and sum up all predictions to get the demand in the next hour or should we train one single model on all time series to get the global demand for the next hour?

Training one model on a single time series is easier and probably more accurate. However, training 5,000 models (and probably more in real life) can pose a few technical problems. Training one single model on all time series might not be that accurate. As expected, a compromise solution was implemented. Smart energy meters have been clustered based on energy usage profile, and the average time series of hourly energy usage for each cluster has been calculated. The goal now is to calculate the energy demand in the next hour for each clustered time series, weight it by the cluster size, and then sum up all contributions to find the final total energy demand for the next hour.

Thirty smart meter clusters have been detected based on the energy used on business days versus the weekend, at different times over the 24 hours, and the average hourly consumption.

More details on this data preparation procedure can be found in the *Data Chef ETL Battles. What can be prepared with today's data? Ingredient Theme: Energy Consumption Time Series* blog post, available at `https://www.knime.com/blog/EnergyConsumptionTimeSeries`, and in the *Big Data, Smart Energy, and Predictive Analytics* whitepaper, available at `https://files.knime.com/sites/default/files/inline-images/knime_bigdata_energy_timeseries_whitepaper.pdf`.

The final dataset contains 30 time series of average energy usage by the 30 clusters. Each time series shows the electrical profile of a given cluster of smart meters: from stores (high energy consumption from 9 a.m. to 5 p.m. on business days) to nightly business customers (high energy consumption from 9 p.m. to 6 a.m. every day), from family households (high energy consumption from 7 a.m. to 9 a.m. and then again from 6 p.m. to 10 p.m. every business day) to other unclear entities (using energy across 24 hours on all 7 days of the week). For example, cluster 26 refers to stores (*Figure 6.7*). Here, electrical energy is used mainly between 9 a.m. and 5 p.m. on all business days:

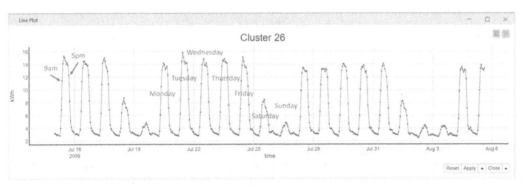

Figure 6.7 – Plot of energy usage by the hour for cluster 26

On the opposite side, cluster 13 includes a number of restaurants (*Figure 6.8*), where the energy usage is pushed to the evening, mainly from 6 p.m. to midnight, every day of the week:

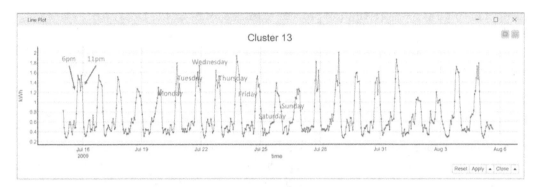

Figure 6.8 – Plot of energy usage by the hour for cluster 13

Notice that cluster 26 is the poster child for time series analysis, with a clear seasonality on the 24 hours in a day and the 7 days of the week series. In this chapter, we will continue with an autoregressive analysis of cluster 26's time series. The goal will be to predict the average energy usage in the next hour, based on the average energy usage in the past n hours, for cluster 26.

Now that we have a set of time series describing the usage of electrical energy by the hour for clusters of users, we will try to perform some predictions of future usage for each cluster. Let's focus first on the data preparation for this time series problem.

Data Preparation – Creating the Past

Let's now implement in practice a demand prediction application, using the time series for cluster 26. Again, we will have two separate workflows: one to train the LSTM-based RNN and one to deploy it in production. Both applications will include a data preparation phase, which must be exactly the same for both. In this section, we will go through this data preparation phase.

Dealing with **time series**, the **data preparation** steps are slightly different from what is implemented in other classification or clustering applications. Let's go through these steps:

- **Data loading**: Read from the file the time series of the average hourly used energy for the 30 identified clusters and the corresponding times.

- **Date and time standardization**: Time is usually read as a string from the file. To make sure that it is processed appropriately, it is best practice to transform it into a **Date&Time** object. A number of nodes are available to deal with Date&Time objects in an appropriate and easy way, but especially in a standardized way.

- **Timestamp alignment**: Once the time series has been loaded, we need to make sure that its sampling has been consistent with no time holes. Possible time holes need to be filled with missing values. We also need to make sure that the data of the time series has been time-sorted.

- **Partitioning**: Here, we need to create a training set to train the network and a test set to evaluate its performance. Differently from classification problems, here we need to respect the time order so as not to mix the past and future of the time series in the same set. Past samples should be reserved for the training set and future samples for the test set.

- **Missing value imputation**: Missing value imputation for time series is also different from missing value imputation in a static dataset. Since what comes after depends on what was there before, most techniques of missing value imputation for time series are based on previous and/or the following sample values.

- **Creating the input vector of past samples**: Once the time series is ready for analysis, we need to build the tensors to feed the network. The tensors must consist of n past samples that the network will use to predict the value for the next sample in time. So, we need to produce sequences of n past m-dimensional vectors (the n past samples) for all training and test records.

- **Creating the list to feed the network**: Finally, the input tensors of past samples must be transformed into a list of values, as this is the input format required by the network.

Let's start with data loading.

Data Loading and Standardization

The dataset is read from a **CSV** file via the **File Reader** node: 30 time series and one date column. The date column is imported by the File Reader node as a string and must be converted into a Date&Time object to make sure it is processed – for example, sorted – appropriately in the next steps. **Date&Time** is the internal standard object to represent date and time entities in KNIME Analytics Platform. In order to convert a string into a Date&Time object, we use the **String to Date&Time** node:

Figure 6.9 – The String to Date&Time node and its configuration window

In the configuration window (*Figure 6.9*), you must select the string input columns containing the date and/or time information and define the date/time format. You can do this manually, by providing a string format – for example, as dd.mm.yyyy, where dd indicates the day, mm the month, and yyyy the year.

For example, if you have date format of day(2).month(2).year(4), you can manually add the option dd.MM.yyyy, if this is not available in the **Date format** options. When manually adding the date/time type, you must select the appropriate **New type** option: **Date or Time** or **Date&time**.

Alternatively, you can provide the date/time format automatically, by pressing the **Guess data type and format** button. With this last option, KNIME Analytics Platform will parse your string to find out the date/time format. It works most of the time! If it does not, you can always revert to manually entering the date/time format.

> **Tip**
> In the node description of the **String to Data&Time** node, you can find an overview of possible placeholders in the format structures. The most important ones are **y** for year, **M** for month in year, **d** for day of month, **H** for hour of day (between 0 and 23), **m** for minute of hour, and **s** for second of minute. Many more placeholders are supported – for example, **W** for week of month or **D** for day of year.

The String to Date&Time node is just one of the many nodes that deals with Date&Time objects, all contained in the **Other Data Types/Time Series** folder in the **Node Repository** panel. Some nodes manipulate Date&Time objects, such as, for example, to calculate a time difference or produce a time shift; other nodes are used to convert Date&Time objects from one format to another.

After that, the Column Filter node is inserted to isolate the time series for cluster 26 only. The only required standardization here was about the date conversion from a string to a Date&Time object. We can now move on to data cleaning.

Data Cleaning and Partitioning

The **Timestamp Alignment** component is inserted to check for time holes in the time series. This component checks whether the selected timestamp column is uniformly sampled in the selected time scale. Missing values will be inserted at skipped sampling times. In this case, it checks whether the **rowID** column, containing the timestamps, has missing sampling times considering an hourly sampling rate.

The Timestamp Alignment component is part of the time series-dedicated component set available in EXAMPLES/00_Components/Time Series. To create an instance in your workflow, just drag and drop it into the workflow editor or double-click it.

After that, we partition the data into a training set and test set, to train the LSTM-based RNN and evaluate it. We have not provided an additional validation set here to evaluate the network performance throughout the training process. We decided to keep things simple and just provide a training set to the Keras Network Learner node and a test set to measure the error on the time series prediction task:

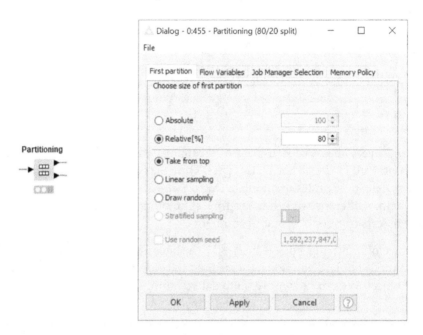

Figure 6.10 – The Partitioning node and its configuration window. Notice the Take from top data extraction mode for time series analysis

To separate the input dataset into training and test sets, we use again a **Partitioning** node. Here, we decided to implement an 80%–20% split: 80% of the input data will be directed toward training and 20% toward testing. In addition, we set the extraction procedure to **Take from top** (*Figure 6.10*). In a time series analysis problem, we want to keep the intrinsic time order of the data: we use the past to train the network and the future to test it. When using the **Take from top** data extraction option, the top percentage of the data is designated to the top output port, while the remaining at the bottom to the lower output port. If the data is time-sorted from past to future, then this data extraction modality preserves the time order of the data.

> **Important note**
>
> In a time series analysis problem, partitioning should use the **Take from top** data extraction modality, in order to preserve the time order of the data and use the past for training and the future for testing.

As for every dataset, the operation for missing value imputation is an important one; first, because neural networks cannot deal with missing values and second, because choosing the right missing value imputation technique can affect your final results.

> **Important note**
>
> Missing value imputation must be implemented after the Timestamp Alignment component since this component, by definition, creates missing values.

In *Chapter 4, Building and Training a Feedforward Network*, we already introduced the **Missing Value** node and its different strategies to impute missing values. Some of these strategies are especially useful when it comes to sequential data, as they take the previous and/or following values in a time series into account. Possible strategies are as follows:

- **Average/linear interpolation**, replacing the missing value with the average value of previous and next sample
- **Moving average**, replacing the missing value with the mean value of the sample window
- **Next**, replacing the missing value with the value of the next sample
- **Previous**, replacing the missing value with the value of the previous sample

We went for linear interpolation between the previous and next values to impute missing values in the time series (*Figure 6.11*):

Figure 6.11 – The Missing Value node and its configuration window

The formula to use for missing value imputation is calculated in the **Missing Value** node on the training data, applied to the test data with the **Missing Value (Apply)** node, and saved to a file through the Model Writer node. The pure application on the test set of the formula defined on the training set prevents the test data from interfering with the implementation of any transformation required for model training.

Let's focus next on the creation of input tensors for the neural network.

Creating the Input Tensors

We have read the data, converted the date cells into Date&Time objects, isolated the time series for cluster 26, assigned missing values to missing sampling steps, partitioned the data into 80% for the training set and 20% for the test set, applied a linear interpolation between previous and next value for missing value imputation. The data is ready, it is now time to create the input tensors for the neural network.

> **Important note**
> A key node to create vectors of past samples that is so often needed in time series analysis is the Lag Column node.

Figure 6.12 shows the Lag Column node and its configuration window:

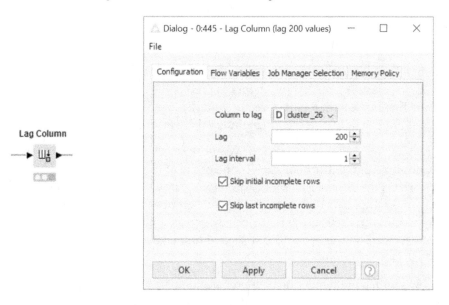

Figure 6.12 – The Lag Column node and its configuration window

The **Lag Column** node makes copies of the selected column and shifts them down a number, i, of cells, where $i = 1$, k, $2k$, $3k, ..., nk$ cells, where k is the lag interval and n is the **Lag** setting in the configuration window.

The Lag Column node is a very simple yet very powerful node that comes in handy in a lot of situations. If the input column is time-sorted, then shifting down the cells corresponds to moving them into the past or the future, depending on the time order.

In *Figure 6.13*, we explain this concept:

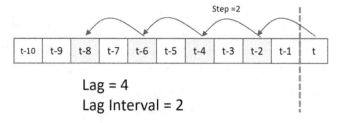

Figure 6.13 – The Lag Column node takes snapshots of the same column at different times, as defined by the Lag and Lag interval settings

Considering Lag = 4 and Lag Interval = 2, the Lag Column node produces four copies of the selected column, each copy moving backward with a step of 2. That is, besides the selected column at current time t, we will also have four snapshots of the same column at time t-2, t-4, t-6, and t-8 (*Figure 6.13*).

For our demand prediction problem, we used the values for the average energy used by cluster 26 in the immediate 200 past hours to predict the average energy need at the current hour. That is, we built an input vector with the 200 immediate past samples, using a Lag Column node with Lag=200 and Lag Interval=1 (*Figure 6.12*).

For space reasons, we then transformed the vector of cells into a collection of cells using the **Column Aggregator** node, as it is one of the possible formats to feed the neural network via the Keras Network Learner node. The Column Aggregator node is another way to produce **lists** of data cells. The node groups the selected columns per row and aggregates their cells using the selected aggregation method. In this case, the **List** aggregation method was selected and applied to the 200 past values of cluster 26, as created via the Lag Column node.

The workflow snippet, implementing data preparation part to feed the upcoming RNN for the demand prediction problem, is shown in *Figure 6.14*:

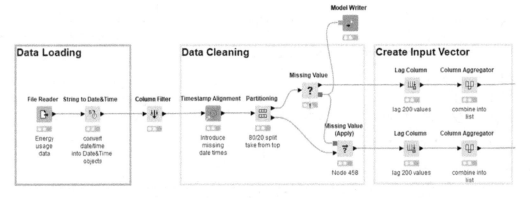

Figure 6.14 – Data preparation for demand prediction: date and time standardization, time alignment, missing value imputation, creating the input vector of past samples, and partitioning

The data is ready. Let's now build, train, and test the LSTM-based RNN to predict the average demand of electrical energy for cluster 26 at the current hour given the average energy used in the previous 200 hours by the same cluster 26.

Building, Training, and Deploying an LSTM-Based RNN

Let's proceed with the next step: building a simple LSTM-based RNN for demand prediction. First, we will train the network, then we will test it, and finally, we will deploy it. In this case study, we used no validation set for the network and we performed no optimization on the static hyperparameters of the network, such as, for example, the size of the LSTM layer.

A relatively simple network is already achieving good error measures on the test set for our demand prediction task, and therefore, we decided to focus this section on how to test a model for time series prediction rather than on how to optimize the static parameters of a neural network. We looked at the optimization loop in *Chapter 5, Autoencoder for Fraud Detection*. In general, this optimization loop can also be applied to optimize network hyperparameters. Let's begin by building an LSTM-based RNN.

Building the LSTM-Based RNN

For this case study, we went for the simplest possible LSTM-based RNN: an RNN with just one hidden LSTM layer. So, the final network consists of the following:

- One input layer accepting tensors of 200 past vectors – each past vector being just the previous sample, that is, with size 1 – obtained through a Keras Input Layer node with Shape = 200, 1.

- One hidden layer with 100 LSTM units, accepting the previous tensor as the only input, through the **Keras LSTM Layer** node

- A classic dense layer as output with just one neuron producing the predicted value for the next sample in the time series, obtained through the Keras Dense Layer node with the ReLU activation function.

The nodes used to build this neural architecture are shown in *Figure 6.15*:

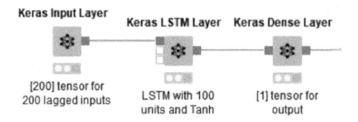

Figure 6.15 – Building a very basic, very simple LSTM-based RNN

> **Important note**
>
> The size of the input tensor was [200,1], which is a sequence of 200 1-sized vectors. If the length of the input sequence is not known, we can use *?* to indicate unknown sequence length. The NLP case studies in the next chapter will show you some examples of this.

We have already described the Keras Input Layer node and the Keras Dense Layer node in previous chapters. Let's explore, in this section, just the Keras LSTM Layer node.

> **Important note**
>
> Until now, we have used the term vector when we've talked about the input, the cell state, and the output. A tensor is a more generalized form, representing a vector stretching along k-dimensions. A rank 0 tensor is equal to a scalar value, a rank 1 tensor is equal to a vector, and a rank 2 tensor is equal to a matrix.

Notice that the Keras LSTM Layer node accepts up to three input tensors: one with the input values of the sequence and two to initialize the hidden state tensors, $s(t)$ and $h(t)$.

If the previous neural layer produces more than one tensor as output, in the configuration window of the current LSTM layer, via a drop-down menu, you can select which tensor should be used as input or to initialize the hidden states.

We will explore more complex neural architectures in the next chapters. Here, we have limited our architecture to the simplest classic LSTM layer configuration, accepting just one input tensor from the input layer. The one input tensor accepted as input can be seen in the configuration window of the LSTM Layer node in *Figure 6.16*:

Keras LSTM Layer

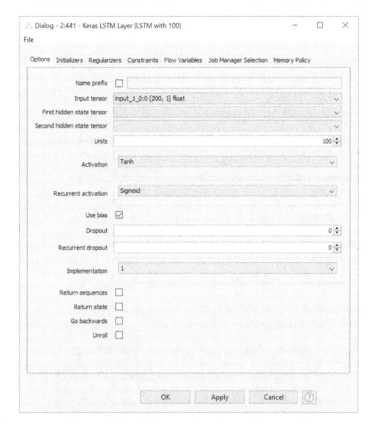

Figure 6.16 – The Keras LSTM Layer node and its configuration window

For the LSTM layer, we can set two activation functions, called **Activation** and **Recurrent activation**. The **Recurrent activation** function is used by the gates to filter the input components. The function selected as **Activation** is used to create the candidates for the cell state, $\tilde{s}(t)$, and to normalize the new cell state, $s(t)$, before applying the output gate. This means that for the standard LSTM unit, which we introduced in this chapter, the setting for **Activation** is the tanh function and for **Recurrent activation** the sigmoid function.

We set the layer to add biases to the different layers of the LSTM unit but decided to not use the dropout.

The **Implementation** and **Unroll** setting options don't have any impact on the results but can improve the performance depending on your hardware and the sequence length. When activating the **Unroll** checkbox, the network will be unrolled before training, which can speed up the learning process, but it is memory-expensive and only suitable for short input sequences. If unchecked, a so-called symbolic loop is used in the TensorFlow backend.

You can choose whether to return the intermediate output tensors $[h(t + 1), h(t + 2), ..., h(t + n)]$ as a full sequence or just the last output tensor, $h(t + n)$ (the **Return sequences** option). In addition, you can also output the hidden cell state tensor as output (the **Return state** option). In the energy demand prediction case study, only the final output tensor of the LSTM unit is used to feed the next dense layer with the ReLU activation function. Therefore, the two checkboxes are not activated.

The other three tabs in the node configuration window set the regularization terms, initialization strategies, and constraints on the learning algorithm. We set no regularizations and no constraints in this layer. Let's train this network.

Training the LSTM-Based RNN

The Keras Network Learner node then follows to train this LSTM-based RNN on the training set. We know about this node already. Let's summarize the specs used in its configuration window for this case study here:

- The input tensor is accepted with conversion to **From Collection of Number (double)**.

- The output vector is produced with conversion to **Number (double)**.

- The loss function is set to **Mean Squared Error (MSE)** in the **Target** tab.

- The number of epochs is set to 50, the training batch size to 256, and the training algorithm to **Adam** – an optimized version of backpropagation – in the **Options** tab.

- The learning rate is set to be 0.001 with no learning rate decay.

For this network, with just one neuron in the output layer, the MSE loss function on a training batch takes on a simpler form and becomes the following:

$$E = \frac{1}{N} \sum_{k=1}^{N} (y_k - \hat{y}_k)^2$$

Here, N is the batch size, y_k is the output value for training sample k, and $\hat{y}_k$ is the corresponding target answer.

Since we are talking about number prediction and MSE as the loss function, the plot in the **Loss** tab of the **Learning Monitor** view is the one to take into account to evaluate the learning process. Since we are trying to predict exact numbers, the accuracy is not meaningful in this case. *Figure 6.17* shows the **Learning Monitor** view of the Keras Network Learner node for this demand prediction example:

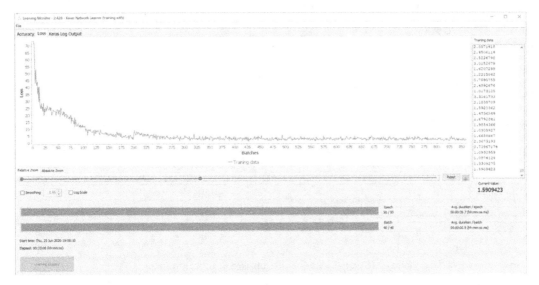

Figure 6.17 – Plot of the MSE loss function over training epochs in the Loss tab of
the Learning Monitor view

The screenshot in *Figure 6.17* shows that after just a few batch training iterations, we reach an acceptable prediction error, at least on the training set. After training, the network should be applied to the test set, using the **Keras Network Executor** node, and saved for deployment as a Keras file using the **Keras Network Writer** node.

Let's now apply the trained LSTM network to the test set.

Testing the LSTM-Based RNN

In theory, to test the performance of the network, we just need to apply the network to the input tensors in the test set. This is easily done with a **Keras Network Executor** node.

Figure 6.18 shows the inside of the **In-sample testing** component:

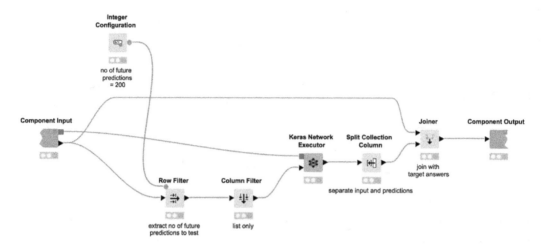

Figure 6.18 – Inside of the In-sample testing component

The In-sample testing component selects the number of input sequences to test on (the **Row Filter** node), then passes them through the **Keras Network Executor** node, and joins the predictions with the corresponding target answers.

After that, and outside of the **In-sample testing** component, the **Numeric Scorer** node calculates some error metrics and the **Line Plot (Plotly)** node shows the original time series and the reconstructed time series (final workflow in *Figure 6.25*). The numeric error metrics quantify the error, while the line plot gives a visual idea of how faithful the predictions are. Predictions generated with this approach are called **in-sample** predictions.

The Numeric Scorer node calculates six error metrics (*Figure 6.19*): R^2, **Mean Absolute Error (MAE)**, MSE, **Root Mean Squared Error (RMSE)**, **Mean Signed Difference (MSD)**, and **Mean Absolute Percentage Error (MAPE)**. The corresponding formulas are shown here:

$$R^2 = 1 - \frac{\sum_{k=1}^{N}(y_k - \hat{y}_k)^2}{\sum_{k=1}^{N}(y_k - \overline{y})^2}$$

$$MAE = \frac{1}{N}\sum_{k=1}^{N}|y_k - \hat{y}_k|$$

$$MSE = \frac{1}{N}\sum_{k=1}^{N}(y_k - \hat{y}_k)^2$$

$$RMSE = \sqrt{\frac{1}{N}\sum_{k=1}^{N}(y_k - \hat{y}_k)^2}$$

$$MSD = \frac{1}{N}\sum_{k=1}^{N}(y_k - \hat{y}_k)$$

$$MAPE = \frac{1}{N}\sum_{k=1}^{N}\frac{|y_k - \hat{y}_k|}{|y_k|}$$

Here, N is the number of predictions from the test set, y_k is the output value for the test sample k, and $\hat{y}_k$ is the corresponding target answer. We chose to apply the network on a test set of 600 tensors, generated the corresponding predictions, and calculated the error metrics. This is the result we got:

△ Statis... — □ ✕	
File	
R²:	0.968
Mean absolute error:	0.529
Mean squared error:	0.645
Root mean squared error:	0.803
Mean signed difference:	0.02
Mean absolute percentage error:	0.093

Figure 6.19 – Error measures between in-sample predicted 600 values and
the corresponding target values

Each metric has its pros and cons. Commonly adopted errors for time series predictions are MAPE, MAE, or MSE. MAPE, for example, shows just 9% error on the next 600 values of the predicted time series, which is a really good result. The plot in *Figure 6.20* proves it:

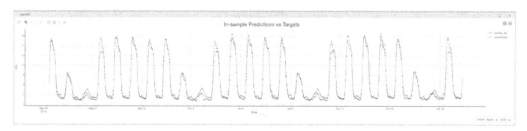

Figure 6.20 – The next 600 in-sample predicted values against the next 600 target values
in the time series

This is an easy test. For each value to predict, we feed the network with the previous history of real values. This is a luxury situation that we cannot always afford. Often, we predict the next 600 values, one by one, based just on past predicted values. That is, once we have trained the network, we trigger the next prediction with the first 200 real past values in the test set. After that, however, we predict the next value based on the latest 199 real values plus the currently predicted one; then again based on the latest 198 real values plus the previously predicted one and the currently predicted one, and so on. This is a suboptimal, yet more realistic, situation. Predictions generated with this approach are called **out-sample** predictions and this kind of testing is called out-sample testing.

To implement out-sample testing, we need to implement the loop that feeds the current prediction back into the vector of past samples. This loop has been implemented in the deployment workflow as well. Let's have a look at the details of this implementation.

Building a Deployment Loop

To implement out-sample testing, we need to implement the loop described in the previous section, where the currently predicted value becomes part of the tensor of past values for the next prediction. This is done in the component named **Deployment Loop** (*Figure 6.21*), which is also inside the out-sample testing component in the final workflow (*Figure 6.25*):

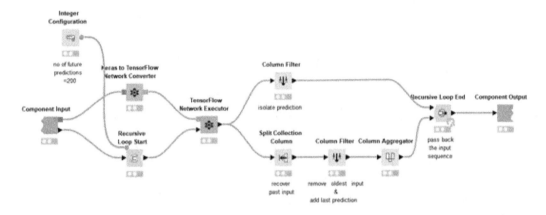

Figure 6.21 – The deployment loop. Notice the recursive loop to pass back
the new input sequence at each iteration

Here, a **recursive loop**, formed by a **Recursive Loop Start** node and a **Recursive Loop End** node, predicts, at each iteration, the next value and forms the new input sequence for the network, by eliminating the oldest sample and adding the latest prediction. The **Recursive Loop Start** node requires no configuration, while the **Recursive Loop End** node requires the ending condition for the loop. We parameterized this ending condition (600 predictions) through the flow variable, named no_preds, created in the **Integer Configuration** node (no_preds=600).

The Integer Configuration node belongs to a special group of configuration nodes, so its configuration window transfers into the configuration window of the component that contains it. As a consequence, the **Deployment Loop** component has a configuration setting for the number of predictions to create with the recursive loop, as shown in *Figure 6.22*:

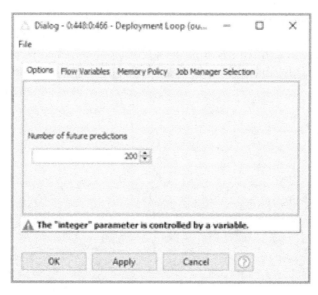

Figure 6.22 – The configuration window of the Deployment Loop component

> **Important note**
> The recursive loop is one of the few loops in KNIME Analytics Platform that allows you to pass the results back to be consumed in the next iteration.

The **Deployment Loop** component uses two more new important nodes:

- **The Keras to TensorFlow Network Converter node**: The Keras to TensorFlow Converter node converts a Keras deep learning model with a TensorFlow backend into a TensorFlow model. TensorFlow models are executed using the TensorFlow Java API, which is usually faster than the Python kernel available via the Keras Python API. If we use the Keras Network Executor node within the recursive loop, a Python kernel must be started at each iteration, which slows down the network execution. A TensorFlow model makes the network execution much faster.

- **The TensorFlow Network Executor node**: The configuration window of the TensorFlow Network Executor node is similar to the configuration window of the Keras Network Executor node, the only difference being the backend engine, which in this case is TensorFlow.

For out-sample testing, the deployment loop is triggered with the first tensor in the test set and from there it generates 600 predictions autonomously. In the out-sample testing component, these predictions are then joined with the target values and outside of the out-sample testing component, the Numeric Error node calculates the selected error metrics.

Obviously, for out-sample testing, the error values become larger (*Figure 6.23*), since the prediction error is influenced by the prediction errors in the previous steps. MAPE, for example, reaches 18%, which is practically double the result from in-sample testing:

Statis... — ☐ ✕	
File	
R²:	0.836
Mean absolute error:	0.939
Mean squared error:	3.309
Root mean squared error:	1.819
Mean signed difference:	0.245
Mean absolute percentage error:	0.178

Figure 6.23 – Error measures between the out-sample predicted 600 values and
the corresponding target values

In *Figure 6.24*, we can see the prediction error when visualizing the predicted time series and comparing it with the original time series for the first 600 out-sample predictions:

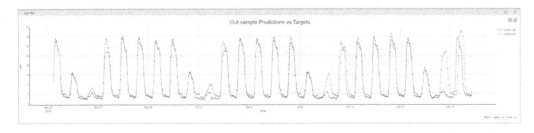

Figure 6.24 – The next 600 out-sample predicted values (orange) against the next 600
target values (blue) in the time series

There, we can see that the first predictions are quite correct, but they start deteriorating the further we move from the onset of the test set. This effect is, of course, not present for in-sample predictions. Indeed, the error values on the first out-sample predictions are comparable to the error values for the corresponding in-sample predictions.

We have performed here a pretty crude time series prediction since we have not taken into account the seasonality prediction as a separate problem. We have somehow let the network manage the whole prediction by itself, without splitting seasonality and residuals. Our results are satisfactory for this use case. However, for more complex use cases, the seasonality index could be calculated, the seasonality subtracted, and predictions performed only on the residual values of the time series. Hopefully, this would be an easier problem and would lead to more accurate predictions. Nevertheless, we are satisfied with the prediction error, especially considering that the network had to manage the prediction of the seasonality as well.

The final workflow, building, training, and in-sample testing the network, is shown in *Figure 6.25*:

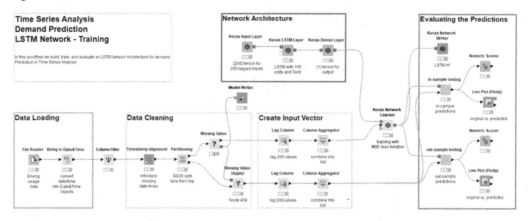

Figure 6.25 – The final workflow to prepare the data and build, train, and test the LSTM-based network on a time series prediction problem

This workflow is available in the book's GitHub space. Let's now move on to the deployment workflow.

Deploying the LSTM-Based RNN

Deployment at this point is easy. We read the deployment data, for example, from a `.table` file; then, we apply the same data preparation steps as for the training and test data. We isolate the first input sequence with 200 past samples; we apply the deployment loop to generate n new samples (here, we went for $n = 670$); we apply the trained LSTM-based RNN inside the deployment loop; and finally, we visualize the predictions with a Line Plot (Plotly) node. Notice that this time there are no predictions versus target values, since the deployment data is real-world data and not lab data, and as such does not have any target values to be compared to.

The deployment workflow is shown in *Figure 6.26* and is available on KNIME Hub at `https://hub.knime.com/kathrin/spaces/Codeless%20Deep%20Learning%20with%20KNIME/latest/Chapter%206/`:

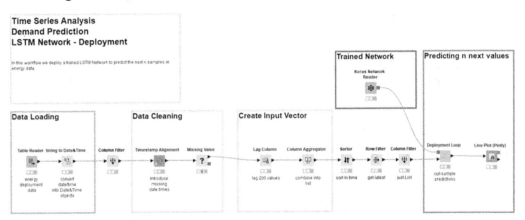

Figure 6.26 – The deployment workflow for a demand prediction problem

This is the deployment workflow, including data reading, the same data preparation as for the data in the training workflow, network reading, and a deployment loop to generate the predictions.

In this last section, we have learned how to apply the deployment loop to a deployment workflow to generate new predictions in real life.

Summary

In this chapter, we introduced a new recurrent neural unit: the LSTM unit. We showed how it is built and trained, and how it can be applied to a time series analysis problem, such as demand prediction.

As an example of a demand prediction problem, we tried to predict the average energy consumed by a cluster of users in the next hour, given the energy used in the previous 200 hours. We showed how to test in-sample and out-sample predictions and some numeric measures commonly used to quantify the prediction error. Demand prediction applied to energy consumption is just one of the many demand prediction use cases. The same approach learned here could be applied to predict the number of customers in a restaurant, the number of visitors to a web site, or the amount of a type of food required in a supermarket.

In this chapter, we also introduced a new loop in KNIME Analytics Platform, the recursive loop, and we mentioned a new visualization node, the Line Plot (Plotly) node.

In the next chapter, we will continue with RNNs, focusing on different text-related applications.

Questions and Exercises

Check your level of understanding of the concepts explored in this chapter by answering the following questions:

1. Why are LSTM units suitable for time series analysis?

    a). Because they are faster than classic feedforward networks

    b). Because they can remember past input tensors

    c). Because they use gates

    d). Because they have hidden states

2. What is the data extraction option to use for partitioning in time series analysis?

    a). Draw randomly

    b). Take from top

    c). Stratified Sampling

    d). Linear Sampling

3. What is a tensor?

   a). A tensor is a two-dimensional vector.

   b). A tensor is a k-dimensional vector.

   c). A tensor is just a number.

   d). A tensor is a sequence of numbers.

4. What is the difference between in-sample and out-sample testing?

   a). In-sample testing uses the real past values from the test set to make the predictions. Out-sample testing uses past prediction values to make new predictions.

   b). In-sample testing is more realistic than out-sample testing.

   c). In-sample testing is more complex than out-sample testing.

   d). In-sample testing applies the trained network while out-sample testing uses rules.

7
Implementing NLP Applications

In *Chapter 6, Recurrent Neural Networks for Demand Prediction*, we introduced **Recurrent Neural Networks** (**RNNs**) as a family of neural networks that are especially powerful to analyze sequential data. As a case study, we trained a **Long Short-Term Memory** (**LSTM**)-based RNN to predict the next value in the time series of consumed electrical energy. However, RNNs are not just suitable for strictly numeric time series, as they have also been applied successfully to other types of time series.

Another field where RNNs are state of the art is **Natural Language Processing** (**NLP**). Indeed, RNNs have been applied successfully to text classification, language models, and neural machine translation. In all of these tasks, the time series is a sequence of words or characters, rather than numbers.

In this chapter, we will run a short review of some classic NLP case studies and their RNN-based solutions: a sentiment analysis application, a solution for free text generation, and a similar solution for the generation of name candidates for new products.

We will start with an overview of text encoding techniques to prepare the sequence of words/characters to feed our neural network. The first case study, then, classifies text based on its sentiment. The last two case studies generate new text as sequences of new words, and new words as sequences of new characters, respectively.

In this chapter we will cover the following topics:

- Exploring Text Encoding Techniques for Neural Networks

- Finding the Tone of your Customers' Voice – Sentiment Analysis

- Generating Free Text with RNNs

- Generating Product Names with RNNs

Exploring Text Encoding Techniques for Neural Networks

In *Chapter 4, Building and Training a Feedforward Neural Network*, you learned that feedforward networks – and all other neural networks as well – are trained on numbers and don't understand nominal values. In this chapter, we want to feed words and characters into neural networks. Therefore, we need to introduce some techniques to encode sequences of words or characters – that is, sequences of nominal values – into sequences of numbers or numerical vectors. In addition, in NLP applications with RNNs, it is mandatory that the order of words or characters in the sequence is retained throughout the text encoding procedure.

Let's have a look at some **text encoding** techniques before we dive into the NLP case studies.

Index Encoding

In *Chapter 4, Building and Training a Feedforward Neural Network*, you learned about **index encoding** for nominal values. The idea was to represent each nominal class with an integer value, also called an index.

We can use this same idea for text encoding. Here, instead of encoding each class with a different index, we encode each word or each character with a different index. First, a dictionary must be created to map all words/characters in the text collection to an index; afterward, through this mapping, each word/character is transformed into its corresponding index and, therefore, each sequence of words/characters into the sequence of corresponding indexes. In the end, each text is represented as a sequence of indexes, where each index encodes a word or a character. The following figure gives you an example:

The quick brown fox jumped over the brown dog

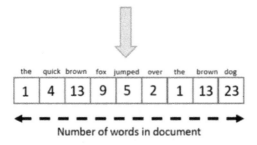

Figure 7.1 – An example of text encoding via indexes at the word level

Notice that index 1, for the word *the*, and index 13, for the word *brown*, are repeated twice in the sequence, as the words appear twice in the example sentence, *the quick brown fox jumped over the brown dog.*

Later in this chapter, in the *Finding the Tone of Your Customers' Voice – Sentiment Analysis* section, we'll use index encoding on words to represent text.

In the *Free Text Generation with RNNs* section, on the other hand, we'll use one-hot vectors as text encoding on characters. Let's explore what one-hot vector encoding is.

One-Hot Vector Encoding

The sequence of indexes has the disadvantage that it introduces an artificial distance between words/characters. For example, if *apple* is encoded as 1, *shoe* as 2, and *pear* as 3, *apple* and *pear* are further away from each other (distance = 2) than *shoe* and *pear* (distance = 1), which semantically might not make sense. In this way, as words don't have an ordered structure, we would introduce an artificial distance/similarity between words that might not exist in reality. We also encountered this problem in *Chapter 4, Building and Training a Feedforward Neural Network*, and we solved it by introducing the concept of one-hot vectors.

The idea of **one-hot vector encoding** is to represent each feature with a vector, where the distance across all vectors is the same. In the case of word or character encoding, the features are the different words/characters and each word/character is represented by a one-hot vector. A one-hot vector consists of as many binary components as the number of different words/characters in the dataset. Each component is associated with one word/character and it is set to 1 to encode a specific word/character, or otherwise to 0. This means that each word/character is represented as a one-hot vector and therefore, each text is a sequence of one-hot vectors. The following figure shows an example of one-hot vector encoding for the sentence *the quick brown fox jumped over the brown dog*.

Notice, in *Figure 7.2*, that the one-hot vectors for the words *the* and *brown* repeat twice in the sequence:

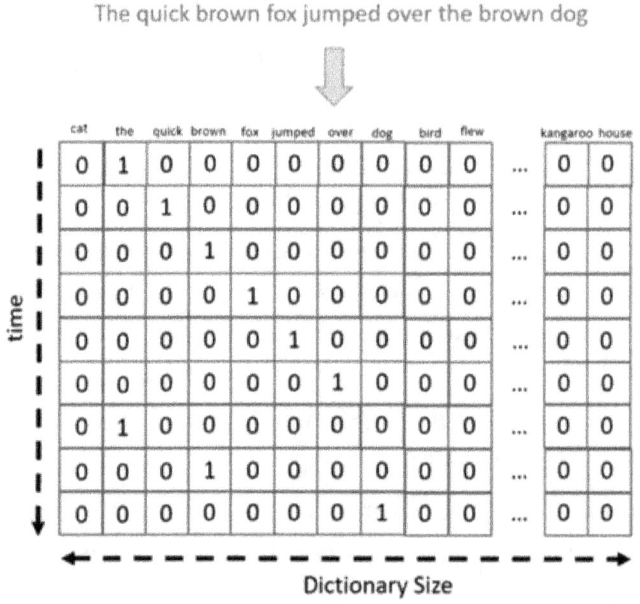

The quick brown fox jumped over the brown dog

cat	the	quick	brown	fox	jumped	over	dog	bird	flew		kangaroo	house
0	1	0	0	0	0	0	0	0	0	...	0	0
0	0	1	0	0	0	0	0	0	0	...	0	0
0	0	0	1	0	0	0	0	0	0	...	0	0
0	0	0	0	1	0	0	0	0	0	...	0	0
0	0	0	0	0	1	0	0	0	0	...	0	0
0	0	0	0	0	0	1	0	0	0	...	0	0
0	1	0	0	0	0	0	0	0	0	...	0	0
0	0	0	1	0	0	0	0	0	0	...	0	0
0	0	0	0	0	0	0	1	0	0	...	0	0

time

Dictionary Size

Figure 7.2 – An example of text encoding via one-hot vectors at the word level

> **Tip**
> Remember that the **Keras Learner** node can convert index-based encodings into one-hot vectors. Thus, to train a neural network on one-hot-vectors, it is sufficient to feed it with an index-based encoding of the text document.

A commonly used text encoding – similar to one-hot vectors but that doesn't retain the word order – are **document vectors**. Here, a vector is built from all the words available in the document collection and each word becomes a component in the vector space. Thus, each text is transformed into a vector of 0s and 1s, encoding the presence (1) or absence (0) of the words. One vector represents one text document and contains multiple 1s. Notice that this encoding does not retain the word order because all of the text is encoded within the same vector structure regardless of the word order.

Working with words, the dimension of one-hot vectors is equal to the dictionary size – that is, to the number of words available in the document corpus. If the document corpus is large, the dictionary size quickly becomes the number of words in the whole language. Therefore, one-hot vector encoding on a word level can lead to very large and sparse representations.

Working with characters, the dictionary size is the size of the character set, which, even including punctuation and special signs, is much smaller than in the previous case. Thus, one-hot vector encoding fits well for character encoding but might lead to dimensionality explosion on word encoding.

To encode a document at the word level, a much more appropriate method is embeddings.

Embeddings for Word Encoding

The goal of word embeddings is to map words into a geometric space. This is done by associating a numeric vector to every word in a dictionary in a way that words with similar meanings have similar vectors and the distance between any two vectors captures part of the semantic relationship between the two associated words. The geometric space formed by these vectors is called the *embedding space*. For word encoding, the embedding space has a lower dimension (only a few tens or hundreds) than the vector space for one-hot vector encodings (in the order of many thousands).

To learn the projection of each word into the continuous vector space, a dedicated neural network layer is used, which is called the embedding layer. This layer learns to associate a vector representation with each word. The best-known word embedding techniques are **Word2vec** and **GloVe**.

There are two ways that words embeddings can be used (J. Brownlee, *How to Use Word Embedding Layers for Deep Learning with Keras*, Machine Learning Mastery Blog, 2017, `https://machinelearningmastery.com/use-word-embedding-layers-deep-learning-keras/`):

- Adopting a ready-to-go layer previously trained on some external text corpus
- Training a new embedding layer as part of your neural network

If trained jointly with a neural network, the input to an embedding layer is an index-based encoded sequence. The number of output units in the embedding layer defines the dimension of the embedding space. The weights of the embedding layer, which are used to calculate the embedding representation of each index, and therefore of each word, are learned during the training of the network.

Now that we are familiar with different text encoding techniques, let's move on to our first NLP use case.

Finding the Tone of Your Customers' Voice – Sentiment Analysis

A common use case for NLP is **sentiment analysis**. Here, the goal is to identify the underlying emotion in some text, whether positive or negative, and all the nuances in between. Sentiment analysis is implemented in many fields, such as to analyze incoming messages, emails, reviews, recorded conversations, and other similar texts.

Generally, sentiment analysis belongs to a bigger group of NLP applications known as text classification. In the case of sentiment analysis, the goal is to predict the sentiment class.

Another common example of text classification is language detection. Here, the goal is to recognize the text language. In both cases, if we use an RNN for the task, we need to adopt a *many-to-one architecture*. A many-to-one neural architecture accepts a sequence of inputs at different times, t, and uses the final state of the output unit to predict the one single class – that is, sentiment or language.

Figure 7.3 shows an example of a many-to-one architecture:

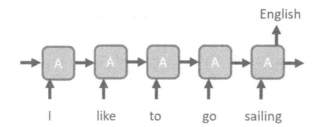

Figure 7.3 – An example of a many-to-one neural architecture: a sequence of many inputs at different times and only the final status of the output

In our first use case in this chapter, we want to analyze the sentiment of movie reviews. The goal is to train an RNN at a word level, with an embedding layer and an LSTM layer.

For this example, we will use the IMDb dataset, which contains two columns: the text of the movie reviews and the sentiment. The sentiment is encoded as 1 for positive reviews and as 0 for negative reviews.

Figure 7.4 shows you a small subset with some positive and some negative movie reviews:

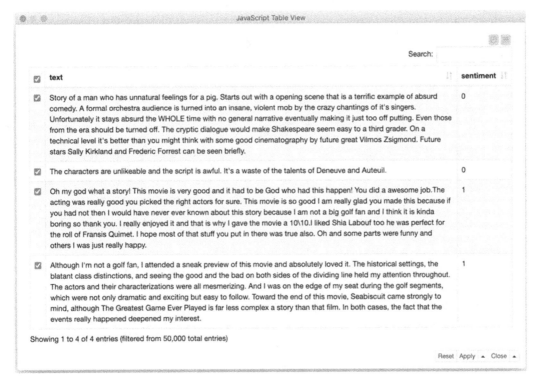

Figure 7.4 – Extract of the IMDb dataset, showing positive- and negative-labeled reviews

Let's start with reading and encoding the texts of the movie reviews.

Preprocessing Movie Reviews

The embedding layer expects index-based encoded input sequences. That is, each review must be encoded as a sequence of indexes, where each index (an integer value) represents a word in the dictionary.

As the number of words available in the IMDb document corpus is very high, we decided to reduce them during the text preprocessing phase, by removing stop words and reducing all words to their stems. In addition, only the n most frequent terms in the training set are encoded with a dedicated index, while all others receive just the default index.

In theory, RNNs can handle sequences of variable length. In practice, though, the sequence length for all input samples in one training batch must be the same. As the number of words per review might differ, we define a fixed sequence length and we zero-pad too-short sequences – that is, we add 0s to complete the sequence – and we truncate too-long sequences.

All these preprocessing steps are applied to the training set and the test set, with one difference. In the preprocessing of the training set, the dictionary with the n most frequent terms is created. This dictionary is then only applied during the preprocessing of the test set.

In summary, we perform the following preprocessing steps:

1. Read and partition the dataset into training and test sets.

2. Tokenize, clean, and stem the movie reviews in the training set and the test set.

3. Create a dictionary of all the terms. The n most frequent terms in the training set are represented by dedicated indexes and all other terms by a default index.

4. Map the words in the training and test set to the corresponding dictionary indexes.

5. Truncate too-long word sequences in the training set and test set.

6. Zero-pad too-short sequences in the training set and test set.

The workflow in *Figure 7.5* performs all these steps:

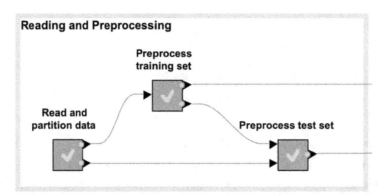

Figure 7.5 – Preprocessing workflow snippet for the sentiment analysis case study

The first metanode, **Read and partition data**, reads the table with the movie reviews and sentiment information and partitions the dataset into a training set and a test set. The **Preprocessing training set** metanode performs the different preprocessing steps on the training set and creates and applies the dictionary, which is available at the second output port. The last metanode, **Preprocess test set**, applies the created dictionary to the test set and performs the different preprocessing steps on the test set.

Let's see how all these steps are implemented in KNIME Analytics Platform.

Reading and Partitioning the Dataset

The first part, reading and partitioning the dataset, is performed by the **Read and partition data** metanode.

Figure 7.6 shows you the workflow snippet inside the metanode:

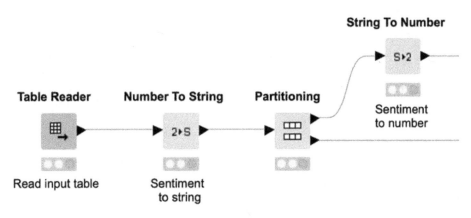

Figure 7.6 – Workflow snippet inside the Read and partition metanode

The **Table Reader** node reads the table with the sentiment information as an integer value and the movie reviews as a string value. Next, the sentiment information is transformed into a string with the **Number To String** node. This step is necessary to allow stratified sampling in the **Partitioning** node. In the last step, the data type of the column sentiment is transformed back into an integer using the **String To Number** node so that it can be used as the target column during training by the Keras Learner node.

Now that we have a training set and a test set, let's continue with the preprocessing of the training set.

Preprocessing the Training Set and Dictionary Creation

The preprocessing of the training set and the creation of the dictionary is performed in the **Preprocess training set** metanode.

Figure 7.7 shows you the inside of the metanode:

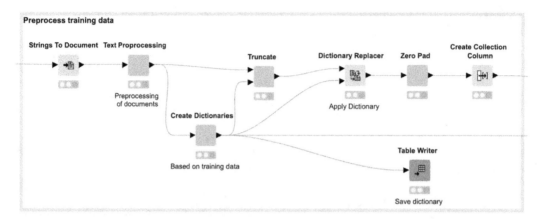

Figure 7.7 – Workflow snippet inside the Preprocess training set metanode

For the preprocessing of the movie reviews, the **KNIME Text Processing** extension is used.

> **Tip**
> The KNIME Text Processing extension includes nodes to read and write documents from and to a variety of text formats; to transform words; to clean up sentences of spurious characters and meaningless words; to transform a text into a numeric table; to calculate all required text statistics; and finally, to explore topics and sentiment.

The KNIME Text Processing extension relies on a new data type: **Document object**. Raw text becomes a document when additional metadata, such as title, author(s), source, and class, are added to it. Text in a document is tokenized following one of the many available language-specific tokenization algorithms. **Document tokenization** produces a hierarchical structure of the text items: sections, paragraphs, sentences, and words. Words are often referred to as tokens or terms.

To make use of the preprocessing nodes of the KNIME Text Processing extension, we need to transform the movie reviews into documents, via the **Strings To Document** node. This node collects values from different columns and turns them into a document object, after tokenizing the main text.

Figure 7.8 shows you the configuration window of the **Strings To Document** node:

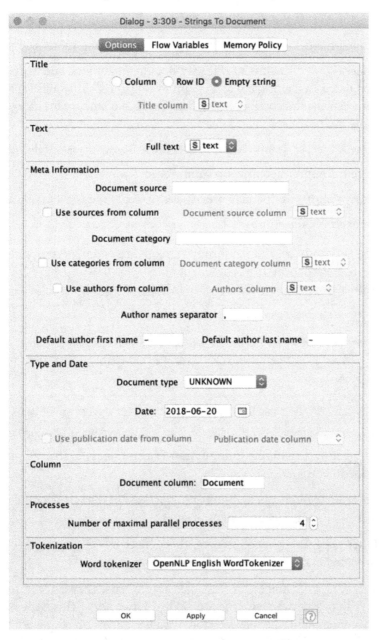

Figure 7.8 – Configuration window of the Strings To Document node

The node gives you the opportunity to define the following:

- The document text via the **Full text** option.

- The document title, as a **Column**, **Row ID**, or **Empty string** value.

- The document source, document category, document authors, and document publication date as a fixed string or a column value. If column values are used, remember to enable the corresponding flag. Often, the **Document category** field is used to store the task class.

- The document type, as **Transaction**, **Proceeding**, **Book**, or just **UNKNOWN**.

- The name of the output document column.

- The maximum number of parallel processes to execute the word tokenizer.

- The word tokenizer algorithm.

Next, the document objects are cleaned through a sequence of text preprocessing nodes, contained in the **Text Preprocessing** component of the workflow in *Figure 7.7*. The inside of the **Text Preprocessing** component is shown in *Figure 7.9*:

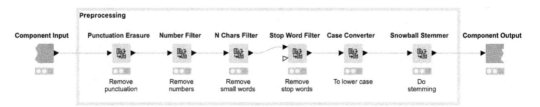

Figure 7.9 – Workflow snippet showing the inside of the Preprocessing component

The workflow snippet starts with the **Punctuation Erasure** node, to strip all punctuation from the input documents.

The **Number Filter** node filters out all numbers, expressed as digits, including decimal separators (, or .) and possible leading signs (+ or -).

The **N Chars Filter** node filters out all terms with less than N – in our case, $N = 3$ – characters, as specified in the configuration window of the node.

Filler words, such as *so*, *thus*, and so on, are called **stop words**. They carry little information and can be removed with the **Stop Word Filter** node. This node filters out all terms that are contained in the selected stop word list. A custom stop word list can be passed to the node via the second input port, or a default built-in stop word list can be adopted. A number of built-in stop word lists are available for various languages.

The **Case Converter** node converts all terms into upper or lowercase. In this case study, they are converted into lowercase.

Lastly, the **Snowball Stemmer** node reduces words to their stem, removing the grammar inflection, using the Snowball stemming library (`http://snowball.tartarus.org/`).

> **Important note**
> The goal of stemming is to reduce inflectional forms and derivationally related forms to a common base form. For example, *look*, *looking*, *looks*, and *looked* are all replaced by their stem, *look*.

Now that we have cleaned up the text of the movie reviews of the training set, we can create the dictionary.

Creating the Dictionary Based on the Training Set

The dictionary must assign two indexes to each word:

- **Index**: A progressive integer index to each of the n most frequent terms in the training set and the same default index to all other terms.

- **Counter**: A progressive eight-digit index to each of the words. This eight-digit index is just a temporary index that will help us deal with truncation.

Figure 7.10 shows you a subset of the dictionary we want to create:

Term	Integer Index	8-Digit Index
movie	0	1000 0000
film	1	1000 0001
...		
peerless	20001	1011 8142
overseen	20001	1011 8143
zipper	20001	1011 8144

Figure 7.10 – A small subset of the dictionary, where each word is represented by a progressive integer index and another progressive eight-digit integer index

Both indexes are created in the **Create Dictionary** component and *Figure 7.11* shows you the workflow snippet inside the component:

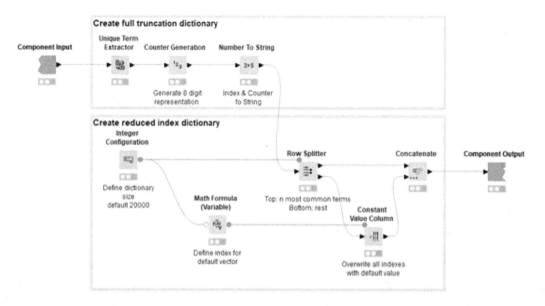

Figure 7.11 – Workflow snippet contained in the Create Dictionary component

The **Create Dictionary** component has a configuration window, which you can see in *Figure 7.12*. The input option in the configuration window is inherited from the **Integer Configuration** node and requests the dictionary size as the number of the n most frequent words in the document collection. The default is $n = 20000$:

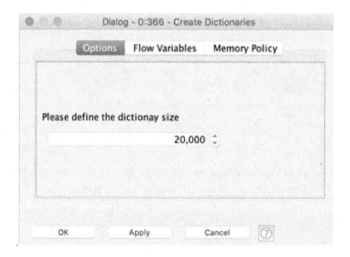

Figure 7.12 – Configuration window of the Create Dictionary component

The workflow inside the component first creates a global set of unique terms over all the documents by using the **Unique Term Extractor** node:

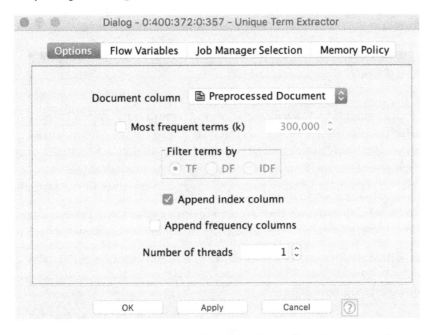

Figure 7.13 – Configuration window of the Unique Term Extractor node

This node allows us to create an index column and a frequency column, as shown in the preceding screenshot. The index column contains a progressive integer number starting from 1, where 1 is assigned to the most frequent term.

The node optionally provides the possibility to filter the top *k* most frequent terms. For that, three frequency measures are available: the **term frequency**, the **document frequency**, and the **inverse document frequency**. For now, we want to select all terms and we will work on the dictionary size later.

> **Important note**
>
> **Term frequency (TF):** The number of occurrences of a term in all documents
>
> **Document frequency (DF):** The number of documents in which a term occurs
>
> **Inverse document frequency (IDF):** Logarithm of the number of documents divided by DF

The eight-digit index is created via the **Counter Generation** node. This node adds a new **Counter** column to the input data table, starting from a minimum value (**Min Value**) of 10,000,000 and using 1 as the step size. This minimum value guarantees the eight-digit format.

The **Index** and **Counter** columns are then converted from integers into strings with the **Number To String** node.

Next comes the reduction of the dictionary size. The top n most frequent terms keep the progressive index assigned by the **Unique Term Extractor** node, while all other terms get a default index of $n + 1$. Remember that n can be changed via the component's configuration window. For this example, n was set to 20,000. In the lower part of the component sub-workflow, the **Row Splitter** node splits the input data table into two sub-tables: the top n rows (top output port) and the rest of the rows (lower output port).

The **Constant Value Column** node then replaces all index values with the default index value $n + 1$ in the lower sub-table. Lastly, the two sub-tables are concatenated back together.

Now that the dictionary is ready, we can continue with the truncation of the movie reviews.

Truncating Too-Long Documents

We have stated that we will work with fixed-size documents – that is, with a maximum number of words for each document. If a document has more words than allowed, it will be truncated. If it has fewer words than allowed, it will be zero-padded. Let's see how the **truncation** procedure works – that is, how we remove the last words from a too-long document. This all happens in the **Truncation** component. *Figure 7.14* shows you the workflow snippet inside the component:

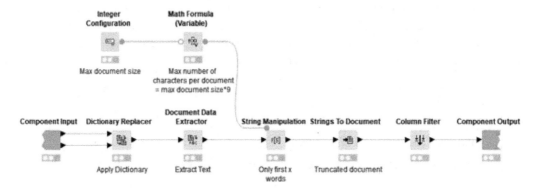

Figure 7.14 – Workflow snippet inside the Truncation component

First, we set the maximum number, m, of terms allowed in a document. Again, this is a parameter that can be changed through the component's configuration window, shaped via the **Integer Configuration** node. We set the maximum number of terms in a document – that is, the maximum document size – as $m = 80$ terms. If a document is too long, we should just keep the first m terms and throw away the rest.

It is not easy to count the number of words in a text. Since words have variable lengths, we should detect the spaces separating the words within a loop and then count the words. Loops, however, often slow down execution. So, an alternative trick is to use the eight-digit representation of the words inside the text.

Within the text, each word is substituted by its eight-digit code via the **Dictionary Replacer** node. The **Dictionary Replacer** node matches terms in the input documents at the top input port with dictionary terms at the lower input port and then replaces them with the corresponding value in the dictionary table.

The **Dictionary Replacer** node has two input ports:

- The upper input port for the documents containing the terms to be replaced

- The lower input port with the dictionary table for the matching and replacement operation

> **Important note**
> The dictionary table must consist of at least two string columns. One string column contains the terms to replace (keys) and the other string column contains the replacement strings (values). In the configuration window, we can set both columns from the data table at the lower input port.

At this point, we have text with terms of fixed length (8 digits + 1 <space>) and not words of variable length. So, limiting a text to m words is the same as limiting a text to $m * (8 + 1)$ characters, if $m = 80$, to 720 characters. This operation is much easier to carry out without loops or complex node structures, but just with a **String Manipulation** node. However, the **String Manipulation** node works on string objects and not on documents. To use it, we need to move temporarily back to text as strings.

The text is extracted from the document as a simple string with the **Document Data Extractor** node. This node extracts information, such as, for example, the text and title, from a document cell.

The **Math Formula (Variable)** node takes the flow variable for the maximum document size and calculates the maximum number of characters allowed in a document.

The **String Manipulation** node extracts the substring from the text starting from the first character (at position 0) until the maximum number of characters allowed, using the substr() function. This effectively keeps only the top m terms and removes all others.

Lastly, the text is transformed back into a document, called **Truncated Document**, and all superfluous columns are removed in the **Column Filter** node.

At this point, the eight-digit indexes have exhausted their task and can be substituted with the progressive integer index for the encoding. This is done in the **Dictionary Replacer** node, once again.

With that, we have truncated too-long documents to the maximum number of terms allowed. Next, we need to zero-pad too-short documents.

Zero-Padding Too-Short Documents

When sequences are too short with respect to a set number of values, **zero-padding** is often applied. Zero-padding means that 0s are added to the sequence until the set number of values is reached. In our case, if a document has fewer words than the set number, we fill the remaining empty spaces with 0s. This happens in the **Zero Pad** component.

Figure 7.15 shows you the workflow snippet inside the Zero Pad component:

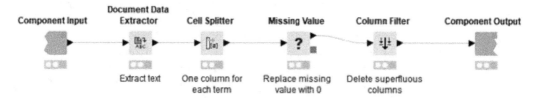

Figure 7.15 – Workflow snippet inside the Zero Pad component

Zero-padding is again performed at the string level, and not at the document level. After the text has been extracted as a string from the input document using the **Document Data Extractor** node, the **Cell Splitter** node splits the input text at each <space> and creates one new column for each index.

Remember that all truncated text now has a maximum length of m indexes from the previous step. So, from those texts, the number of newly generated columns is surely m. For all other texts with shorter-term sequences, the **Cell Splitter** node will fill the empty columns with missing values. It is enough to turn these missing values into 0s and the zero-padding procedure is complete. This replacement of missing values with 0s is performed by the **Missing Value** node.

Lastly, all superfluous columns are removed within the **Column Filter** node.

Now that all term sequences – that is, all text – have the same length, collection cells are created with the **Create Collection Cell** node to feed the Keras Learner node.

Next, we need to perform the same preprocessing on the test and apply the created dictionary.

Preprocessing the Test Set

The preprocessing of the test set is performed in the **Preprocess test set** metanode. This metanode has two input ports: the upper port for the dictionary created in the **Preprocess training set** metanode and the lower port for the test set.

Figure 7.16 shows you the workflow snippet inside the Preprocess test set metanode:

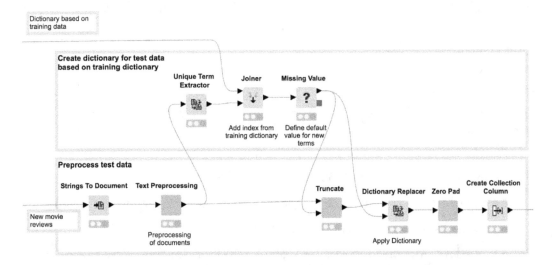

Figure 7.16 – Workflow snippet inside the Preprocess test set metanode

The lower part of the workflow is similar to the workflow snippet inside the **Preprocess training set** metanode, only the part including the creation of the dictionary is different. Here, the dictionary for the test set is based on the dictionary from the training set. All terms available in the training set dictionary receive the corresponding index encoding; all remaining terms receive the default index.

Therefore, first a list of all terms in the test set is created using the **Unique Term Extractor** node. Next, this list is joined with the list of terms in the training set dictionary using a right outer join. A right outer join allows us to keep all the rows from the lower input port – that is, all terms in the test set – and to add the indexes from the training dictionary, if available. For all terms that are not in the training dictionary, the joiner node creates missing values in the index columns. These missing values are then replaced with the default index value using the **Missing Value** node.

All other steps, such as truncation and zero-padding, are performed in the same way as in the preprocessing of the training set.

We have finished the preprocessing phase and we can now continue with the definition of the network architecture and its training.

Defining and Training the Network Architecture

In this section, we will define and train the network architecture for this sentiment classification task.

Network Architecture

We want to use an LSTM-based RNN, where we train the embedding as well. The embedding is trained by an embedding layer. Therefore, we create a neural network with four layers:

- An **input layer** to define the input size
- An **embedding layer** to produce an embedding representation of the term space
- An **LSTM layer** to exploit the sequential property of the text
- A **dense layer** with one unit with the sigmoid activation function, as we have a binary classification problem at hand

The embedding layer expects a sequence of index-based encoded terms as input. Therefore, the input layer must accept sequences of m integer indexes (in our case, $m = 80$). This means Shape = 80 and data type = Int 32 in the configuration window of the **Keras Input Layer** node.

Next, the **Keras Embedding Layer** node must learn to embed the integer indexes into an appropriate high-dimensional vector space. *Figure 7.17* shows its configuration window. The input tensor is directly recovered from the output of the previous input layer:

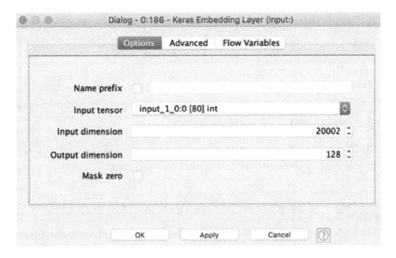

Figure 7.17 – Configuration window of the Keras Embedding Layer node

There are two important configuration settings for the **Keras Embedding Layer** node. For the **Input dimension** setting, we need to provide the dictionary size – that is, the number of unique indexes. The number of unique indexes is the maximum index value plus 1 since the counter started from 0. For **Output dimension**, we provide the dimension of the final embedding space. We have arbitrarily chosen an embedding dimension of 128. The output tensor of the **Keras Embedding Layer** node then has the dimension [sequence length m, embedding dimension]. In our case, this is [80, 128].

Next, the **Keras LSTM Layer** node is used to add an LSTM-based recurrent layer to the network. This node is used with the default settings and 128 units, which means Units = 128, Activation = Tanh, Recurrent activation = Hard sigmoid, Dropout = 0.2, Recurrent dropout = 0.2, and return sequences, return state, go backward, and unroll all unchecked.

Lastly, a **Keras Dense Layer** node with one unit with the sigmoid activation function is used to predict the final binary sentiment classification.

Now that we have our preprocessed data and the neural architecture, we can start training the network.

Training the Recurrent Network with Embeddings

The network is trained, as usual, with the **Keras Network Learner** node.

In the first tab, **Input Data**, the **From Collection of Number (integer)** conversion is selected, as our input is a collection cell of integer values (the indexes), encoding our movie reviews. Next, the collection cell is selected as input.

In the second tab, **Target Data**, the **From Number (integer)** conversion type and the column with the sentiment class are selected. In the lower part, the binary cross-entropy is selected as the loss function since it is a binary classification task.

In the third tab, **Options**, the following training parameters are set: Epochs = 30, Training batch size = 100, shuffle training data before each epoch is activated, and Optimizer = Adam (with the default settings).

Now that the network is trained, we can apply it to the test set and evaluate how good its performance is at predicting the sentiment behind a review text.

Executing and Evaluating the Network on the Test Set

To execute the network on the test set, the **Keras Network Executor** node is used.

In the configuration window, we again select **From Collection of Number (integer)** as the conversion type and the collection cell as input.

As output, we are interested in the output of the last dense layer, as this gives us the probability for sentiment being equal to 1 (positive). Therefore, we click on the **add output** button, select the sigmoid layer, and make sure that the **To Number (double)** conversion is used.

The **Keras Network Executor** node adds one new column to the input table with the probability for the positive class encoded as 1.

Next, the **Rule Engine** node translates this probability into a class prediction with the following expression:

```
$dense_1/Sigmoid:0_0$ > 0.5 => 1
TRUE => 0
```

Here, $dense_1/Sigmoid:0_0$ is the name of the output column from the network.

The expression transforms all values above 0.5 into 1s, and into 0s otherwise.

> **Important note**
> Remember that the different instruction lines in a **Rule Engine** node are executed sequentially. Execution stops when the antecedent in one line is verified.

Lastly, the **Scorer** node evaluates the performance of the model and the **Keras Network Writer** node saves the trained network for deployment. *Figure 7.18* shows the network performance, in the view of the **Scorer** node, achieving a respectable 83% of correct sentiment classification on the movie reviews:

Confusion Matrix - 4:367 - Scorer		
File Hilite		
sentiment ... 0	1	
0 10007	2493	
1 1645	10855	

Correct classified: 20,862	Wrong classified: 4,138
Accuracy: 83.448 %	Error: 16.552 %
Cohen's kappa (κ) 0.669	

Figure 7.18 – Performance of the LSTM and embedding-based network on sentiment classification

With this, we have finished our first NLP case study. *Figure 7.19* displays the complete workflow used to implement the example. You can download the workflow from the KNIME Hub at `https://hub.knime.com/kathrin/spaces/Codeless%20 Deep%20Learning%20with%20KNIME/latest/Chapter%207/`:

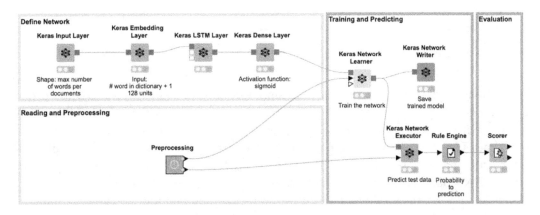

Figure 7.19 – Complete workflow to prepare the text and build, train, and evaluate the neural network for sentiment analysis

For now, we offer no deployment workflow. In *Chapter 10, Deploying a Deep Learning Network*, we will come back to this trained network to build a deployment workflow.

Let's now move on to the next NLP application: free text generation with RNNs.

Generating Free Text with RNNs

Now that we have seen how RNNs can be used for text classification, we can move on to the next case study. Here, we want to train an RNN to generate new free text in a certain style, be it Shakespearean English, a rap song, or mimicking a Brothers Grimm fairy tale. We will focus on the last application: training a network to generate free text in the style of Brothers Grimm fairy tales. However, the network and the process can be easily adjusted to produce a new rap song or a text in old Shakespearean English.

So, how can we train an RNN to generate new text?

The Dataset

First of all, you need a text corpus to train the network to generate new text. Any text corpus is good. However, keep in mind that the text you use for training will define the style of the text automatically generated. If you train the network on Shakespearean theater, you will get new text in old Shakespearean English; if you train the network on rap songs, you will get urban-style text, maybe even with rhyme; if you train the network on fairy tales, you will get text in the fairy tale style.

Thus, for a network to generate new fairy tales, it must be trained on existing fairy tales. We downloaded the Brothers Grimm corpus from the Gutenberg project, from `https://www.gutenberg.org/ebooks/2591`.

Predicting Words or Characters?

The second decision to make is whether to train the network at the word or character level. Both options have their pros and cons.

Training a network at the word level sounds more logical since languages are structured by words and not by characters. Input sequences (sequences of words) are short but the dictionary size (all words in the domain) is large. On the other hand, training the network at a character level relies on much smaller and more manageable dictionaries, but might lead to very long input sequences. According to Wikipedia, the English language, for example, has around 170,000 different words and only 26 different letters. Even if we distinguish between uppercase and lowercase, and we add numbers, punctuation signs, and special characters, we have a dictionary with less than 100 characters.

We want to train a network to generate text in the Brothers Grimm style. In order to do that, we train the network with a few Brothers Grimm tales, which already implies a very large number of words in the dictionary. So, to avoid the problem of a huge dictionary and the consequent possibly unmanageable network size, we opt to train our fairy tale generator at the character level.

Training at the character level means that the network must learn to predict the next character after the past n characters have passed through the input. The training set, then, must consist of many samples of sequences of n characters together with the next character to predict (the target value).

During deployment, a start sequence of n characters must trigger the network to generate the new text. Indeed, this first sequence predicts the next character; then in the next step, the $n - 1$ most recent initial characters and the predicted character will make the new input sequence to predict the next character, and so on.

In the next section, we will explain how to clean, transform, and encode the text data from the Grimms' fairy tales to feed the network.

Preprocessing and Encoding

We populate the training set using the sliding window approach – that is, with partially overlapping sequences. To make this clearer, let's include the sentence Once upon a time in the training set using a window length of $m = 5$ and a sliding step of 1. The five characters Once<space> should predict u; then we slide the window one step to the right, and nce<space>u should predict p. Again, we slide the window one character to the right and ce<space>up should predict o, and so on.

On the left of *Figure 7.20*, you can see the created input sequences and the target values:

Input sequence	Target	Input sequence	Target
Once<space>	u	41 14 3 5 57	21
nce<space>u	p	14 3 5 57 21	16
ce<space>up	o	3 5 57 21 16	17
e<space>upo	n	5 57 21 16 17	14

Figure 7.20 – Example of overlapping sequences used for training

Next, we need to encode the character sequences. In order to avoid introducing an artificial distance among characters, we opted for one-hot vector encoding. We will perform the one-hot encoding in two steps. First, we perform an index-based encoding; then we convert it into one-hot encoding in the **Keras Network Learner** node via the **From Collection of Number (integer)** conversion option to **One-Hot Tensor**. The resulting overlapping index-encoded sequences for the training set are shown on the right of *Figure 7.20*.

The workflow snippet in the next figure reads and transforms the fairy tales into overlapping index-based encoded character sequences and their associated target character. Both the input sequence and target character are stored in a collection-type column:

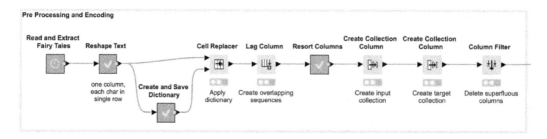

Figure 7.21 – Preprocessing workflow snippet reading and transforming text from Brothers Grimm fairy tales

The workflow performs the following steps:

- Reads all the fairy tales from the corpus and extracts five fairy tales for training and Snow white and Rose red as the seed for deployment

- Reshapes the text, placing one character per row in a single column

- Creates and applies the index-based dictionary, consisting, in this case, of the character set, including punctuation and special signs

- Using the **Lag Column** node, creates the overlapping sequences and then re-sorts them from the oldest to the newest character in the sequence

- Encapsulates the input sequence and target character into collection-type columns

Let's have a look at these steps in detail.

Reading and Extracting Fairy Tales

The workflow snippet, in the **Read and Extract Fairy Tales** metanode, first reads the fairy tales using a **File Reader** node. The table has one column, where the content of each row corresponds to one line of a fairy tale.

Then, a **Row Filter** node removes the unnecessary meta-information at the top and the bottom of the file, such as the author, title, table of contents, and license agreement. We will not use any of this meta-information during training or deployment.

The **Row Splitter** node splits the collection of fairy tales into two subsets: at the lower output port, only Snow white and Rose red and at the top output port, all the other fairy tales. We'll save Snow white and Rose red for deployment.

Next, a **Row Filter** node is used to extract the first five fairy tales, which are used for training.

The next step is the reshaping of the text into a sequence of characters with one single column.

Reshaping the Text

Before we can create the overlapping sequences of characters to feed the network, we need to transform all the fairy tales text into a long sequence (column) of single characters: one character in each row. This step is called **reshaping** and it is implemented in the **Reshape Text** metanode. *Figure 7.22* shows its contents:

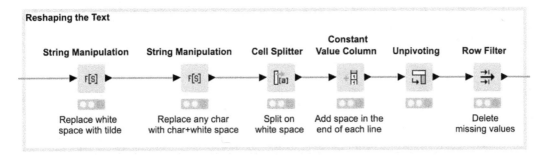

Figure 7.22 – Workflow snippet inside the Reshape Text metanode

It starts with two **String Manipulation** nodes. The first one replaces each white space with a tilde character. The second one replaces each character with the character itself plus a `<space>` character, by using the `regexReplace()` function. `regexReplace()` takes advantage of regular expressions, such as `"[^\\s]"` to match any character in the input string and `"$0 "` for the matched character plus `<space>`. The final syntax for the `regexReplace()` function, used within the **String Manipulation** node and applied to the input column, `$Col0$`, is then the following:

```
regexReplace($Col0$,"[^\\s]" ,"$0 ")
```

Next, the **Cell Splitter** node splits the text at each `<space>` character, producing many columns with one character per cell.

Notice that the last character in the paragraph (the newline) has not received the `<space>` character afterward. To solve this problem, a constant column with a `<space>` character is added using the **Constant Value Column** node.

The **Unpivoting** node reshapes the data table from many columns into one column only with a sequence of single characters. Let's spend a bit of time on the **Unpivoting** node and its unsuspected tricks for reshaping data tables. The **Unpivoting** node performs a disaggregation of the input data table. *Figure 7.23* shows you an example. It distinguishes between value columns and retaining columns. The selected value columns are then rotated to become rows and attached to the corresponding values in the retaining columns. Since the rotation of the value columns might result in more than one row, a duplication of the rows with the retaining column values might be necessary:

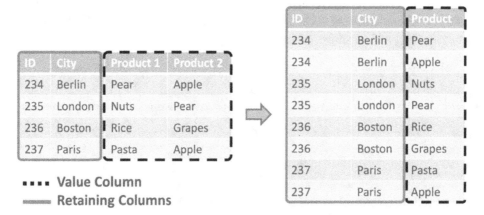

Figure 7.23 – Example for the unpivoting operation, where Product 1 and Product 2 are the selected Value columns, and ID and City are the selected retaining columns

For the reshaping of the text, we set all columns as value columns and none as retaining columns. The result is the representation of the fairy tale as a long sequence of characters within one column.

At last, some cleaning up: all rows with missing values are removed with the **Row Filter** node.

Creating and Applying the Dictionary

We now need to create the dictionary and the index-based mapping for the index-based encoding. Since we work at the character level, the dictionary here is nothing more than the character set – that is, the list of unique characters in the fairy tales corpus. To get this list, we remove all duplicate characters from the reshaped text using the **Remove Duplicate Filter** node.

> **Tip**
> The **Remove Duplicate Filter** node is a powerful node when it comes to detecting and handling duplicate records in the dataset.

Next, we assign an index to each row – that is, to each unique character – with the **Counter Generation** node, which we introduced already in the first case study of this chapter. Here, we use 0 for **Min Value** and 1 for **Scale Unit**.

Now that we have the dictionary ready, we apply it with the **Cell Replacer** node, already introduced in *Chapter 4, Building and Training a Feedforward Neural Network*.

Creating and Resorting the Overlapping Sequences

To create the overlapping sequences of characters, we use the **Lag Column** node, which we already introduced and explained in the previous chapter, *Chapter 6, Recurrent Neural Networks for Demand Prediction*. In this case study, we use sequences of $m = 100$ consecutive characters to predict the next character. Therefore, in the **Lag Column** node, **Lag** is set to 100, **Lag interval** is set to 1, and incomplete rows at the beginning and end of the output table are skipped.

According to the way the **Lag Column** node works, we end up with a data table sorted on a growing time from right to left. The oldest character of each sequence (col-100) is in the farthest column to the right; the current character to predict (col) is in the farthest column to the left. Basically, the time of the sequence is sorted backward with respect to what the network is expecting.

The following figure shows you an example:

col	col-1	col-2	col-3	col-4	col-5	col-6	col-7
o	p	u		e	c	n	O
n	o	p	u		e	c	n
	n	o	p	u		e	c

Figure 7.24 – Resulting output of the Lag Column node, where the time is sorted in ascending order from right to left

We need to reorder the columns to follow an ascending order from left to right, in order to have the oldest character on the left and the most recent character on the right. This re-sorting is performed by the **Resort Columns** metanode.

Figure 7.25 shows you the inside of the metanode:

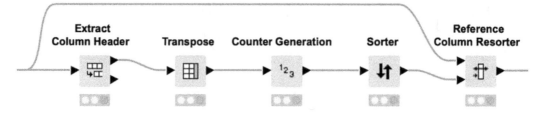

Figure 7.25 – Workflow snippet contained in the Resort Columns metanode

Here, the **Reference Column Resorter** node changes the order of the data columns in the table at the top input port according to the order established in the data table at the lower input port. The reference data table at the lower input port must contain a string-type column with the column headers from the first input table in a particular order. The columns in the first data table are then sorted according to the row order of the column names in the second data table.

To create the table with sorted column headers, we extract the column headers with the **Extract Column Header** node. The **Extract Column Header** node separates the column headers from the table content and outputs the column headers at the top output port and the content at the lower output port.

Then, the row of column headers is transposed into a column with the **Transpose** node.

Finally, we assign an increasing integer number to each column header via the **Counter Generation** node and we sort them by counter value in descending order using the **Sorter** node.

Now that we have the column headers from the first table sorted correctly in time, we can input it at the lower port of the **Reference Column Resorter** node. The result is a data table where each row is a sequence of $m = 100$ characters, time is sorted from left to right, and subsequent rows contain overlapping character sequences. At this point, we can create the collection cells for the input and target data of the network.

> **Important note**
> Even though the target data consists of only one single value, we still need to transform it into a collection cell so that the index can be transformed into a one-hot vector by the **Keras Network Learner** node.

Let's move on to the next step: defining and training the network architecture.

Defining and Training the Network Architecture

Let's now design and train an appropriate neural network architecture to deal with time series, character encoding, and overfitting, and to predict the next character in the sequence.

Defining the Network Architecture

For this case study, we decided to use a neural network with four layers:

- A **Keras input layer**, to define the input shape
- A **Keras LSTM layer**, to deal with time series
- A **Keras dropout layer**, to prevent overfitting
- A **Keras dense layer**, to output the probability of the next character

As usual, we define the input shape of the neural network using a **Keras Input Layer** node. The input here is a second-order tensor: the first dimension is the sequence length ($m = 100$, but we will allow a variable length ?) and the second dimension is the size of the one-hot vectors – that is, the size of the character set (65). So, the input shape is ?, 65.

As we don't need the intermediate hidden states, we leave most of the settings as default in the **Keras LSTM Layer** node. We just set the number of units to 512.

Free text generation can be seen as a multi-class classification application, where the characters are the classes. Therefore, the **Keras Dense Layer** node at the output of the network is set to have 65 units (one for each character in the character set) with the softmax activation function, to score the probability of each character to be the next character.

Let's proceed with training this network on the encoded overlapping sequences.

Training the Network

Again, to train the network, we use the by-now-familiar **Keras Network Learner** node.

In the first configuration tab, **Input Data**, we select **From Collection of Number (integer) to One-Hot-Tensor** to handle encoding conversion and the collection column with the character sequence as input.

In the second configuration tab, **Target Data**, we select **From Collection of Number (integer) to One-Hot-Tensor** again on the collection column containing the target value. As this is a multi-class classification problem, we set the loss function to **Categorical Cross Entropy**.

In the third configuration tab, **Options**, we provide the training parameters: 50 epochs, training batch size 256, shuffling option on, and optimizer as Adam with default settings for the learning rate.

The network is finally saved in **Keras format** with the **Keras Network Writer** node. In addition, the network is converted into a TensorFlow network with the **Keras to TensorFlow Network Converter** node and saved with the **TensorFlow Network Writer** node. The TensorFlow network is used in deployment to avoid a time-consuming Python startup, required by the Keras network.

Figure 7.26 shows the full workflow implementing all the described steps to train a neural network to generate fairy tales. This workflow and the used dataset are available on KNIME Hub at https://hub.knime.com/kathrin/spaces/Codeless%20 Deep%20Learning%20with%20KNIME/latest/Chapter%207/:

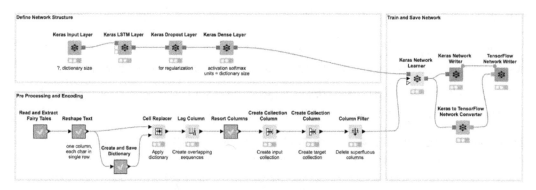

Figure 7.26 – Workflow to train a neural network to generate fairy tales

Now that we have trained and saved the network, let's move on to deployment to generate a new fairy tale's text.

Building a Deployment Workflow

To trigger the generation of new text during deployment, we start with an input sequence of the same length as each of the training sequences ($m = 100$). We feed the network with that sequence to predict the next character; then, we delete the oldest character in the sequence, add the predicted one, and apply the network again to our new input sequence, and so on. This is exactly the same procedure that we used in the case study for demand prediction. So, we will implement it here again with a recursive loop (*Figure 7.27*):

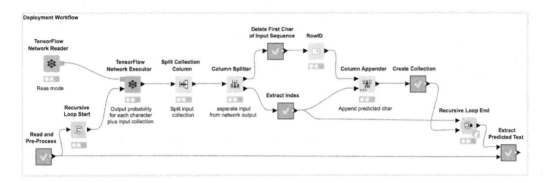

Figure 7.27 – Deployment workflow to generate new free text

The trigger sequence was taken from the **Snow white and Rose red** fairy tale. The text for the trigger sequence was preprocessed, sequenced, and encoded as in the workflow used to train the network. This is done in the **Read and Pre-Process** metanode, shown in *Figure 7.28*:

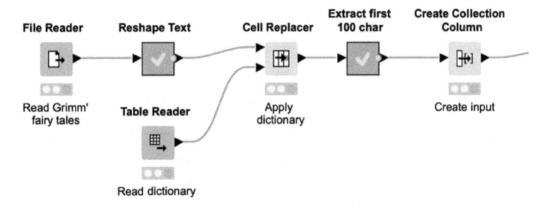

Figure 7.28 – Workflow content in the Read and Pre-Process metanode to read and preprocess the trigger sequence

The workflow reads the **Snow white and Rose red** fairy tale as well as the dictionary from the files created in the training workflow. Then, the same preprocessing steps as in the training workflow are applied.

After that, we read the trained TensorFlow network and apply it to the trigger sequence with the **TensorFlow Network Executor** node.

The output of the network is the probability of each character to be the next. We can pick the predicted character following two possible strategies:

- The character with the highest probability is assigned to be the next character, known as the greedy strategy.

- The next character is picked randomly according to the probability distribution.

We have implemented both strategies in the **Extract Index** metanode in two different deployment workflows.

Figure 7.29 shows the content of the **Extract Index** metanode when implementing the first strategy:

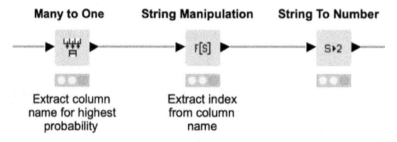

Figure 7.29 – Workflow snippet to extract the character with the highest probability

This metanode takes as input the output probabilities from the executed network and extracts the character with the highest probability. The key node here is the **Many to One** node, which extracts the cell with the highest score (probability) from the network output.

Figure 7.30 shows the content of the **Extract Index** metanode when implementing the second strategy:

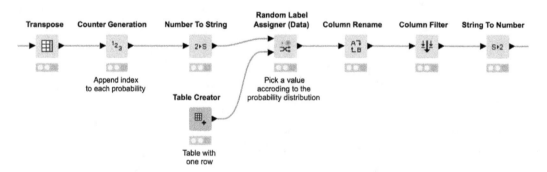

Figure 7.30 – Workflow snippet to pick the next character based on a probability distribution

This workflow snippet expects as input the probability distribution for the characters and picks one according to it. The key node here is the **Random Label Assigner (Data)** node, which assigns a value based on the input probability distribution.

The **Random Label Assigner (Data)** node assigns one index to each data row at the lower input port based on the probability distribution at the upper input port. The data table at the upper input port must have two columns: one column with the class values – in our case, the index-encoded characters in string format – and one column with the corresponding probabilities. Therefore, the first part of the workflow snippet in *Figure 7.30* prepares the data table for the top input port of the **Random Label Assigner (Data)** node, from the network output, using the **Transpose** node, the **Counter Generation** node, and the **Number To String** node, while the **Table Creator** node creates a new table with only one row using the **Table Creator** node. This means the **Random Label Assigner (Data)** node then picks one index, based on the probability distribution defined by the table at the first input port.

> **Tip**
> The idea of the recursive loop and its implementation are explained in detail in *Chapter 6, Recurrent Neural Networks for Demand Prediction*.

You can download the deployment workflow, implementing both options, from the KNIME Hub: `https://hub.knime.com/kathrin/spaces/Codeless%20Deep%20Learning%20with%20KNIME/latest/Chapter%207/`.

The New Fairy Tale

At last, I am sure you want to see the kind of free text that the network was able to produce. The following is an example of free generated text, using the first strategy.

The trigger sequence of 100 characters (not italics) comes from the first sentence of the fairy tale, *Snow white and Rose red*. The remaining text has been automatically generated by the network.

> *SNOW-WHITE AND ROSE-RED There was once a poor widow who lived in a lonely cottage. In front of the cas, and a hunbred of wine behind the door of the; and he said the ansmer: 'What want yeurnKyow yours went for bridd, like is good any, or cries, and we will say I only gave the witeved to the brood of the country to go away with it.' But when the father said, 'The cat soon crick.' The youth, the old ...*

The network has successfully learned the structure of the English language. Although the text is not perfect, you can see sensible character combinations, full words, some correct usage of quotation marks, and other similarly interesting features that the network has assimilated from the training text.

Generating Product Names with RNNs

This last NLP case study is similar to the previous one. There, we wanted the network to create new free text based on a start sequence; here, we want the network to create new free words based on a start token. There, we wanted the network to create new sequences of words; here, we want the network to create new sequences of characters. Indeed, the goal of this product name generation case study is to create new names – that is, new words. While there'll be some differences, the approaches will be similar.

In this section, we will explore the details of this new approach.

The Problem of Product Name Generation

Normally, we don't associate artificial intelligence with creativity, as it is usually used to predict the outcome based on previously seen examples. The challenge for this case study is to use artificial intelligence to create something new, which is thought to be in the domain of creative minds.

Let's take a classic creative marketing example: product naming. Before a new product can be launched to the market, it actually needs a name. To find the name, the most creative minds of the company come together to generate a number of proposals for product names, taking different requirements into account. For example, the product name should sound familiar to the customers and yet be new and fresh too. Of all those candidates, ultimately only one will survive and be adopted as the name for the new product. Not an easy task!

Now, let's take one of the most creative industries: fashion. A company specializing in outdoor wear has a new line of clothes ready for the market. The task is to generate a sufficiently large number of name candidates for the new line of clothing. Names of mountains were proposed, as many other outdoor fashion labels have. Names of mountains evoke the feeling of nature and sound familiar to potential customers. However, new names must also be copyright free and original enough to stand out in the market.

Why not use fictitious mountain names then? Since they are fictitious, they are copyright free and differ from competitor names; however, since they are similar to existing mountain names, they also sound familiar enough to potential customers. Could an artificial intelligence model help generate new fictitious mountain names that still sound realistic enough and are evocative of adventure? What kind of network architecture could we use for such a task?

As we want to be able to form new words that are somehow reminiscent of mountain names, the network must be trained on the names of already-existing mountains.

To form the training set, we use a list of 33,012 names of US mountains, as extracted from Wikipedia through a Wikidata query.

Figure 7.31 shows you a subset of the training data:

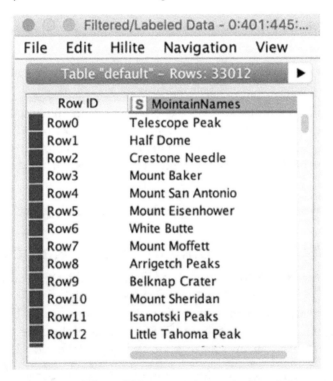

Figure 7.31 – Subset of US mountain names in the training set

Now that we have some training data, we can think about the network architecture. This time, we want to train a **many-to-many** LSTM-based RNN (see *Figure 7.32*). This means that during training, we have a sequence as input and a sequence as output. During deployment, the RNN, based on some initialized hidden states and the start token, must predict the first character of the new name candidate; then at the next step, based on the predicted character and on the updated hidden states, it must predict the next character – and so on until an end token is predicted and the process of generating the new candidate name is concluded:

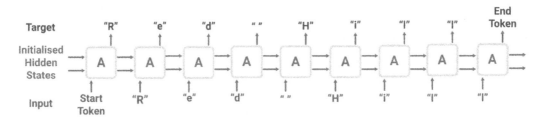

Figure 7.32 – Simplified, unrolled visualization of the many-to-many RNN architecture for the product name generation case study

To train the LSTM unit for this task, we need two sequences: an input sequence, made of a start token plus the mountain name, and a target sequence, made of the mountain name plus an end token. Notice that, at each training iteration, we feed the correct character into the network from the training set and not its prediction. This is called the **teacher forcing** training approach.

Let's focus first on preprocessing and encoding input and target sequences.

Preprocessing and Encoding Mountain Names

The goal of the preprocessing is to create and encode input and target sequences, including the start and end tokens. As in the previous case study, we want to use one-hot encoding. Therefore, we create an index-based encoding, and we use the **From Collection of Number (integer) to One-Hot Tensor in the Keras Network Learner** node conversion option. We also want to use 1 as the start token index and 0 as the end token index.

In the last case study, you learned that during training, the lengths of the sequences in one batch have to be the same. Therefore, we take the number of characters of the longest mountain name (58) plus 1 as the sequence length. Since this is the length of the longest mountain name, there is no need for truncation, but all shorter sequences will be zero-padded by adding multiple end tokens:

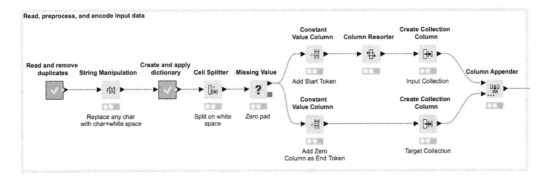

Figure 7.33 – Workflow to read, encode, and create the input and target sequences for mountain name generation

The workflow snippet in the preceding figure creates the input and target sequences by doing the following:

1. Reading the mountain names and removing duplicates by using the **Table Reader** node and the **Duplicate Row Filter** node

2. Replacing each `<space>` with a tilde character and afterward, each character with the character itself and `<space>`, using two **String Manipulation** nodes (this step is described in detail in the preprocessing of the previous case study, *Free text generation with RNNs*)

3. Creating and applying a dictionary (we will have a close look at this step in the next sub-section)

4. Character splitting based on `<space>` and replacing all missing values with end tokens, to zero pad too-short sequences

5. Creating input and target sequences as collection type cells

Most of the steps are similar to the preprocessing steps in the case study of free text generation with RNNs. We will only take a closer look at *step 3* and *step 5*. Let's start with *step 3*.

Creating and Applying a Dictionary

Creating and applying the dictionary is implemented in the **Create and apply dictionary** metanode. *Figure 7.34* shows its contents. The input to this metanode is mountain names with spaced characters:

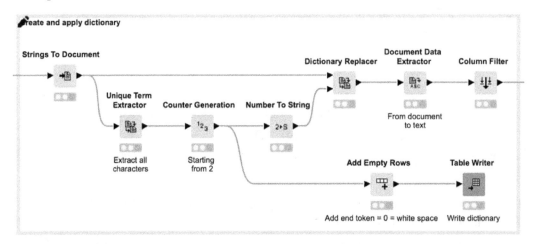

Figure 7.34 – Workflow snippet inside the Create and apply dictionary metanode

In this metanode, we again use nodes from the KNIME Text Processing extension. The **Strings To Document** node tokenizes these names with spaced characters so that each character becomes its own term. Then, the **Unique Term Extractor** node gives us the list of unique characters in all documents – that is, the character set. The **Counter Generation** node assigns an index to each character starting from 2, as we want to use indexes 0 and 1 for the end and start tokens. To use it as a dictionary in the next step, the created numerical indexes are transformed into strings by the **Number To String** node. Finally, the dictionary is applied (the **Dictionary Replacer** node), to transform characters into indexes in the original mountain names, and the text is extracted from the document (the **Document Data Extractor** node).

> **Tip**
>
> The KNIME Text Processing extension and some of their nodes, such as **Strings To Document**, **Unique Term Extractor**, **Dictionary Replacer**, and **Document Data Extractor**, were introduced more in detail in the first case study of this chapter, *Finding the Tone of Your Customers' Voice – Sentiment Analysis*.

In the separate, lower branch of the workflow snippet, we finalize the dictionary for the deployment by adding one more row for the end token, using the **Empty Table Row** node (see *Figure 7.35*). This node adds a number of rows to the input data table, either with missing values or with predefined constant values for each cell type. In our case, we add one additional row, and we use 0 as the default value for the integer cells and an empty string for the string cells. This adds one new row to our dictionary table, with 0 in the index column and empty strings in the character columns. We need this additional row in the deployment workflow to remove the end token(s):

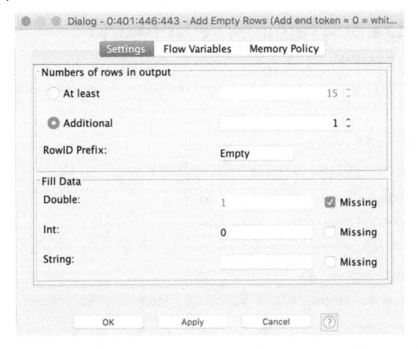

Figure 7.35 – Configuration window of the Add Empty Rows node

Let's move on to the last step of the preprocessing.

Creating the Input and Target Sequences

After the **Missing Value** node in the workflow in *Figure 7.35*, we have the zero-padded, encoded sequences. What is missing, though, is the start token at the beginning of the input sequence and the end token at the end of the target sequence, to make sure that the input and target sequence have the same length.

The additional values are added with **Constant Values Column** nodes, where the constant value 1 is used for the start token in the input sequence and the value 0 for the end token in the target sequence. In the case of the input sequence, the new column with the start token must be at the beginning. This is taken care of by the **Column Resorter** node. Now, the sequences can be aggregated and transformed into collection cells, using the **Create Collection Column** node.

Let's now design and train the appropriate network architecture.

Defining and Training the Network Architecture

The process of designing and training the network is similar to the process used in the previous NLP case studies.

Designing the Network

In this case, we want to use a network with five layers:

- A **Keras input layer** to define the input shape
- A **Keras LSTM layer** for the sequence analysis
- A **Keras dropout layer** for regularization
- A **Keras dense layers** with linear activation
- A **Keras softmax layer** to transform the output into a probability distribution

The number of unique characters in the training set – that is, the character set size – is 95. Since we allow sequences of variable length, the shape of the input layer is ?, 95. The ? stands for a variable sequence length.

Next, we have the **Keras LSTM Layer** node. This time, it is important to activate the **Return sequences** and **Return state** checkboxes, as we need the intermediate output states during the training process and the cell state in the deployment. We also set 256 units for this layer and we have left all other settings unchanged.

In this case study, we want to add even more randomization to the character pick at the output layer, to increment the network creativity. This is done by introducing the τ **temperature** parameter in the softmax function of the trained output layer.

Remember, the softmax function is defined as follows:

$$P(y = j|x) = \frac{e^{z_j}}{\sum_{k=1}^{K} e^{z_k}} \text{ with } z_i = x^T w_i$$

If we now introduce the additional τ **temperature** parameter, the formula for the activation function changes to the following:

$$P(y = j|x) = \frac{e^{z_j/\tau}}{\sum_{k=1}^{K} e^{z_k/\tau}} \text{ with } z_i = x^T w_i.$$

This means we divide the linear part by τ before applying the softmax function.

To be able to insert the temperature parameter after training, we split the output layer into two layers: one **Keras Dense Layer** node with a linear activation function for the linear part and one **Keras Softmax Layer** node to apply the activation function.

> **Important note**
>
> Temperature is a parameter that can be added after training to control the confidence of the network output.
>
> $\tau < 1$ makes the network more confident but also more conservative. This often leads to generating the same results at every run.
>
> $\tau > 1$ implements softer probability distributions over the different outputs. This leads to more diversity but, at the same time, also to more mistakes, such as in this case, character combinations that are impossible in English.

Training and Postprocessing the Network

The network is trained using the **Keras Network Learner** node. For the input data and the target data, the **From Collection of Number (integer)** conversion to **One-Hot Tensor** is selected. The different characters are again like different classes in a multi-class classification problem; therefore, the **Categorical Cross Entropy** loss function is adopted for training.

In the third tab, **Options**, the training phase is set to run for 30 epochs, with a batch size of 128 data rows, shuffling the data before each epoch, and using Adam as the optimizer algorithm with the default settings. So far, this is all the same as in the previous NLP case studies.

After training the network, the temperature, τ, is added by using the **DL Python Editor** node with the following lines of Python code:

```
from keras.models import Model
from keras.layers import Input, Lambda
from keras import backend as K
# Define Inputs
state1=Input((256,))
state2=Input((256,))
new_input=Input((1,95))
# Extract layers
lstm=input_network.layers[-4]
dense_softmax=input_network.layers[-1]
dense_linear=input_network.layers[-2]
# Apply LSTM Layer on new Inputs
x, h1, h2=lstm(new_input, initial_state=[state1, state2])
# Apply the linear layer
linear=dense_linear(x)
# Add lambda
linear_div_temp=Lambda(lambda x: x*0.9)(linear)
# Apply Softmax activation
probabilities = dense_softmax(linear_div_temp)
output_network = Model(inputs=[new_input, state1, state2],
outputs=[probabilities, h1, h2])
```

Remember that the hidden states of the previous LSTM unit are always used as input in the next LSTM unit. Therefore, three inputs are defined in the code: two for the two hidden states and one for the last predicted character encoded as a one-hot vector.

Finally, the network is transformed into a TensorFlow network object and saved for deployment. The final training workflow is shown in *Figure 7.36*:

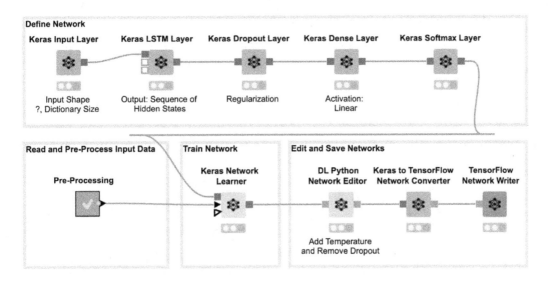

Figure 7.36 – Training workflow for the product name generation case study

The workflow is available on the KNIME Hub: `https://hub.knime.com/kathrin/`
`spaces/Codeless%20Deep%20Learning%20with%20KNIME/latest/`
`Chapter%207/`.

Let's continue with the deployment workflow.

Building a Deployment Workflow

The deployment workflow again uses the recursive loop approach, similar to the deployment workflow of the NLP and the demand prediction case studies. This time, though, there is one big difference.

In the last two case studies, the hidden state vectors were re-initialized at each iteration, as we always had m previous characters or m previous values as input. In this case study, we pass back, from the loop end node to the loop start node, not only the predicted index but also the two hidden state tensors from the LSTM layer.

In *Figure 7.37*, you can see the deployment workflow, which is also available on the KNIME Hub: `https://hub.knime.com/kathrin/spaces/Codeless%20 Deep%20Learning%20with%20KNIME/latest/Chapter%207/`. Let's look at the setting differences in detail:

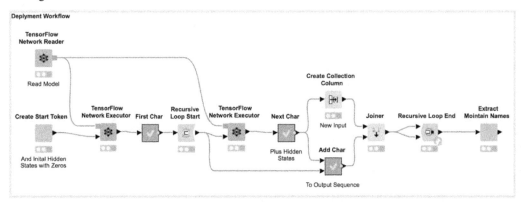

Figure 7.37 – Deployment workflow to create multiple possible product names

The first component, **Create Start Token**, sets the number, k, of new fictitious mountain names to generate. Then, it creates a table with three columns and k rows. One column contains only start tokens – that is, a collection cell with the value 1. The other two columns contain the initial hidden states – that is, collection cells with 256 zeros in both columns.

The **TensorFlow Network Executor** node executes the network one first time, producing as output the probability distribution over the indexes. In the configuration window of **TensorFlow Network Executor**, we have selected as input the columns with the first hidden state, the second hidden state, and the input collection. In addition, we set three output columns: one output column for the probability distribution, one output column for the first hidden state, and one output column for the second hidden state. We then pick the next index-encoded character according to the output probability distribution using the **Random Label Assigner (Data)** node in the **First Char** metanode. All these output values, predicted indexes, and hidden states make their way to the loop start node to predict the second index-encoded character.

Then, we start the recursive loop to generate one character after the next. At each iteration, we apply the network to the last predicted index and hidden states. We then pick the next character, again with the **Random Number Assigner (Data)** node, and we feed the last predicted value and the new hidden states into the lower input port of the **Recursive Loop End** node so that they can reach back to the loop start node.

In the **Extract Mountain Names** component, we finally apply the dictionary – created in the training workflow – and we remove all the mountain names that appeared already in the training set.

In *Figure 7.38*, you can see some of the generated mountain names. Indeed, they are new, copyright-free, evocative of mountains, and nature-feeling, and can be generated automatically in a number k as high as desired:

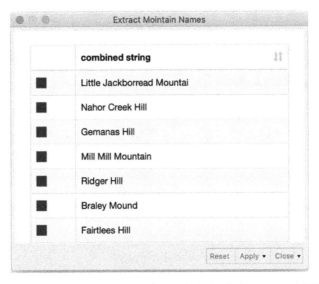

Figure 7.38 – Mountain names generated by the deployment workflow

One of them will eventually be chosen as the new product name.

Summary

We have reached the end of this relatively long chapter. Here, we have described three NLP case studies, each one solved by training an LSTM-based RNN applied to a time series prediction kind of problem.

The first case study analyzed movie review texts to extract the sentiment hidden in it. We dealt there with a simplified problem, considering a binary classification (positive versus negative) rather than considering too many nuances of possible user sentiment.

The second case study was language modeling. Training an RNN on a given text corpus with a given style produced a network capable of generating free text in that given style. Depending on the text corpus on which the network is trained, it can produce fairy tales, Shakespearean dialogue, or even rap songs. We showed an example that generates text in fairy tale style. The same workflows can be easily extended with more success to generate rap songs (R. Silipo, *AI generated rap songs*, CustomerThink, 2019, `https://customerthink.com/ai-generated-rap-songs/`) or Shakespearean dialogue (R. Silipo, *Can AI write like Shakespeare?*, Towards data Science, 2019, `https://towardsdatascience.com/can-ai-write-like-shakespeare-de710befbfee`).

The last case study involved the generation of candidates for new product names that must be innovative and copyright-free, stands out in the market, and be evocative of nature. So, we trained an RNN to generate fictitious mountain names to be used as name candidates for a new outdoor clothing line.

In the next chapter, we will describe one more NLP example: neural machine translation.

Questions and Exercises

1. What is a word embedding?

    a) An encoding functionality that can be trained within the neural network

    b) A text cleaning procedure

    c) A training algorithm for an RNN

    d) A postprocessing technique to choose the most likely character

2. Which statement regarding sentiment analysis is true?

    a) Sentiment analysis can only be solved with RNNs.

    b) Sentiment analysis is the same as emotion detection.

    c) Sentiment analysis identifies the underlying sentiment in a text.

    d) Sentiment analysis is an image processing task.

3. What does a many-to-many architecture mean?

    a) An architecture with an input sequence and an output sequence

    b) An architecture with an input sequence and a vector as output

    c) An architecture with many hidden units and many outputs

    d) An architecture with one input feature and an output sequence

4. Why do I need a trigger sequence for free text generation?

    a) To calculate the probabilities

    b) To compare the prediction with the target

    c) To initialize the hidden states before predicting the next character

    d) To save the network in TensorFlow format

8
Neural Machine Translation

In the previous chapter, *Chapter 7, Implementing NLP Applications*, we introduced several text encoding techniques and used them in three **Natural Language Processing** (**NLP**) applications. One of the applications was for free text generation. The result showed that it is possible for a network to learn the structure of a language, so as to generate text in a certain style.

In this chapter, we will build on top of this case study for free text generation and train a neural network to automatically translate sentences from a source language into a target language. To do that, we will use concepts learned from the free text generation network, as well as from the autoencoder introduced in *Chapter 5, Autoencoder for Fraud Detection*.

We will start by describing the general concept of machine translation, followed by an introduction to the encoder-decoder neural architectures that will be used for neural machine translation. Next, we will discuss all the steps involved in the implementation of the application, from preprocessing to defining the network structure to training and applying the network.

The chapter is organized into the following sections:

- Idea of Neural Machine Translation

- Encoder-Decoder Architecture

- Preparing the Data for the Two Languages

- Building and Training an Encoder-Decoder Architecture

Idea of Neural Machine Translation

Automatic translation has been a popular and challenging task for a long time now. The flexibility and ambiguity of the human language make it still one of the most difficult tasks to implement. The same word or phrase can have different meanings depending on the context and, often, there might not be just one correct translation, but many possible ways to translate the same sentence. So, how can a computer learn to translate text from one language into another? Different approaches have been introduced over the years, all with the same goal: to automatically translate sentences or text from a source language into a target language.

The development of automatic translation systems started in the early 1970s with **Rule-Based Machine Translation** (**RBMT**). Here, automatic translation was implemented through hand-developed rules and dictionaries by specialized linguists at the lexical, syntactic, and semantic levels of sentences.

In the 1990s, **statistical machine translation** models became state of the art, even though the first concepts for statistical machine translation were introduced in 1949 by Warren Weaver. Instead of using dictionaries and handwritten rules, the idea became to use a vast corpus of examples to train statistical models. This task can be described as modeling the probability distribution, $p(t|s)$, that a string, t, in the target language (for example, German) is the translation of a string, s, in the source language (for example, English). Different approaches have been introduced to model this $p(t|s)$ probability distribution, the most popular of which came from the Bayes theorem and modeled $p(t|s)$ as $p(s|t)p(t)$. Thus, in this approach, the task is split into two subtasks: training a language model, $p(t)$, and modeling the probability, $p(s|t)$. More generally, several subtasks can be defined, and several models are trained and tuned for each subtask.

More recently, neural machine translation gained quite some popularity in the task of automatic translation. Also, here, a vast corpus of example sentences in a source and target language is required to train the translation model. The difference between classical statistical-based models and neural machine translation is in the definition of the task: instead of training many small sub-components and tuning them separately, one single network is trained in an end-to-end fashion.

One network architecture that can be used for neural machine translations is an encoder-decoder network. Let's find out what this is.

Encoder-Decoder Architecture

In this section, we will first introduce the general concept of an encoder-decoder architecture. Afterward, we will focus on how the encoder is used in neural machine translation. In the last two subsections, we will concentrate on how the decoder is applied during training and deployment.

One of the possible structures for neural machine translation is the **encoder-decoder** network. In *Chapter 5, Autoencoder for Fraud Detection*, we introduced the concept of a neural network consisting of an encoder and a decoder component. Remember, in the case of an autoencoder, the task of the encoder component is to extract a dense representation of the input, while the task of the decoder component is to recreate the input based on the dense representation given by the encoder.

In the case of encoder-decoder networks for neural machine translation, the task of the encoder is to extract the context of the sentence in the source language (the input sentence) into a dense representation, while the task of the decoder is to create the corresponding translation in the target language from the dense representation of the encoder.

Figure 8.1 visualizes this process:

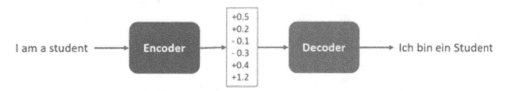

Figure 8.1 – The general structure of an encoder-decoder network for neural machine translation

Here, the source language is English, and the target language is German. The goal is to translate the sentence I am a student from English into German, where one correct translation could be Ich bin ein Student. The encoder consumes the I am a student sentence and produces as output a dense vector representation of the content of the sentence. This dense vector representation is fed into the decoder, which then outputs the translation.

In this case study, the input and the output of the network are sequences. Therefore, **Recurrent Neural Network (RNN)** layers are commonly used in the encoder and decoder parts, to capture the context information and to handle input and output sequences of variable length.

In general, encoder-decoder RNN-based architectures are used for all kinds of sequence-to-sequence analysis tasks – for example, question-and-answer systems. Here, the question is first processed by the encoder, which creates a dense numerical representation of it, then the decoder generates the answer.

Let's focus now on the encoder part of the neural translation network, before we move on to the decoder, to understand what kind of data preparation is needed.

Applying the Encoder

The goal of the encoder is to extract a dense vector representation of the context from the input sentence. This can be achieved by using a **Long Short-Term Memory (LSTM)** layer where the encoder reads the input sentence (in English) either word by word or character by character.

> Tip
>
> In *Chapter 6, Recurrent Neural Networks for Demand Prediction*, we introduced LSTM layers. Remember that an LSTM layer has two hidden states, one being the cell state and the other being a filtered version of it. The cell state contains a summary of all previous inputs.

In a classic encoder-decoder network architecture, the vectors of the hidden states of the LSTM layer are used to store the dense representation. *Figure 8.2* shows how the LSTM-based encoder processes the input sentence:

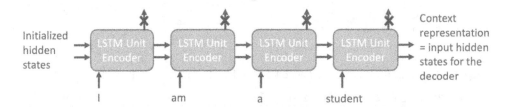

Figure 8.2 – Example of how the encoder processes the input sentence

The encoder starts with some initialized hidden state vectors. At each step, the next word in the sequence is fed into the LSTM unit and the hidden state vectors are updated. The final hidden state vectors, after processing the whole input sequence in the source language, contain the context representation and become the input for the hidden state vectors in the decoder.

The intermediate output hidden states of the encoder are not used.

Now that we have a dense representation of the context, we can use it to feed the decoder. While the way the encoder works during training and deployment stays the same, the way the decoder works is a bit different during training and deployment.

Let's first concentrate on the training phase.

Applying the Decoder during Training

The task of the decoder is to generate the translation in the target sequence from the dense context representation, either word by word or character by character, using again an RNN with an LSTM layer. This means that, in theory, each predicted word/character should be fed back into the network as the next input. However, during training, we can skip the theory and apply the concept of **teacher forcing**. Here, the actual word/character is fed back into the LSTM unit instead of the predicted word/character, which greatly benefits the training procedure.

Figure 8.3 shows an example of teacher forcing during the training phase of the decoder:

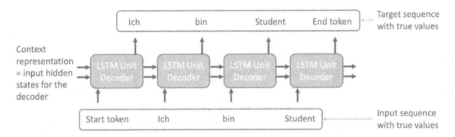

Figure 8.3 – Example of teacher forcing while training of the decoder

The dense context representation of the encoder is used to initialize the hidden states of the decoder's LSTM layer. Next, two sequences are used by the LSTM layer to train the decoder: the input sequence with the true word/character values, starting with a **start token**, and the target sequence, also with the true word/character values.

> **Important note**
> The target sequence, in this case, is the input sequence shifted by one character and with an end token at the end.

To summarize, three sequences of words/characters are needed during training:

- The input sequence for the encoder
- The input sequence for the decoder
- The output sequence for the decoder

During deployment, we don't have the input and output sequence for the decoder. So, let's find out how the trained decoder can be used during deployment.

Applying the Decoder during Deployment

When we apply the trained network, we don't know the true values of the translation sequence. So, we feed only the dense context representation from the encoder and a start token into the decoder. Then, the decoder applies the LSTM unit multiple times, always feeding the last predicted word/character back into the LSTM unit as input for the next step. *Figure 8.4* visualizes the usage of the decoder during deployment:

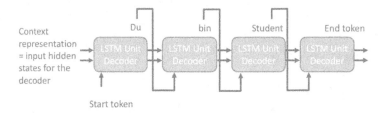

Figure 8.4 – Usage of the decoder during deployment

In the first step, the dense context representation from the encoder forms the input hidden state vectors and the **start token** forms the input value for the decoder. Based on this, the first word is predicted, and the hidden state vectors are updated. In the next steps, the updated hidden state vectors and the last predicted word are fed back into the LSTM unit, to predict the next word. This means that if a wrong word has been predicted once; the error accumulates in this kind of sequential prediction.

In this section, you learned what encoder-decoder neural networks are and how they can be used for neural machine translation.

In the next sections, we will go through the steps required to train a neural machine translation network to translate sentences from English into German. As usual, the first step is data preparation.

So, let's start by creating the three sequences required to train a neural machine translation network using an encoder-decoder structure.

Preparing the Data for the Two Languages

In *Chapter 7, Implementing NLP Applications*, we talked about the advantages and disadvantages of training neural networks at the character and word levels. As we already have some experience with the character level, we decided to also train this network for automatic translation at the character level.

To train a neural machine translation network, we need a dataset with bilingual sentence pairs for the two languages. Datasets for different language combinations can be downloaded for free at www.manythings.org/anki/. From there, we can download a dataset containing a number of sentences in English and German that are commonly used in everyday life. The dataset consists of two columns only: the original short text in English and the corresponding translation in German.

Figure 8.5 shows you a subset of this dataset to be used as the training set:

	JavaScript Table View	
Hug Tom.	Umarmen Sie Tom!	
Hug Tom.	Umarmt Tom!	
Hug Tom.	Drückt Tom!	
Hug Tom.	Drücken Sie Tom!	
Hug Tom.	Drück Tom!	
I agree.	Ich bin einverstanden.	
I'll go.	Ich gehe.	
I'm fat.	Ich bin fett.	
I'm fat.	Ich bin dick.	
I'm old.	Ich bin alt.	
I'm sad.	Ich bin traurig.	
I'm shy.	Ich bin schüchtern.	
It's me!	Ich bin's.	
It's me.	Ich bin's.	
Kiss me.	Küsst mich.	
Lock it.	Schließ es ab.	
Lock it.	Schließe sie ab.	

Reset Apply ▲ Close ▲

Figure 8.5 – Subset of the training set with English and German sentences

As you can see, for some English sentences, there is more than one possible translation. For example, the sentence Hug Tom can be translated to Umarmt Tom, Umarmen Sie Tom, or Drücken Sie Tom.

Remember that a network doesn't understand characters, only numerical values. Thus, character input sequences need to be transformed into numerical input sequences. In the first part of the previous chapter, we introduced several encoding techniques.

As for the free text generation case study, we adopted **one-hot encoding** as the encoding scheme, which will be implemented in two steps. First, an **index-based encoding** is produced; then, this index-based encoding is converted into a one-hot encoding inside the **Keras Network Learner** node during training and the **Keras Network Executor** node when applying the trained network.

In addition, a dictionary mapping for the English and German characters with their index is also needed. In the previous chapter, for product name generation, we resorted to the **KNIME Text Processing Extension** to generate the index-based encoding for the character sequences. We will do the same here.

For the training of the neural machine translation, three index-encoded character sequences must be created:

- The input sequence to feed the encoder. This is the index-encoded input character sequence from the source language – in our case, English.

- The input sequence to feed the decoder. This is the index-encoded character sequence for the target language, starting with a start token.

- The target sequence to train the decoder, which is the input sequence to the decoder shifted by one step in the past and ending with an end token.

The workflow in *Figure 8.6* reads the bilingual sentence pairs, extracts the first 10,000 sentences, performs the index-encoding for the sentences in English and German separately, and finally, partitions the dataset into a training and a test set:

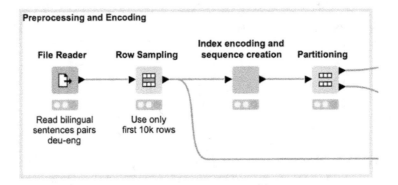

Figure 8.6 – Preprocessing workflow snippet to prepare the data to train the
network for neural machine translation

Most of the work of the preprocessing happens inside the component named **Index encoding and sequence creation**. *Figure 8.7* shows its content:

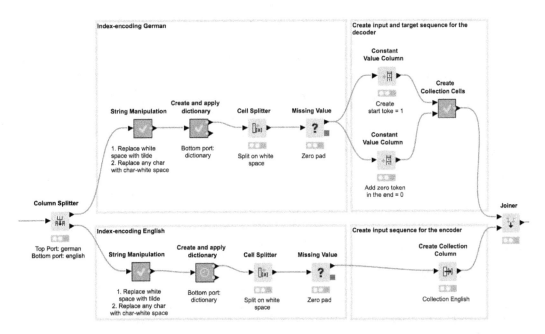

Figure 8.7 – Workflow snippet inside the component named Index encoding and sequence creation

The workflow snippet inside the component first separates the English text from the German text, then produces the index-encoding for the sentences – in the upper part for the German sentences and the lower part for the English sentences. Then, finally, for each language, a dictionary is created, applied, and saved.

After the index-encoding of the German sentences, the two sequences for the decoder are created: in the upper branch by adding a start token at the beginning and in the lower branch by adding an end token at the end of the sequence.

All sequences from the German and English languages are then transformed into collection cells so that they can be converted to one-hot encoding before training.

Building and Training the Encoder-Decoder Architecture

Now that the three sequences are available, we can start defining the network structure within a workflow. In this section, you will learn how to define and train an encoder-decoder structure in KNIME Analytics Platform. Once the network is trained, you will learn how the encoder and decoder can be extracted into two networks. In the last section, we will discuss how the extracted networks can be used in a deployment workflow to translate English sentences into German.

Defining the Network Structure

In the encoder-decoder architecture, we want to have both the encoder and the decoder as LSTM networks. The encoder and the decoder have different input sequences. The English one-hot-encoded sentences are the input for the encoder and the German one-hot-encoded sentences are the input for the decoder. This means two input layers are needed: one for the encoder and one for the decoder.

The **encoder** network is made up of two layers:

- An input layer implemented via the **Keras Input Layer** node: The shape of the input tensor is $[?, n]$, where n is the dictionary size for the source language. $?$ in the input tensor shape represents variable length sequences, while n indicates one-hot vectors with n components. In our example, $n = 71$ for the English language, and the shape of the input tensor is $[?, 71]$.

- An LSTM Layer via a **Keras LSTM Layer** node: In this node, we use 256 units and enable the *return state* checkbox to pass the hidden states to the upcoming decoder network.

The **decoder network** is made of three layers:

- First, a **Keras Input Layer** node to define the input shape. Again, the input shape $[?, m]$, is a tuple, where $?$ represents a variable length and m the size of each vector in the input sequence – that is, the dictionary size of the target language (German). In our example, the input tensor for German has a shape of $[?, 85]$.

- An LSTM layer via a Keras **LSTM Layer** node. This time, the optional input ports are used to feed the hidden states from the encoder into the decoder. This means the output port of the first LSTM layer in the encoder network is connected to both optional input ports in the decoder network. In addition, the output port of the Keras Input Layer node for the German input sequences is connected to the top input port. In its configuration window, it is important to select the correct input tensors as well as the hidden tensors. The *return sequence* and *return state* checkboxes must be activated to return the intermediate output hidden states, which are used in the next layer to extract the probability distribution for the next predicted character. As in the encoder LSTM, 256 units are used.

- Last, a softmax layer is added via a **Keras Dense Layer** node to produce the probability vector of the characters in the dictionary in the target language (German). In the configuration window, the softmax activation function is selected to have 85 units, which is the size of the dictionary of the target language.

The workflow in *Figure 8.8* defines this encoder-decoder network structure:

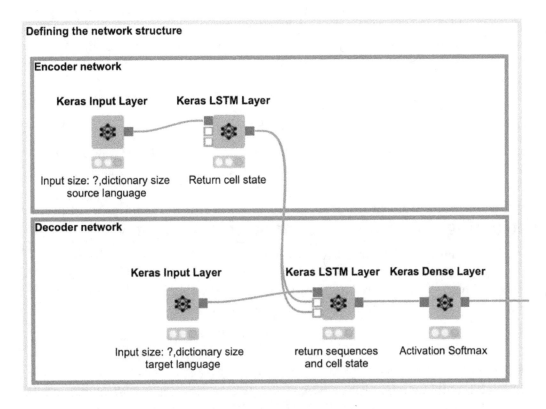

Figure 8.8 – The workflow snippet that defines the encoder-decoder network

The upper part of the workflow defines the encoder with a **Keras Input Layer** and **Keras LSTM Layer** node. In the lower part, the decoder is defined as described previously.

Now that we have defined the encoder-decoder architecture, we can train the network.

Training the Network

As in all other examples in this book, the **Keras Network Learner** node is used to train the network.

In the first tab of the configuration window, named **Input Data**, the input columns for both input layers are selected: in the upper part for the source language, which means the input for the encoder, and in the lower part for the target language, which means the input for the decoder. To convert the index-encoded sequences into one-hot-encoded sequences, the **From Collection of Number (integer) to One-Hot Tensor** conversion type is used for both columns.

In the next tab of the configuration window, named **Target Data**, the column with the target sequence for the decoder is selected and the **From Collection of Number (integer) to One-Hot Tensor** conversion type is enabled again. Characters are again considered like classes in a multi-class classification problem; therefore, the Categorical Cross Entropy loss function is adopted for the training process.

In the third tab, **Options**, the training phase is set to run for a maximum of 120 epochs, with a batch size of 128 data rows, shuffling the data before each epoch and using Adam as the optimizer algorithm with the default settings.

During training, we monitor the performance using the **Learner Monitor** view of the Keras Network Learner node and decide to stop the learning process when an accuracy of 94% has been reached.

Extracting the Trained Encoder and Decoder

To apply the trained model to translate new sentences, we need to split the encoder and decoder apart. To do so, each part is extracted from the complete network using a few lines of Python code in a **DL Python Network Editor** node. This node allows us to edit and modify the network structure using the **Python libraries** directly.

Remember that the output of the decoder is the probability distribution across all characters in the target language. In *Chapter 7, Implementing NLP Applications*, we introduced two approaches for the prediction of the next character based on this output probability distribution. Option one picks the character with the highest probability as the next character. Option two picks the next character randomly according to the given probability distribution.

In this case study, we use option one and implement it directly in the decoder via an additional **lambda layer**. To summarize, when postprocessing, we need to perform the following steps:

- Separate the encoder and decoder parts of the network.

- Introduce a lambda layer with an argmax function that selects the character with the highest probability in the softmax layer.

> **Important note**
> Lamba layers allow you to use arbitrary TensorFlow functions when constructing sequential and functional API models using TensorFlow as the backend. Lambda layers are best suited for simple operations or quick experimentation.

Let's start with extracting the encoder.

Extracting the Encoder

In the following code, you can see the Python code used to extract the encoder:

1. Load packages:

    ```
    from keras.models import Model
    from keras.layers import Input
    ```

2. Define input:

    ```
    new_input = Input((None,70))
    ```

3. Extract trained encoder LSTM and define model:

    ```
    encoder = input_network.layers[-3]
    output = encoder(new_input)
    output_network = Model(inputs=new_input, outputs=output)
    ```

It starts with defining the input, feeding it into the encoder's LSTM layer, and then defining the output.

In more detail, in the first two lines, the required packages are loaded. Next, an input layer is defined; then, the -3 layer – the trained LSTM layer of the encoder – is extracted. Finally, the network output is defined as the output of the trained encoder LSTM layer

Now that we have extracted the encoder, let's see how we can extract the decoder.

Extracting the Decoder and Adding a Lambda Layer

In the following code snippet, you can see the code used in the **DL Python Network Editor** node to extract the decoder part and add the lambda layer to it:

1. Load the packages:

```
from keras.models import Model
from keras.layers import Input, Lambda
from keras import backend as K
```

2. Define the inputs:

```
state1 = Input((256,))
state2 = Input((256,))
new_input = Input((1,85))
```

3. Extract the trained decoder LSTM layer and softmax layer:

```
decoder_lstm = input_network.layers[-2]
decoder_dense = input_network.layers[-1]
```

4. Apply the LSTM and dense layer:

```
x, out_h, out_c = decoder_lstm(new_input, initial_
state=[state1, state2])
probability_output = decoder_dense(x)
```

5. Add the lambda layer and define the output:

```
argmax_output = Lambda(lambda x: K.argmax(x, axis=-1))
(probability_output)
output_network = Model(inputs=[new_input, state1,
state2], outputs=[probability_output, argmax_output,
out_h, out_c])
```

The code again first loads the necessary packages, then defines three inputs – two for the input hidden states and one for the one-hot-encoded character vector. Next, it extracts the trained LSTM layer and the softmax layer in the decoder. Finally, it introduces the lambda layer with the argmax function and defines the output.

For faster execution during deployment, the encoder and the decoder are converted into TensorFlow networks using the **Keras to TensorFlow Network Converter** node.

Now that we have trained the neural machine translation network and we have separated the encoder and the decoder, we want to apply them to the sentences in the test set.

The full training workflow is available on the KNIME Hub: `https://hub.knime.com/kathrin/spaces/Codeless%20Deep%20Learning%20with%20KNIME/latest/Chapter%208/`.

Applying the Trained Network for Neural Machine Translation

To apply the encoder and decoder networks to the test data, we need a workflow that first applies the encoder to the index-encoded English sentences to extract the context information, and then applies the decoder to produce the translation.

The decoder should be initialized with the first hidden states from the encoder and with the start token from the input sequence, to trigger the translation character by character in the recursive loop. *Figure 8.9* visualizes the process:

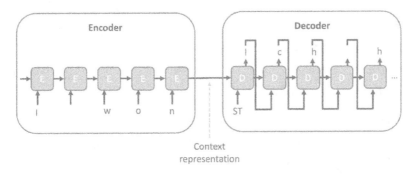

Figure 8.9 – The idea of applying the encoder and decoder model during deployment

The workflow snippet in *Figure 8.10* performs exactly these steps:

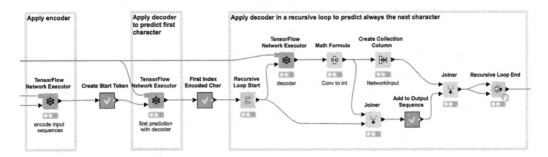

Figure 8.10 – This workflow snippet applies the trained encoder-decoder neural architecture to translate English sentences into German sentences

It starts with a **TensorFlow Network Executor** node (the first one on the left in *Figure 8.10*). This node takes the encoder and the index-encoded English sentences as input. In its configuration window, two outputs are defined from the LSTM hidden states.

Next, we create a start token and transform it into a collection cell. To this start token, we apply the decoder network using another **TensorFlow Network Executor** node (the second one from the left). In the configuration window, we make sure that the hidden states from the encoder produced in the previous **TensorFlow Network Executor** node are used as input. As output, we again set the hidden states, as well as the next predicted character – that is, the first character of the translated sentence.

Now, we enter the recursive loop, where this process is repeated multiple times using the updated hidden states from the last iteration and the last predicted character as input.

Finally, the German dictionary is applied to the index-encoded predicted characters and the final translation is obtained. The following is an excerpt of the translation results:

English	German	Translation
You run.	Du läufst.	Sie laufen.
You won.	Du hast gewonnen.	Sie gens!
She blushed.	Sie errötete.	Sie lief rot an.
Sit with me.	Setz dich zu mir!	Wirgen Sie mir!
Start again.	Fang noch einmal an.	Beginnen Sie noch einmal.
Stop trying.	Probieren Sie es nicht länger.	Probier es nicht länger.
Take a walk.	Geh spazieren!	Geht spazieren!
Talk to Tom.	Sprich mit Tom!	Rune mir es Tom!
That's cool.	Das ist cool.	Das ist geil.
Be brave.	Sei tapfer!	Seid tapfer!

Figure 8.11 – Final results of the deployed translation network on new English sentences

In the first column, we have the new English sentences, in the second column, the correct translations, and in the last column, the translation generated by the network. Most of these translations are actually correct, even though they don't match the sentences in column two, as the same sentence can have different translations. On the other hand, the translation of the `Talk to Tom` sentence is not correct as `rune` is not a German word.

The described deployment workflow is available on the KNIME Hub: `https://hub.knime.com/kathrin/spaces/Codeless%20Deep%20Learning%20with%20KNIME/latest/Chapter%208/`.

In this section, you have learned how you can define, train, and apply encoder-decoder architectures based on the example of neural machine translation at the character level.

Summary

In this chapter, we explored the topic of neural machine translation and trained a network to produce English-to-German translations.

We started with an introduction to automatic machine translation, covering its history from rule-based machine translation to neural machine translation. Next, we introduced the concept of encoder-decoder RNN-based architectures, which can be used for neural machine translation. In general, encoder-decoder architectures can be used for sequence-to-sequence prediction tasks or question-answer systems.

After that, we covered all the steps needed to train and apply a neural machine translation model at the character level, using a simple network structure with only one LSTM unit for both the encoder and decoder. The joint network, derived from the combination of the encoder and decoder, was trained using a **teacher forcing** paradigm.

At the end of the training phase and before deployment, a **lambda layer** was inserted in the decoder part to predict the character with the highest probability. In order to do that, the structure of the trained network was modified after the training process with a few lines of Python code in a DL Python Network Editor node. The Python code split the decoder and the encoder networks and added the lambda layer. This was the only part involving a short, simple snippet of Python code.

Of course, this network could be further improved in many ways – for example, by stacking multiple LSTM layers or by training the model at the word level using additional embeddings.

This is the last chapter on RNNs. In the next chapter, we want to move on to another class of neural networks, **Convolutional Neural Networks (CNNs)**, which have proven to be very successful for image processing.

Questions and Exercises

1. An encoder-decoder model is a:

   a.) Many-to-one architecture

   b.) Many-to-many architecture

   c.) One-to-many architecture

   d.) CNN architecture

2. What is the task of the encoder in neural machine translation?

   a.) To encode the characters

   b.) To generate the translation

   c.) To extract a dense representation of the content in the target language

   d.) To extract a dense representation of the content in the source language

3. What is another application for encoder-decoder LSTM networks?

   a.) Text classification

   b.) Question-answer systems

   c.) Language detection

   d.) Anomaly detection

9

Convolutional Neural Networks for Image Classification

In the previous chapters, we talked about **Recurrent Neural Networks (RNNs)** and how they can be applied to different types of sequential data and use cases. In this chapter, we want to talk about another family of neural networks, called **Convolutional Neural Networks (CNNs)**. CNNs are especially powerful when used on data with grid-like topology and spatial dependencies, such as images or videos.

We will start with a general introduction to CNNs, explaining the basic idea behind a convolution layer and introducing some related terminology such as padding, pooling, filters, and stride.

Afterward, we will build and train a CNN for image classification from scratch. We will cover all required steps: from reading and preprocessing of the images to defining, training, and applying the CNN.

To train a neural network from scratch, a huge amount of labeled data is usually required. For some specific domains, such as images or videos, such a large amount of data might not be available, and the training of a network might become impossible. Transfer learning is a proposed solution to handle this problem. The idea behind transfer learning consists of using a state-of-the-art neural network trained for a task A as a starting point for another, related, task B.

In this chapter, we will cover the following topics:

- Introduction to CNNs
- Classifying Images with CNNs
- Introduction to Transfer Learning
- Applying Transfer Learning for Cancer Type Prediction

Introduction to CNNs

CNNs are commonly used in image processing and have been the winning models in several image-processing competitions. They are often used, for example, for image classification, object detection, and semantic segmentation.

Sometimes, CNNs are also used for non-image-related tasks, such as recommendation systems, videos, or time-series analysis. Indeed, CNNs are not only applied to two-dimensional data with a grid structure but can also work when applied to one- or three-dimensional data. In this chapter, however, we focus on the most common CNN application area: **image processing**.

A CNN is a neural network with at least one **convolution layer**. As the name states, convolution layers perform a convolution mathematical transformation on the input data. Through such a mathematical transformation, convolution layers acquire the ability to detect and extract a number of features from an image, such as edges, corners, and shapes. Combinations of such extracted features are used to classify images or to detect specific objects within an image.

A convolution layer is often found together with a **pooling layer**, also commonly used in the feature extraction part of image processing.

The goal of this section is thus to explain how convolution layers and pooling layers work separately and together and to detail the different setting options for the two layers.

As mentioned, in this chapter we will focus on CNNs for image analysis. So, before we dive into the details of CNNs, let's quickly review how images are stored.

How are Images Stored?

A grayscale image can be stored as a matrix, where each cell represents one pixel of the image and the cell value represents the gray level of the pixel. For example, a black and white image, with size 5 x 5 pixels, can be represented as a matrix with dimensions 5 x 5, where each value of the matrix ranges between 0 and 1. 0 is a black pixel, 1 is a white pixel, and a value in between corresponds to a level of gray in the grayscale.

Figure 9.1 here depicts an example:

0	0	0	0	0
0	0	0.5	1	0
0	0.5	1	0.5	0
0	1	0.5	0	0
0	0	0	0	0

Figure 9.1 – Matrix representation of a grayscale 5 x 5 image

As each pixel is represented by one gray value only, one **channel** (matrix) is sufficient to represent this image. For color images, on the other hand, more than one value is needed to define the color of each pixel. One option is to use the three values specifying the intensity of red, green, and blue to define the pixel color. In the following screenshot, to represent a color image, three channels are used instead of one: (*Figure 9.2*):

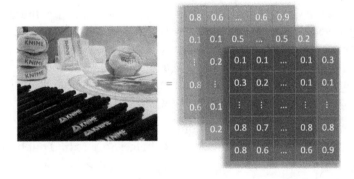

Figure 9.2 – Representing a 28 x 28 color image using three channels for RGB

Moving from a grayscale image to a **red, green, and blue** (RGB) image, the more general concept of **tensor**—instead of a simple matrix—becomes necessary. In this way, the grayscale image can be described as a tensor of $5 x 5 x 1$, while a color image with $28 x 28$ pixels can be represented with a $28 x 28 x 3$ tensor.

In general, a tensor representing an image with n pixels height, m pixels width, and k channels has the dimension n x m x k.

But why do we need special networks to analyze images? Couldn't we just **flatten** the image, represent each image as a long vector, and train a standard fully connected feedforward neural network?

> **Important note**
> The process of transforming a matrix representation of an image into a vector is called **flattening**.

Why do we need CNNs?

For basic binary images, flattening and fully connected feedforward networks might yield acceptable performance. However, with more complex images, with strong pixel dependencies throughout the image, the combination of flattening and feedforward neural networks usually fails.

Indeed, the spatial dependency is lost when the image is flattened into a vector. As a result, fully connected feedforward networks are not translation-invariant. This means that they produce different results for shifted versions of the same image. For example, a network might learn to identify a cat in the upper-left corner of an image, but the same network is not able to detect a cat in the lower-right corner of the same image.

In addition, the flattening of an image produces a very long vector, and therefore it requires a very large fully connected feedforward network with many weights. For example, for a $224 x 224$ pixel image with three channels, the network needs $224 * 224 * 3 = 150,528$ inputs. If the next layer has 100 neurons, we would need to train $15,052,800$ weights only in the first layer. You see that the number of weights can quickly become unmanageable, likely leading to overfitting during training.

Convolution layers, which are the main building block of a CNN, allow us to solve this problem by exploiting the spatial properties of the image. So, let's find out how a convolution layer works.

How does a Convolution Layer work?

The idea of CNNs is to use filters to detect patterns—also called features—such as corners, vertical edges, and horizontal edges, in different parts of an image.

For an image with one channel a **filter** is a small matrix, often of size 3 x 3 or 5 x 5, called a **kernel**. Different kernels—that is, matrices with different values—filter different patterns. A kernel moves across an image and performs a convolution operation. That convolution operation gives a name to the layer. The output of such a convolution is called a **feature map**.

> **Important note**
>
> For an input image with three channels (for example, an input tensor with shape 28 x 28 x 3,), a kernel with kernel size 2 has the shape 2x2x3. This means the kernel can incorporate information from all channels but only within a small (2 x 2, in this example) region of the input image.

Figure 9.3 here shows an example of how a convolution is calculated for an image of size 4 x 4 x 1 and a kernel with size 3 x 3:

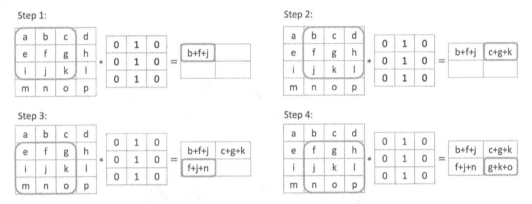

Figure 9.3 – Example of a convolution obtained by applying a 3 x 3 kernel to a 4 x 4 image

In this example, we start by applying the kernel to the upper-left 3 x 3 region of the image. The image values are elementwise multiplied with the kernel values and then summed up, as follows:

$$a * 0 + b * 1 + c * 0 + e * 0 + f * 1 + g * 0 + i * 0 + j * 1 + k * 0 = b + f + j$$

The result of this elementwise multiplication and sum is the first value, in the upper-left corner, in the output feature map. The kernel is then moved across the whole image to calculate all other values of the output feature map.

> **Important note**
>
> The convolution operation is denoted with a * and is different from
> a matrix multiplication. Even though the layer is called convolution,
> most neural network libraries actually implement a related function called
> **cross-correlation**. To perform a correct convolution, according to its
> mathematical definition, the kernel in addition must be flipped. For CNNs this
> doesn't make a difference because the weights are learned anyway.

In a convolution layer, a large number of filters (kernels) are trained in parallel on
the input dataset and for the required task. That is, the weights in the kernel are not
set manually but are adjusted automatically as weights during the network training
procedure. During execution, all trained kernels are applied to calculate the feature map.

The dimension of the feature map is then a tensor of size $n \; x \; m \; x \; \#filters$. In the example
in *Figure 9.3*, we applied only one kernel, and the dimension of the feature map is $2 \; x \; 2 \; x \; 1$.

Historically, kernels were designed manually for selected tasks. For example, the kernel
in *Figure 9.3* detects vertical lines. *Figure 9.4* here shows you the impact of some other
handcrafted kernels:

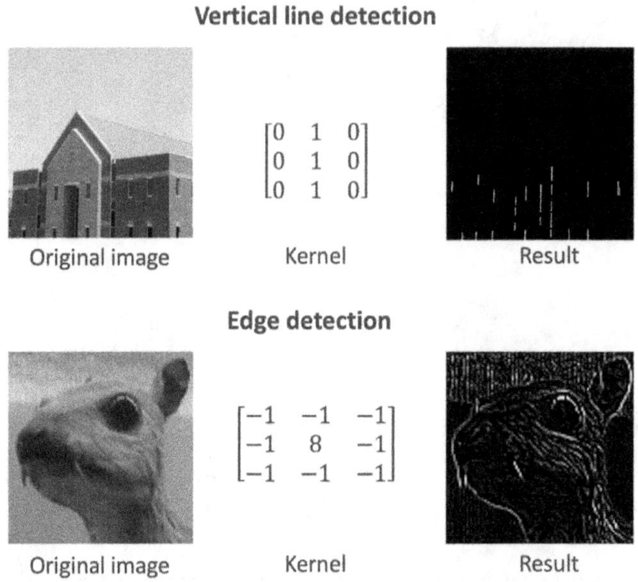

Vertical line detection

$$\begin{bmatrix} 0 & 1 & 0 \\ 0 & 1 & 0 \\ 0 & 1 & 0 \end{bmatrix}$$

Original image   Kernel   Result

Edge detection

$$\begin{bmatrix} -1 & -1 & -1 \\ -1 & 8 & -1 \\ -1 & -1 & -1 \end{bmatrix}$$

Original image   Kernel   Result

Figure 9.4 – Impact of some hand-crafted kernels on the original image

The convolution operation is just a part of the convolution layer. After that, a bias and a
non-linear activation function are applied to each entry in the feature map. For example,
we can add a bias value to each value in the feature map and then apply **rectified liner
unit (ReLU)** as an activation function to set all values below the bias to 0.

> **Important note**
>
> In *Chapter 3*, *Getting Started with Neural Networks*, we introduced dense layers. In a dense layer, the weighted sum of the input is first calculated; then, a bias value is added to the sum, and the activation function is applied. In a convolutional layer, the weighted sum of the dense layer is replaced by the convolution.

A convolution layer has multiple setting options. We have already introduced three of them along the way, and they are listed here:

- The kernel size, which is often 3 *x* 3
- The number of filters
- The activation function, where ReLU is the one most commonly used

There are three more setting options: padding, stride, and dilation rate. Let's continue with padding.

Introducing Padding

When we applied the filter in the example in *Figure 9.3*, the dimension of the feature map shrunk compared to the dimension of the input image. The input image had a size of 4 *x* 4 and the feature map a size of 2 *x* 2.

In addition, by looking at the feature map, we can see that pixels in the inner part of the input image (cells with values f, g, j, and k) are more often considered in the convolution than pixels at corners and borders. This implies that inner values will get a higher weight in further analysis. To overcome this issue, images can be zero-padded by adding zeros in additional external cells (*Figure 9.5*). This is a process called **padding**.

Figure 9.5 here shows you an example of a zero-padded input:

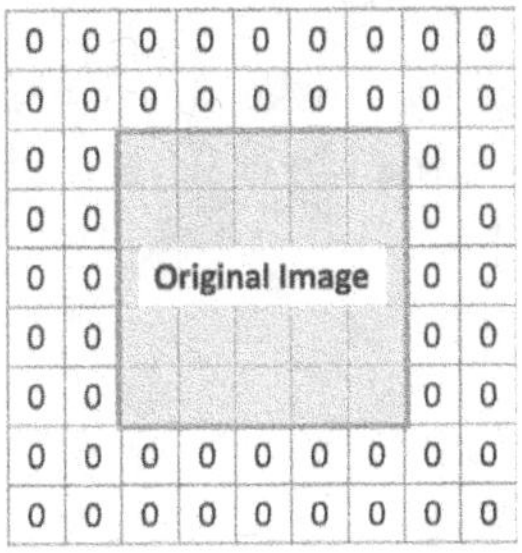

Figure 9.5 – Example of a zero-padded image

Here, two cells with value zero have been added to each row and column, all around the original image. If a kernel of size 3 x 3 is now applied to this padded image, the output dimension of the feature map would be the same as the dimension of the original image. The number of cells to use for zero padding is one more setting available in convolution layers.

Two other settings that influence the output size, if no padding is used, are called **stride** and **dilation rate**.

Introducing Stride and Dilation Rate

In the example in *Figure 9.3*, we applied the filter to every pixel. For images of a large size, it is not always necessary to perform the convolution on every single pixel. Instead of always shifting the kernel by one pixel, we could shift it by more than one horizontal or vertical pixel.

The number of pixels used for the kernel shift is called **stride**. The stride is normally defined by a tuple, specifying the number of cells for the shift in the horizontal and vertical direction. A higher stride value, without padding, leads to a downsampling of the input image.

The top part of *Figure 9.6* shows how a kernel of size 3 x 3 moves across an image with stride 2, 2.

Another setting option for a convolution layer is the **dilation rate**. The dilation rate indicates that only one cell out of n consecutive cells in the input image is used for the convolution operation. A dilation rate of $n = 2$ uses only one every two pixels from the input image for the convolution. A dilation rate of $n = 3$ uses one of three consecutive pixels. As for the stride, a dilation rate is a tuple of values for the horizontal and vertical direction. When using a dilation rate higher than $n = 1$, the kernel gets dilated to a larger field of view on the original image. So, a 3 x 3 kernel with dilation rate 2, 2 explores a field of view of size 5 x 5 in the input image, while using only nine convolution parameters.

For a 2 x 2 kernel and a dilation rate of 1, 1, the kernel scans an area of 3 x 3 on the input image using only its corner values (see the lower part of *Figure 9.6*). This means for a dilation rate of 2, 2, we have a gap of size 1. For a dilation rate of 3, 3, we would have a gap size of 2, and so on:

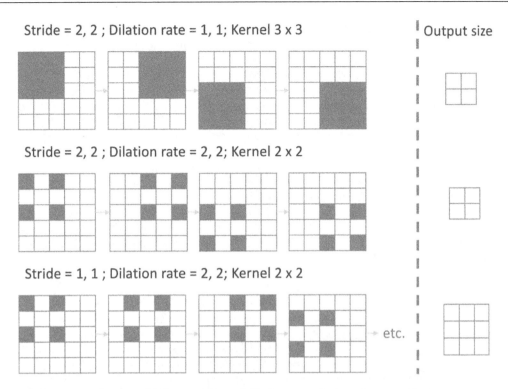

Figure 9.6 – Impact of different stride and dilation rate values on the output feature map

Another commonly used layer in CNNs is the pooling layer.

Introducing Pooling

The idea of **pooling** is to replace an area of the feature map with summary statistics. For example, pooling can replace each 2 x 2 area of the feature map with its maximum value, called **max pooling**, or its average value, called **average pooling** (*Figure 9.7*):

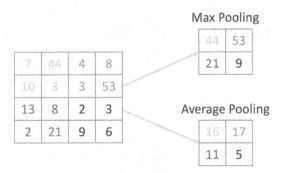

Figure 9.7 – Results of max and average pooling

A pooling layer reduces the dimension of the input image in a more efficient way and allows the extraction of dominant, rotational, and positional-invariant features.

As with a filter, in pooling we need to define the size of the explored area for which to calculate the summary statistics. A commonly used setting is a pooling size of 2 x 2 pixels and a stride of two pixels in each direction. This setting halves the image dimension.

> **Important note**
> Pooling layers don't have any weights, and all settings are defined during the configuration of the layer. They are static layers, and their parameters do not get trained like the other weights in the network.

Pooling layers are normally used after one convolution layer or multiple-stacked convolution layers.

Convolution layers can be applied to input images as well as to feature maps. Indeed, multiple convolution layers are often stacked on top of each other in a CNN. In such a hierarchy, the first convolution layer may extract low-level features, such as edges. The filters in the next layer then work on top of the extracted features and may learn to detect shapes, and so on.

The final extracted features can then be used for different tasks. In the case of image classification, the feature map—resulting from the stacking of multiple convolution layers—is flattened, and a classifier network is applied on top of it.

To summarize, a standard CNN for image classification first uses a series of convolution and pooling layers, then a flattened layer, and then a series of dense layers for the final classification.

Now that we are familiar with convolutional layers and pooling layers, let's see how they can be introduced inside a network for image classification.

Classifying Images with CNNs

In this section, we will see how to build and train from scratch a CNN for image classification.

The goal is to classify handwritten digits between 0 and 9 with the data from the **MNIST database**, a large database of handwritten digits commonly used for training various image-processing applications. The MNIST database contains 60,000 training images and 10,000 testing images of handwritten digits and can be downloaded from this website: http://yann.lecun.com/exdb/mnist/.

To read and preprocess images, KNIME Analytics Platform offers a set of dedicated nodes and components, available after installing the **KNIME Image Processing Extension**.

> **Tip**
>
> The KNIME Image Processing Extension (`https://www.knime.com/community/image-processing`) allows you to read in more than 140 different format types of images (thanks to the Bio-Formats **Application Processing Interface (API)**). In addition, it can be used to apply well-known image-processing techniques such as segmentation, feature extraction, tracking, and classification, taking advantage of the graphical user interface within KNIME Analytics Platform.
>
> In general, the nodes operate on multi-dimensional image data (for example, videos, 3D images, multi-channel images, or even a combination of these), via the internal library `ImgLib2-API`. Several nodes calculate image features (for example, Zernike, texture, or histogram features) for segmented images (for example, a single cell). Machine learning algorithms are applied on the resulting feature vectors for the final classification.

To apply and train neural networks on images, we need one further extension: the **KNIME Image Processing - Deep Learning Extension**. This extension introduces a number of useful image operations—for example, some conversions necessary for image data to feed the **Keras Network Learner** node.

> **Important note**
>
> To train and apply neural networks on images, you need to install the following extensions:
>
> KNIME Image Processing (`https://www.knime.com/community/image-processing`)
>
> KNIME Image Processing – Deep Learning Extension (`https://hub.knime.com/bioml-konstanz/extensions/org.knime.knip.dl.feature/latest`)

Let's get started with reading and preprocessing the handwritten digits.

Reading and Preprocessing Images

For this case study, we use a subset of the MNIST dataset: 10,000 image samples for training and 1,500 for testing. Each image has 28 x 28 pixels and only one channel. The training and testing images are saved in two different folders, with progressive numbers as filenames. In addition, we have a table with the image labels, sorted by the order of the image filenames.

The goal of the reading and preprocessing workflow is to read the images and to match them with their labels. Therefore, the following steps are implemented (also shown in *Figure 9.8*):

1.   Read and sort the images for training.

2.   Import the digit labels for the training images.

3.   Match the labels with the images.

4.   Transform the pixel type from unsigned byte to float.

5.   Convert the labels into a collection cell.

These steps are performed by the workflow shown in the following screenshot:

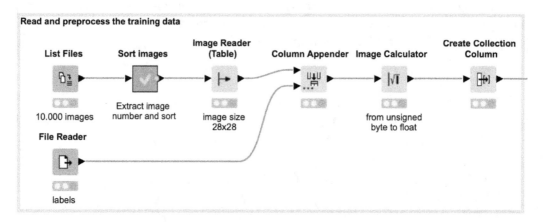

Figure 9.8 – This workflow reads a subset of the MNIST dataset, adds the corresponding labels, and transforms the pixel type from unsigned byte to float

To read the images, we use the **Image Reader (Table)** node. This node expects an input column with the **Uniform Resource Locator (URL)** paths to the image files. To create the sorted list of URLs, the **List Files** node first gets all paths to the image files in the training folder. Then, the **Sort images** metanode is used. *Figure 9.9* here shows you the inside of the metanode:

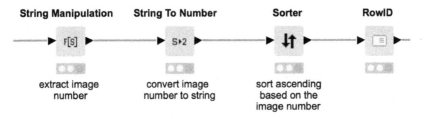

Figure 9.9 – Inside of the Sort images metanode

The metanode extracts the image number from the filename with a **String Manipulation** node and sorts them with a **Sorter** node. The **Image Reader (Table)** node then reads the images.

The **File Reader** node, in the lower branch, reads the table with the image labels.

In the next step, the **Column Appender** node appends the correct label to each image. Since images have been sorted as to match their corresponding label, a simple appending operation is sufficient. *Figure 9.10* here shows a subset of the output of the **Column Appender** node:

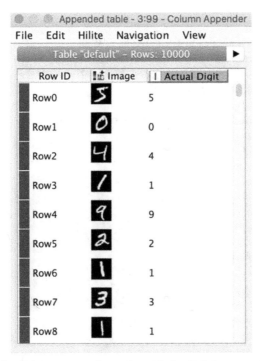

Figure 9.10 – Output of the Column Appender node, with the digit image and the corresponding label

Next, the **Image Calculator** node changes the pixel type from *unsigned byte* to *float*, by dividing each pixel value by 255.

Finally, the **Create Collection Column** node creates a collection cell for each label. The collection cell is required to create the one-hot vector-encoded classes, to use during training.

Now that we have read and preprocessed the training images, we can design the network structure.

Designing the Network

In this section, you will learn how to define a classical CNN for image classification.

A classical CNN for image classification consists of two parts, which are trained together in an end-to-end fashion, as follows:

- **Feature Extraction**: The first part performs the feature extraction of the images, by training a number of filters.

- **Classification**: The second part trains a classification network on the extracted features, available in the flattened feature map resulting from the feature extraction part.

We start with a simple network structure with only one convolution layer, followed by a pooling layer for the feature extraction part. The resulting feature maps are then flattened, and a simple classifier network, with just one hidden layer with the ReLU activation function, is trained on them.

The workflow here in *Figure 9.11* shows this network structure:

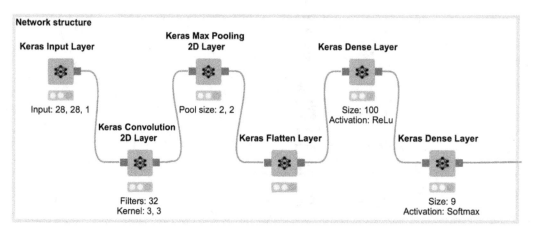

Figure 9.11 – This workflow snippet builds a simple CNN for the classification of the MNIST dataset

The workflow starts with a **Keras Input Layer** node to define the input shape. The images of the MNIST dataset have 28 x 28 pixels and only one channel, as they are grayscale images. Thus, the input is a tensor of shape 28 x 28 x 1, and therefore the input shape is set to 28, 28, 1.

Next, the convolutional layer is implemented with a **Keras Convolution 2D Layer** node. *Figure 9.12* here shows you the configuration window of the node:

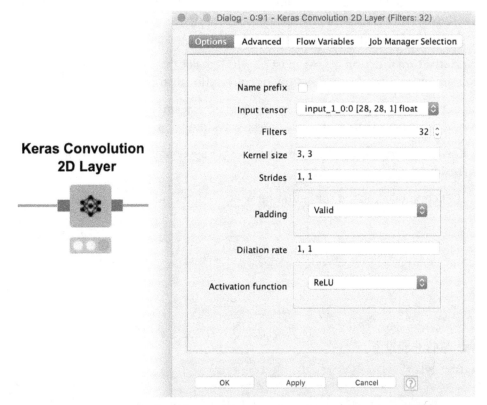

Figure 9.12 – Keras Convolution 2D Layer node and its configuration window

The setting named **Filters** sets the number of filters to apply. This will be the last dimension of the feature map. In this example, we decided to train *32* filters.

Next, you can set the **Kernel size** option in pixels—that is, an integer tuple defining the height and width of each kernel. For the MNIST dataset, we use a kernel size of 3 x 3. This means the setting is 3, 3.50.

Next, you can set the **Strides** option, which is again defined by a tuple of two integers, specifying the strides of the convolution along the height and width of the image. Any stride value greater than 1 is incompatible with any dilation_rate greater than 1.

Next, you can select whether you want to use zero padding or not. The **Padding** option allows you to select between **Valid** and **Same**. **Valid** means no padding is performed. **Same** means zero padding is performed, such that the output dimension of the feature map is the same as the input dimension. As we have mainly black pixels on the border of the images, we decided not to zero-pad the images and selected **Valid**.

Next, you can select the **Dilation rate** option, as an integer tuple. Currently, specifying any dilation rate value greater than 1 is incompatible with specifying any stride value greater than 1. A dilation rate of $1,1$ means that no pixels are skipped. A dilation rate of $2,2$ means every second pixel is used. This means a gap size of 1. We use $1,1$ for the dilation rate .52.

Last, the **Activation function** option must be selected. For this case study, we went for the most commonly used activation function for convolutional layers: **ReLU**.

The output tensor of the convolutional layer (that is, our feature map) has the dimension $26 \times 26 \times 32$, as we have 32 filters and we don't use padding.

Next, a **Keras Max Pooling 2D Layer** node is used to apply max pooling on the two dimensions.

Figure 9.13 here shows you the configuration window of the node:

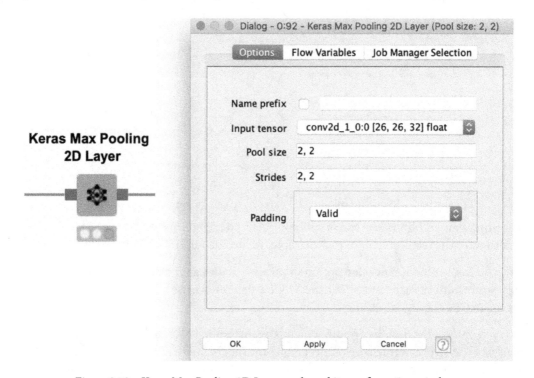

Figure 9.13 – Keras Max Pooling 2D Layer node and its configuration window

In the configuration window of the **Keras Max Pooling 2D Layer** node, you can define the **Pool size**. Again, this is an integer tuple defining the pooling window. Remember, the idea of max pooling is to represent each area of the size of the pooling window with the maximum value in the area.

The **stride** is again an integer tuple, setting the step size to shift the pooling window.

Lastly, you can select whether to apply zero padding by selecting **Valid** for no padding, and **Same** to apply padding.

For this MNIST example, we set **Pool size** as $2, 2$, **Strides** as $2, 2$, and applied no padding. Therefore, the dimension of output of the pooling layer is $13 \times 13 \times 32$.

Next, a **Keras Flatten Layer** node is used to transform the feature map into a vector, with dimension $13 * 13 * 32 = 5408$.

After the **Keras Flatten Layer** node, we build a simple classification network with one hidden layer and one output layer. The hidden layer with the ReLU activation function and 100 units is implemented by the first **Keras Dense Layer** node in *Figure 9.11*, while the output layer is implemented by the second (and last) **Keras Dense Layer** node in *Figure 9.11*. As it is a multiclass classification problem with 10 different classes, here the softmax activation function with 10 units is used. In addition, the **Name prefix** *output* is used so that we can identify the output layer more easily when applying the network to new data.

Now that we have defined the network structure, we can move on to train the CNN.

Training and Applying the Network

To train the CNN built in the previous section, we again use the **Keras Network Learner** node. In the previous chapters, we already saw that this node offers many conversion types for input and target data (such as, for example, the **From Collection of Number (integers) to One-Hot Tensor** option). Installing the **KNIME Image Processing – Deep Learning Extension** adds one more conversion option: **From Image (Auto-mapping)**. This new conversion option allows us to select an image column from the input table and to automatically create the tensor to feed into the network.

Figure 9.14 here shows the **Input Data** tab of the configuration window of the **Keras Network Learner** node, including this additional conversion option:

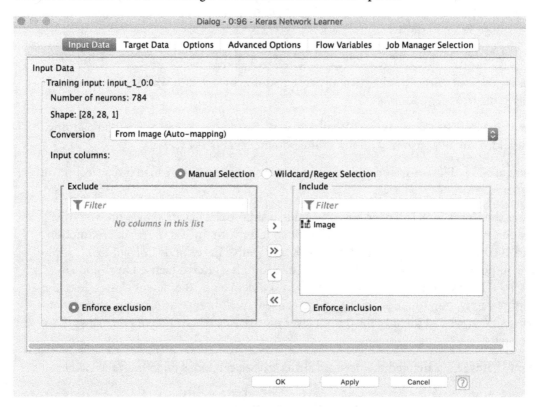

Figure 9.14 – Input Data tab of the configuration window of the Keras Network Learner node with the additional conversion option, From Image (Auto-mapping)

In the **Target Data** tab, the conversion option from **From Collection of Number (integer) to One-Hot Tensor** is selected for the column with the collection cell of the image label.

On the bottom, the *Categorical cross entropy* activation function is selected, as the problem is a multiclass classification problem.

In the **Options** tab, the following training parameters are set:

- **Number of epochs:** 10
- **Training batch size:** 200
- **Optimizer:** Adadelta with the default settings

Figure 9.15 here shows the progress of the training procedure in the **Learning Monitor** view of the **Keras Network Learner** node after node execution:

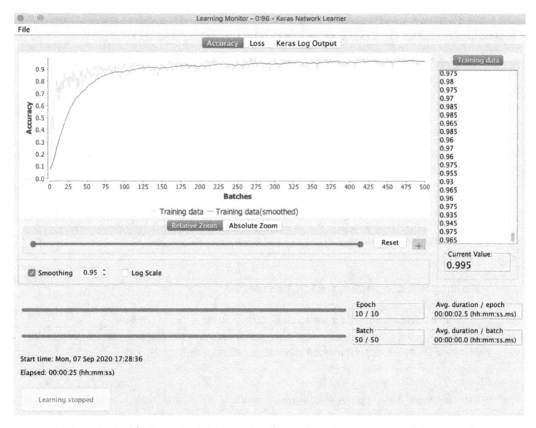

Figure 9.15 – The Learning Monitor view shows the training progress of the network

The **Learning Monitor** view shows the progress of the network during training over the many training batches. On the right-hand side, you can see the accuracy for the last few batches. **Current Value** shows you the accuracy for the last batch, which is in this case **0.995**.

Now that we have a trained CNN satisfactorily performing on the training set, we can apply it to the test set. Here, the same reading and preprocessing steps as for the training set must also be applied on the test set.

The **Keras Network Executor** node applies the trained network on the images in the test set. In the configuration window, the last layer, producing the probability distribution of the different digits, is selected as output.

At this point, a bit of postprocessing is required in order to extract the final prediction from the network output.

Prediction Extraction and Model Evaluation

The output of the **Keras Network Executor** node is a table with 12 columns, comprising the following:

- The image column
- The true class value, named **Actual Value**
- 10 columns with the probability values for the image classes with the column headers: output/Softmax:0_x, where x is a number between 0 and 9 encoding the class

The goal of the postprocessing is to extract the class with the highest probability and then to evaluate the network performance. This is implemented by the workflow snippet shown here in *Figure 9.16*:

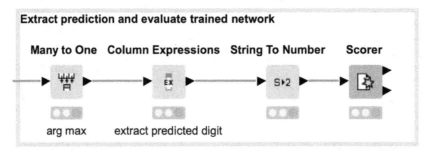

Figure 9.16 – This workflow snippet extracts the digit class with the highest probability and evaluates the network performance on the test set

The **Many to One** node extracts the column header of the column with the highest probability in each row.

Then, the **Column Expression** node extracts the class from the column header.

> **Tip**
>
> The **Column Expression** node is a very powerful node. It provides the possibility to append an arbitrary number of new columns or modify existing columns using expressions.
>
> For each column to be appended or modified, a separate expression can be defined. These expressions can be simply created using predefined functions, similarly to the **Math Formula** and the **String Manipulation** nodes. Nevertheless, there is no restriction on the number of lines an expression can have and the number of functions it can use. Additionally, intermediate results of functions or calculations can be stored within an expression by assigning them to temporary variables (using =).
>
> Available flow variables and columns of the input table can be accessed via the provided access functions variable ("variableName") and column ("columnName").

Figure 9.17 here shows you the configuration window of the **Column Expression** node, with the expression used in the workflow snippet in *Figure 9.16* to extract the class information. In this case, the expression extracts the last character from the strings in the column named **Detected Digit**:

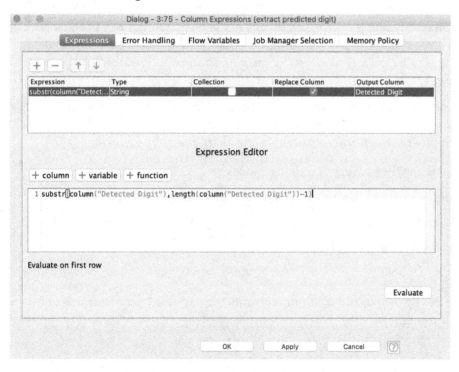

Figure 9.17 – The Column Expression node and its configuration window

Next, the data type of the predicted class is converted from `String` to `Integer` with the **String to Number** node, and the network performance is evaluated on the test set with the **Scorer** node.

Figure 9.18 here shows the view produced by the **Scorer** node:

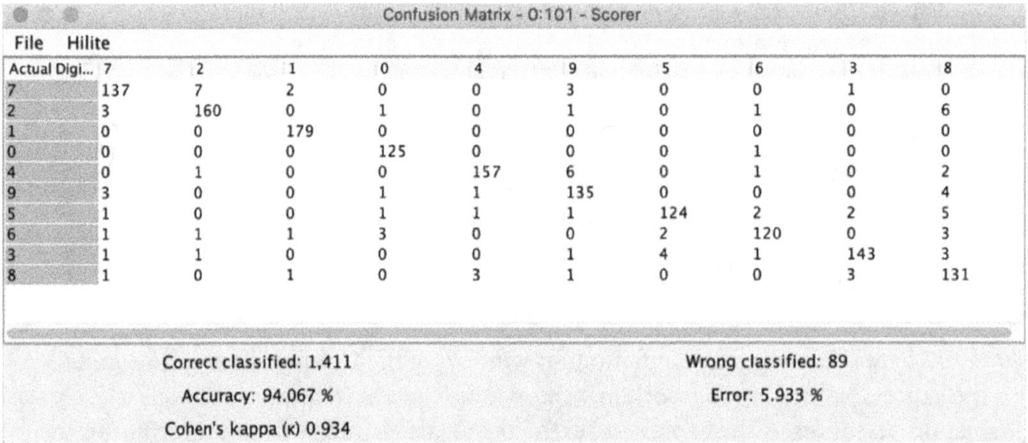

Confusion Matrix - 0:101 - Scorer									
Actual Digi... 7	2	1	0	4	9	5	6	3	8
7 137	7	2	0	0	3	0	0	1	0
2 3	160	0	1	0	1	0	1	0	6
1 0	0	179	0	0	0	0	0	0	0
0 0	0	0	125	0	0	0	1	0	0
4 0	1	0	0	157	6	0	1	0	2
9 3	0	0	1	1	135	0	0	0	4
5 1	0	0	1	1	1	124	2	2	5
6 1	1	1	3	0	0	2	120	0	3
3 1	1	0	0	0	1	4	1	143	3
8 1	0	1	0	3	1	0	0	3	131

Correct classified: 1,411   Wrong classified: 89

Accuracy: 94.067 %   Error: 5.933 %

Cohen's kappa (κ) 0.934

Figure 9.18 – View of the Scorer node, showing the performance of the network on the test set

As you can see, this simple CNN has already reached an accuracy of 94% and a Cohen's kappa of 0.934 on the test set. The complete workflow is available on the KNIME Hub: `https://hub.knime.com/kathrin/spaces/Codeless%20Deep%20 Learning%20with%20KNIME/latest/Chapter%209/`.

In this section, we built and trained from scratch a simple CNN, reaching an acceptable performance for this rather simple image classification task. Of course, we could try to further improve the performance of this network by doing the following:

- Increasing the number of training epochs
- Adding a second convolutional layer together with a pooling layer
- Using batch normalization for training
- Using augmentation
- Using dropout

We leave this up to you, and continue with another way of network learning, called transfer learning.

Introduction to transfer learning

The general idea of **transfer learning** is to reuse the knowledge gained by a network trained for task **A** on another related task **B**. For example, if we train a network to recognize sailing boats (task A), we can use this network as a starting point to train a new model to recognize motorboats (task B). In this case, task A is called the *source task* and task B the *target task*.

Reusing a trained network as the starting point to train a new network is different from the traditional way of training networks, whereby neural networks are trained on their own for specific tasks on specific datasets. *Figure 9.19* here visualizes the traditional way of network training, whereby different systems are trained for different tasks and domains:

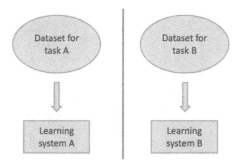

Figure 9.19 – Traditional way of training machine learning models and neural networks

But why should we use transfer learning instead of training models in the traditional, isolated way?

Why use Transfer Learning?

Current state-of-the-art neural networks have shown amazing performance in tackling specific complex tasks. Sometimes, these models are even better than humans, beating world champions at board games or at detecting objects in images. To train these successful networks, usually a huge amount of labeled data is required, as well as a vast amount of computational resources and time.

To get a comprehensive labeled dataset for a new domain, in order to be able to train a network to reach state-of-art-performance, can be difficult or even impossible. As an example, the often-used **ImageNet database**, which is used to train state-of-the-art models, has been developed over the course of many years. It would take time to create a similar new dataset for a new image domain. However, when these state-of-the-art models are applied to other related domains, they often suffer a considerable loss in performance, or, even worse, they break down. This happens due to the model bias toward the training data and domain.

Transfer learning allows us to use the knowledge gained during training on a task and domain where sufficient labeled data was available as a starting point, to train new models in domains where not enough labeled data is yet available. This approach has shown great results in many computer vision and **natural language processing (NLP)** tasks.

Figure 9.20 here visualizes the idea behind transfer learning:

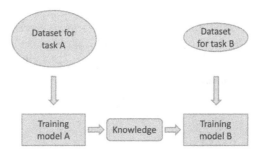

Figure 9.20 – Idea behind transfer learning

Before we talk about how we can apply transfer learning when training a neural network, let's have a quick look at the formal definition of transfer learning and the many scenarios in which it can be applied.

Formal Definition of Transfer Learning

A formal definition of transfer learning and of the related scenarios can be found in the paper by Sinno Jialin Pan and Qiang Yang, *A Survey on Transfer Learning*, IEEE Transactions on Knowledge and Data Engineering, 2009 (`https://ieeexplore.ieee.org/abstract/document/5288526`).

The definition involves the concept of a **domain** and a **task**.

In the paper, a **domain** D is introduced as tuple $\{X, P(X)\}$ where X is the feature space and a $P(X)$ the marginal probability distribution for $X = \{x_1, ..., x_n\} \in X$.

For a given domain, $D = \{X, P(X)\}$, a task $T = \{Y, f(\cdot),\}$ consists of the following two components as well:

- A label space Y
- A predictive function $f(\cdot)$

Here, the predictive function $f(\cdot)$ could be the conditional probability distribution $P(y|X)$. In general, the predictive function is a function trained on the labeled training data to predict the label y for any sample X in the feature space.

Using this terminology, **transfer learning** is defined by Sinno Jialin Pan and Qiang Yang in the following way:

> *"Given a source domain D_S and learning task T_S, a target domain D_T and learning task T_T, transfer learning aims to help improve the learning of the target predictive function $f_T(\cdot)$ in D_T using the knowledge in D_S and T_S, where $D_S \neq D_T$, or $T_S \neq T_T$."*

Sebastian Ruder uses this definition in his article, *Transfer Learning - Machine Learning's Next Frontier, 2017* (`https://ruder.io/transfer-learning/`) to describe the following *four scenarios* in which transfer learning can be used:

1. Different feature spaces: $\mathcal{X}_S \neq \mathcal{X}_T$

    An example in the paper is cross-lingual adaptation, where we have documents in different languages.

2. Different marginal probabilities: $P_S(X) \neq P_T(X)$

    An example comes in the form of documents that discuss different topics. This scenario is called *domain adaption*.

3. Different label spaces: $Y_S \neq Y_T$

    (for example, if we have documents with different labels).

4. Different conditional probabilities $(y|X) \neq P_T(y|X)$.
    This usually occurs together with scenario 3.

Now that we have a basic understanding of transfer learning, let's find out next how transfer learning can be applied to the field of deep learning.

Applying Transfer Learning

In a neural network, the knowledge gained during training is stored in the weights of the layers. For example, in the case of CNNs, a number of filters are trained to extract a number of features. Thus, the knowledge of how to extract such features from an image is stored in the weights of the kernels for the implemented filters.

In a stacked CNN for image classification, the initial convolution layers are responsible for extracting low-level features such as edges, while the next convolution layers extract higher-level features such as body parts, animals, or faces. The last layers are trained to classify the images, based on the extracted features.

So, if we want to train a CNN for a different image-classification task, on different images and with different labels, we must not train the new filters from scratch, but we can use the previously trained convolution layers in a state-of-the-art network as the starting point. Hopefully, the new training procedure will be faster and will require a smaller amount of data.

To use the trained layers from another network as the training starting point, we need to extract the convolution layers from the original network and then build some new layers on top. To do so, we have the following two options:

- We freeze the weights of the trained layers and just train the added layers based on the output of the frozen layers. This approach is often used in NLP applications, where trained embeddings are reused.

- We use the trained weights to initialize new convolution layers in the network and then fine-tune them while training the added layers. In this case, a small training rate is used to not unlearn the learned knowledge from the source task.

For the last case study of this book, we want to train a neural network to predict cancer type from histopathology slide images. To speed up the learning process and considering the relatively small dataset we have, we will apply transfer learning starting from the convolution layers in the popular VGG16 network used here as the source network.

Applying Transfer Learning for Cancer Type Prediction

We will introduce here a new (and final) case study. We will start from the state-of-the-art VGG16 network as a source network to train a new target network on a dataset of images describing three different subtypes of lymphoma, which are **chronic lymphocytic leukemia (CLL)**, **follicular lymphoma (FL)**, and **mantle cell lymphoma (MCL)**.

A typical task for a pathologist in a hospital is to look at histopathology slide images and make a decision about the type of lymphoma. Even for experienced pathologists this is a difficult task and, in many cases, follow-up tests are required to confirm the diagnosis. An assistive technology that can guide pathologists and speed up their job would be of great value.

VGG16 is one of the winner models on the ImageNet Challenge from 2014. It is a stacked CNN network, using kernels of size 3 x 3 with an increasing depth—that is, with an increasing number of filters. The original network was trained on the ImageNet dataset, containing images 224 x 224 x 3, referring to more than 1,000 classes.

Figure 9.21 shows you the network structure of the VGG16 model.

It starts with two convolution layers, each with 64 filters. After a max pooling layer, again two convolution layers are used, this time each with 128 filters. Then, another max pooling layer is followed by three convolution layers, each with 256 filters. After one more max pooling layer, there are again three convolution layers, each with 512 filters, followed by another pooling layer and three convolution layers each with 512 filters. After one last pooling layer, three dense layers are used:

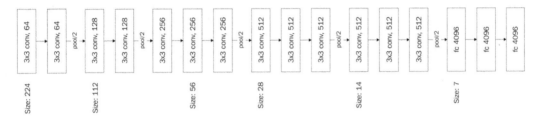

Figure 9.21 – Network structure of the VGG16 model

In this case study, we would like to reuse the trained convolution layers of the VGG16 model and add some layers on top for the cancer cell classification task. During training, the convolution layers will be frozen and only the added layers will be trained.

To do so, we build three separate sub-workflows: one workflow to download the data, one workflow to preprocess the images, and a third workflow to train the neural network, using transfer learning. You can download the workflow with the three sub-workflows from the KNIME Hub: `https://hub.knime.com/kathrin/spaces/` `Codeless%20Deep%20Learning%20with%20KNIME/latest/Chapter%209/`. Let's start with the workflow to download the data.

Downloading the Dataset

The full dataset with images of cancer cells is available as a single `tar.gz` file containing 374 images: `https://ome.grc.nia.nih.gov/iicbu2008/lymphoma/index.html`. The workflow shown in *Figure 9.22* downloads the file and creates a table with the file path and the class information for each image:

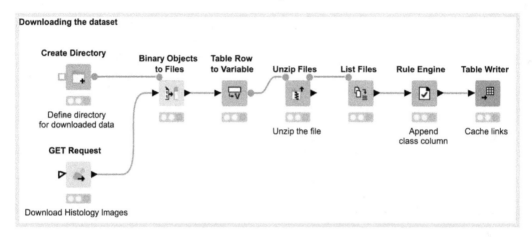

Figure 9.22 – This workflow downloads the full labeled dataset of images of cancer cells

Therefore, the workflow first defines a directory for the downloaded data using the **Create Directory** node. Next, the **GET Request** node and the **Binary Objects to Files** node are used to download and save the `tar.gz` file into the created directory. The **Unzip Files** node unzips the downloaded file. As a result, we get three sub-directories—one for each lymphoma type. Next, the workflow creates a data table that stores the path to the image files using the **List Files** node. Based on the subfolder, the **Rule Engine** node adds the class label according to its class of lymphoma. Finally, the created table is written into a `.table` file.

The next step is to preprocess the images.

Reading and Preprocessing the Images

In the next step, the table created by the workflow in *Figure 9.22* is read and the images are preprocessed. Each image has dimensions 1388px, 1040px, and three-color channels; this means $3x1388x1040$. To reduce the spatial complexity of computation, we use a similar approach as that taken in the paper *Histology Image Classification Using Supervised Classification and Multimodal Fusion* (`https://ieeexplore.ieee.org/document/5693834`), where each image is chopped into 25 blocks. For this use case, we decided to chop each image into blocks of size $3x64x64$.

The loading and preprocessing steps are performed by the workflow shown here in *Figure 9.23*:

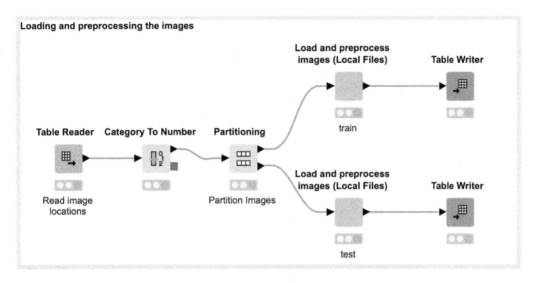

Figure 9.23 – This workflow loads and preprocesses the image

This second workflow starts with reading the table created in the first workflow, including the paths to the images as well as the class information. Next, the **Category To Number** node encodes the different nominal class values (FL, MCL, and CLL) with an index, before the dataset is split into a training set and a test set using the **Partitioning** node. For this case study, we decided to use 60% of the data for training and 40% of the data for testing, using stratified sampling on the **class** column.

In the **Load and preprocess images (Local Files)** component, the images are uploaded and preprocessed.

Figure 9.24 here shows you the inside of this component:

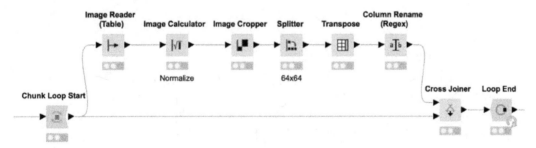

Figure 9.24 – Inside of the Load and preprocess images (Local Files) component

The component uses a loop to load and preprocess one image after the other. The **Chunk Loop Start** node, with one row per chunk, starts the loop, while the **Loop End** node, concatenating the resulting rows from the loop iterations, ends the loop.

In the loop body, one image is always loaded with the **Image Reader (Table)** node. The image is then normalized using the **Image Calculator** node, dividing each pixel value by 255.

Next, the **Image Cropper** node is used to crop the image to a size that is dividable by 64. Since the original size of the images is 1388px 1040px, the first 44 pixels of the left side and the top 16 pixels of each image are cropped.

Figure 9.25 here shows you the configuration window of the node:

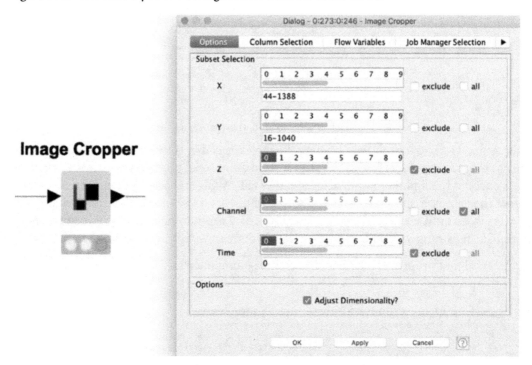

Figure 9.25 – Image Cropper node and its configuration window

Next, the **Splitter** node splits each image into 336 images of size 64 x 64 pixels, storing each new sub-image in a new column, for a total of ~75,000 patches. *Figure 9.26* here shows you the **Advanced** tab of the configuration window of the **Splitter** node, where the maximum size for each dimension of the resulting images has been set:

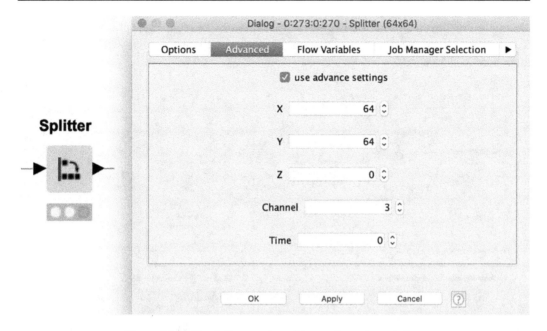

Splitter

Figure 9.26 – The Splitter node and its configuration window

Next, the table is transposed into one column and renamed, before the class information is added to each image with the **Cross Joiner** node.

Now that we have the prepared images, we can continue with the last workflow.

Training the Network

The first step of the training workflow is to define the network structure using *VGG16's convolution layers* as a starting point.

The VGG16 model was originally trained to predict the classes in the ImageNet dataset. Despite the 1,000 classes in the dataset, none of them matches the three cancer types for this study. Therefore, we recycle only the trained convolution layers of the VGG16 network. We will then add some new neural layers on top for the classification task, and finally fine-tune the resulting network to our task.

To train the final network, we will use the **Keras Network Learner** node and the ~75,000 patches created from the training set images. These steps are performed by the workflow shown here in *Figure 9.27*:

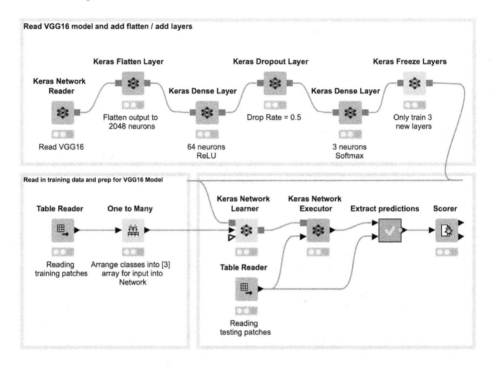

Figure 9.27 – Training workflow to train the new network to classify images of cancer cells

The workflow first reads the VGG16 network with the **Keras Network Reader** node. The **Keras Network Reader** node can read models in three different file formats. Models are saved in a .h5 file with the complete network structure and weights, or networks are saved in .json or .yaml files with just the network structure.

In this case, we read the .h5 file of the trained VGG16 network because we aim to use all of the knowledge embedded inside the network.

The output tensor of the VGG16 network has dimensions $2 \times 2 \times 512$, which is the size of the output of the last max pooling layer. Before we can add some dense layers for the classification task, we flatten the output using the **Keras Flatten Layer** node.

Now, a dense layer with **ReLU** activation and 64 neurons is added using a **Keras Dense Layer** node. Next, a **Dropout Layer** node is introduced, with a dropout rate of 0.5. Finally, one last **Keras Dense Layer** node defines the output of the network. As we are dealing with a classification problem with three different classes, the **softmax** activation function with three units is adopted.

If we were to connect the output of the last **Keras Dense Layer** node to a **Keras Network Learner** node, we would fine-tune all layers, including the trained convolution layers from the VGG16 model. We do not want to lose all that knowledge! So, we decided to not fine-tune the layers of the VGG16 model but to train only the newly added layers. Therefore, the layers of the VGG16 model must be frozen.

To freeze layers of a network, we use the **Keras Freeze Layers** node. *Figure 9.28* here shows you the configuration window of this node:

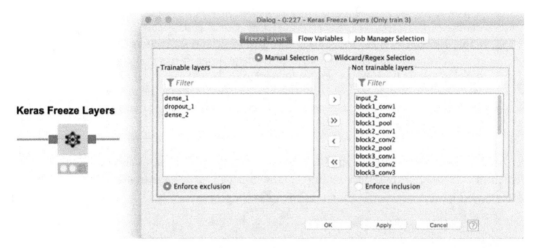

Figure 9.28 – The Keras Freeze Layers node and its configuration window

In the configuration window, you can select the layer(s) to freeze. Later on, when training the network, the weights of the selected layers will not be updated. All other layers will be trained. We froze every layer except the ones we added at the end of the VGG16 network.

In the lower branch of the workflow, we read the training data using the **Table Reader** node and we one-hot encode the class using the **One to Many** node.

Now that we have the training data and the network structure, we can fine-tune it with the **Keras Network Learner** node.

As with all other case studies in this book, the columns for the input data and target data are selected in the configuration window of the **Keras Network Learner** node, together with the required conversion type. In this case, the **From Image** conversion for the input column and from Number (double) for the target column have been selected. Because this is a multiclass classification task, the **Categorical cross entropy** loss function has been adopted. To fine-tune this network, it has been trained for 5 epochs using a training batch size of 64 and RMSProp with the default settings as optimizer.

Once the network has been fine-tuned, we evaluate its performance on the test images. The preprocessed test images, as patches of 64 x 64 px, are read with a **Table Reader** node. To predict the class of an image, we generate predictions for each of the 64 x 64px patches using the **Keras Network Executor** node. Then, all predictions are combined using a simple majority voting scheme, implemented in the **Extract Prediction** metanode.

Finally, the network is evaluated using the **Scorer** node. The classifier has achieved 96% accuracy (fine-tuning for a few more epochs can push the accuracy to 98%).

> **Tip**
> In this use case, the VGG16 model is only used for feature extraction. Therefore, another approach is to apply the convolutional layers of the VGG16 model to extract the features beforehand and to feed them as input into a classic feedforward neural network. This has the advantage that the forward pass through VGG16 would be done only once per image, instead of doing it in every batch update.

We could now save the network and deploy it to allow a pathologist to access those predictions via a web browser, for example. How this can be done using KNIME Analytics Platform and KNIME Server is shown in the next chapter.

Summary

In this chapter, we explored CNNs, focusing on image data.

We started with an introduction to convolution layers, which motivates the name of this new family of neural networks. In this introduction, we explained why CNNs are so commonly used for image data, how convolutional networks work, and the impact of the many setting options. Next, we discussed pooling layers, commonly used in CNNs to efficiently downsample the data.

Finally, we put all this knowledge to work by building and training from scratch a CNN to classify images of digits between 0 and 9 from the MNIST dataset. Afterward, we discussed the concept of transfer learning, introduced four scenarios in which transfer learning can be applied, and showed how we can use transfer learning in the field of neural networks.

In the last section, we applied transfer learning to train a CNN to classify histopathology slide images. Instead of training it from scratch, this time we reused the convolutional layers of a trained VGG16 model for the feature extraction of the images.

Now that we have covered the many different use cases, we will move on to the next step, which is the deployment of the trained neural networks. In the next chapter, you will learn about different deployment options with KNIME software.

Questions and Exercises

1. What is the kernel size in a convolutional layer?

   a) The area summarized by a statistical value

   b) The size of the matrix moving across an image

   c) The number of pixels to shift the matrix

   d) The size of the area used by a layer

2. What is a pooling layer?

   a) A pooling layer is a commonly used layer in RNNs

   b) A pooling layer summarizes an area with a statistical value

   c) A pooling layer is a commonly used layer in feedforward networks

   d) A pooling layer can be used to upsample images

3. When is transfer learning helpful?

   a) To transfer data to another system

   b) If no model is available

   c) If not enough labeled data is available

   d) To compare different models

Section 3:
Deployment and
Productionizing

Deployment is an important and conclusive phase of a whole data analysis project. So, to conclude, we will show different deployment options for our trained neural networks.

This section comprises the following chapters:

- *Chapter 10, Deploying a Deep Learning Network*
- *Chapter 11, Best Practices and Other Deployment Options*

10
Deploying a Deep Learning Network

In the previous sections of this book, we covered the training of deep neural networks for many different use cases, starting with an autoencoder for fraud detection, through **Long Short-Term Memory (LSTM)** networks for energy consumption prediction and free text generation, all the way to cancer cell classification. But training the network is not the only part of a project. Once a deep learning network is trained, the next step is to deploy it.

During the exploration of some of the use cases, a second workflow has already been introduced, to deploy the network to work on real-world data. So, you have already seen some deployment examples. In this last section of the book, however, we focus on the many deployment options for machine learning models in general, and for trained deep learning networks in particular.

Usually, a second workflow is built and dedicated to deployment. This workflow reads the trained model and the new real-world data, it preprocesses this data in exactly the same way as for the training data, then it applies the trained deep learning network on is transformed data and produces the results according to the project's requirements.

This chapter focuses on the reading, writing, and preprocessing of the data in a deployment workflow.

This chapter starts with a review of the features for saving, reading, and converting a trained network. This is followed by two examples of how the preprocessing for our sentiment analysis use case can also be implemented in a deployment workflow. Finally, the chapter shows how to improve execution speed by enabling GPU support.

The chapter consists of the following sections:

Conversion of the Network Structure

Building a Simple Deployment Workflow

Improving Scalability – GPU Execution

Conversion of the Network Structure

The goal of a deployment workflow is to apply a trained network to new real-world data. Therefore, the last step of the training workflow must be to save the trained network.

Saving a Trained Network

All networks described in this book have been trained using the Keras libraries, relying on TensorFlow as the backend. So, the most natural way to save a network is to continue using the Keras libraries and therefore to use the **Keras Network Writer** node. The Keras Network Writer node writes the network, including its weights, in Keras format into a .h5 file.

However, Keras-formatted networks can only be interpreted and executed via the Keras libraries. This is already one level on top of the TensorFlow libraries. Executing the network application on the TensorFlow Java API directly, rather than on a Python kernel via the Keras Python API, makes execution faster. The good news is that KNIME Analytics Platform also has nodes for TensorFlow execution in addition to the nodes based on Keras libraries.

Thus, if faster execution is needed, the Keras network should be converted into a TensorFlow network using the **Keras to TensorFlow Network Converter** node. After conversion, the network can be saved using the **TensorFlow Network Writer** node as a SavedModel file, a compressed zip file. A SavedModel file contains a complete TensorFlow program, including weights and computation. It does not require the original model building code to run, which makes it useful for sharing or deploying.

The first step in a deployment network is to read a trained network.

Reading a Trained Network

KNIME Analytics Platform provides many nodes for reading a trained neural network, such as the following:

- Keras Network Reader

- TensorFlow Network Reader (and TensorFlow 2 Network Reader)

- DL Python Network Creator

- ONNX Network Reader

The **Keras Network Reader** node reads a Keras deep learning network from a file. The file can either contain a full, pre-trained network (`.h5` file) or just a network architecture definition without weights (a `.json` or `.yaml` file). You can use the node to read networks trained with KNIME Analytics Platform or networks trained directly with Keras, such as pretrained Keras networks.

The **TensorFlow Network Reader** (or TensorFlow 2 Network Reader) node reads a TensorFlow (or TensorFlow 2) deep learning network from a directory or from a `zip` file. If reading from a directory, it has to be a valid `SavedModel` folder. If reading from a `zip` file, it must contain a valid `SavedModel` folder.

> **Tip**
> The TensorFlow Network Reader node allows us to select a tag and a signature in its configuration window. Tags are used to identify the meta graph definition to load. Signatures are **concrete functions** specifying the expected input and output. A `SavedModel` can have multiple tags as well as multiple signatures per tag. A network saved with KNIME Analytics Platform has only one tag and one signature. In the **Advanced** tab of the configuration window, you can define your own signature by defining the input and output of the model by selecting one of the hidden layers as output, for example.

Another node, which allows you to read pretrained networks without writing a single line of code, is the **ONNX Network Reader** node. **ONNX** stands for **Open Neural Network Exchange** and is a standard format for neural networks developed by Microsoft and Facebook. Since it is a standard format, it is portable across machine learning frameworks such as PyTorch, Caffe2, TensorFlow, and more. You can download pretrained networks from the ONNX Model Zoo (`https://github.com/onnx/models#vision`) and read them with the ONNX Network Reader node. The ONNX networks can also be converted into TensorFlow networks using the **ONNX to TensorFlow Network Converter** node, and then executed with the TensorFlow Network Executor node.

> **Tip**
>
> To use the ONNX nodes, you need to install the **KNIME Deep Learning –
> ONNX Integration** extension.

Another option for reading a network using Python code is the **DL Python Network
Creator** node, which can be used to read pretrained neural networks using a few lines
of Python code.

> **Tip**
>
> The DL Python Network Creator node can also be used in training workflows
> to define the network architecture using Python code instead of layer nodes.

So far, we have used Keras-based nodes with TensorFlow 1 as the backend. There are also
nodes that use TensorFlow 2 as the backend to implement similar operations.

Using TensorFlow 2

For all the examples in this book, we have used Keras-based nodes that run TensorFlow
1 as the backend. TensorFlow 2 is also supported since the release of KNIME Analytics
Platform 4.2. On the KNIME Hub, you can find many examples of how to use TensorFlow
2 integration.

The TensorFlow 2 integration comes with three nodes:

- **The TensorFlow 2 Network Executor** node
- **The TensorFlow 2 Network Reader** node
- **The TensorFlow 2 Network Writer** node

To train a deep learning model using TensorFlow 2 you can use the **DL Python Network Learner** node.

Now that we have reviewed the many options to save and read neural networks, let's focus on building a simple deployment workflow.

Building a Simple Deployment Workflow

So far, in all the case studies we have explored, we have always performed some kind of preprocessing of the input data, such as encoding categorical features, encoding text, or normalizing data, to name just some of the adopted preprocessing steps. During deployment, the new incoming data must be prepared with the exact same preprocessing as the training data in order to be consistent with the task and with the input that the network expects.

In this section, we use the sentiment analysis case study shown in *Chapter 7, Implementing NLP Applications*, as an example, and we build two deployment workflows for it. The goal of both workflows is to read new movie reviews from a database, predict the sentiment, and write the prediction into the database.

In the first example, the preprocessing steps are implemented manually into the deployment workflow. In the second example, the **Integrated Deployment** feature is used.

Building a Deployment Workflow Manually, without Integrated Deployment

The deployment workflow should access new reviews from a table in a database, apply the trained network, write the reviews with the corresponding predictions into another table in the database, and delete the reviews from the first table.

These steps are performed by the workflow in *Figure 10.1*, which you can download from the KNIME Hub at `https://hub.knime.com/kathrin/spaces/Codeless%20 Deep%20Learning%20with%20KNIME/latest/Chapter_10/`:

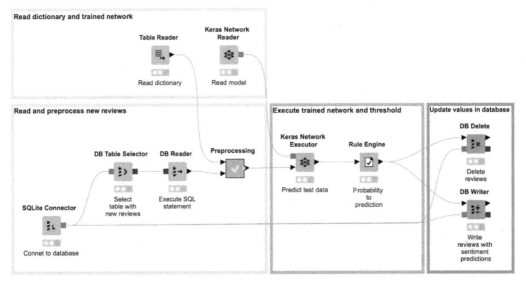

Figure 10.1 – Deployment workflow for the sentiment analysis case study from Chapter 7,
Implementing NLP Applications

The workflow first connects to a SQLite database, where the new movie reviews are stored, using the **SQLite Connector** node.

Next, the **SELECT** SQL statement to read the new reviews from the table named **new_reviews** is implemented by the **DB Table Selector** node.

The SQL statement is then executed through the **DB Reader** node. As a result, we have the new reviews in a data table at the output port of the node.

> **Tip**
>
> In *Chapter 2, Data Access and Preprocessing with KNIME Analytics Platform*, the database extension was introduced in detail. Remember that the database nodes create a SQL statement at their output brown-squared port.

Before applying the network to these new reviews, we need to perform the same transformations as in the training workflow. In the training workflow, reported in *Chapter 7, Implementing NLP Applications*, there was a metanode named **Preprocess test set** where all the required preprocessing steps were applied to the test data. We used this metanode as the basis for creating the preprocessing steps for the incoming data in the deployment workflow.

Figure 10.2 shows the content of this metanode, which is dedicated to the preprocessing of the test set:

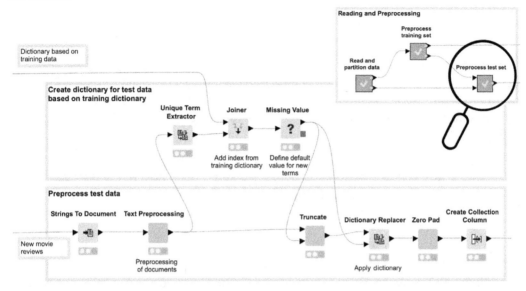

Figure 10.2 – Preprocessing of the test data in the training workflow of the sentiment analysis case study from Chapter 7, Implementing NLP Applications

In the deployment workflow in *Figure 10.1*, the dictionary, created during training is read first; then the preprocessing steps are implemented in the **Preprocessing** metanode.

Figure 10.3 shows you the workflow snippet inside this metanode:

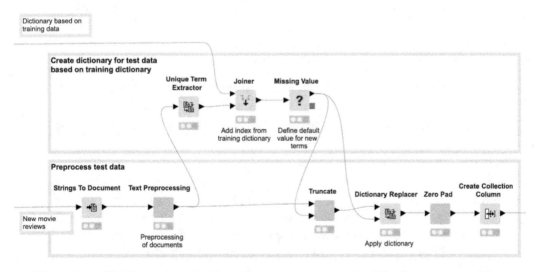

Figure 10.3 – Workflow snippet inside the Preprocessing metanode of the deployment workflow

If we compare the workflow snippets in *Figure 10.2* and *Figure 10.3*, you can see that they contain the same preprocessing steps, as was expected.

Now that the same preprocessing as for the training data has been applied to the deployment data, the trained network can be introduced through the **Keras Network Reader** node (*Figure 10.1*).

Next, the trained network runs on the preprocessed deployment reviews using the **Keras Network Executor** node. The output of the network is the probability of the sentiment being equal to 1, where 1 encodes a positive movie review. The same threshold as during training is also applied here through the **Rule Engine** node: a threshold of 0.5.

In the last step, the tables in the database are updated. First, the **DB Delete** node deletes the reviews we just analyzed from the **new_reviews** table. Then, the **DB Writer** node appends the new movie reviews with their predictions to another table in the database, named **review-with-sentiment**.

This is the first example of the deployment of a neural network using KNIME Analytics Platform. This workflow should be executed on a regular basis to predict the sentiment for all new incoming movie reviews.

> **Tip**
> KNIME Server can schedule the execution of workflows, so you can trigger
> their execution automatically on a regular schedule.

This approach has one disadvantage. If the model is retrained on more data or with different settings (for example, if more or fewer terms are taken into account during training or the threshold for the Rule Engine node is changed) we need to remember to also update the preprocessing steps in the deployment workflow. And since we are forgetful humans, we might forget or make mistakes.

A solution to overcome this issue is the concept of **Integrated Deployment**.

Building a Deployment Workflow Automatically with Integrated Deployment

Until KNIME Analytics Platform 4.2, as well as in other tools, a common approach was to implement data blending, data transformation, and network execution manually in the deployment workflow. This means that you need to copy the different preprocessing snippets, parameters, and network executor nodes from the training workflow to the deployment workflow, making sure that all settings remain unaltered.

This manual step slows down the process and can easily lead to mistakes. Automating the construction of parts of the deployment workflow can be a safer option, especially if the models are changed often, for example, every day or even every hour.

> **Important note**
> Other common names for the training process are data science creation or modeling workflow.

The nodes from the Integrated Deployment extension close the gap between creating and deploying data science.

The Integrated Deployment Extension

The Integrated Deployment extension allows data scientists to combine the model training and deployment into one single workflow. The idea is to capture parts of the training workflow and to automatically write them into the deployment workflow during the execution of the training workflow.

Instead of copying the preprocessing parts manually, one by one, the required parts from the training workflow are captured in between the **Capture Workflow Start** and **Capture Workflow End** nodes. The captured workflow part in the middle can then be written into a new workflow with a **Workflow Writer** node.

Using the Integrated Deployment Extension in the Training Workflow

Let's consider again the deployment workflow for the sentiment analysis case study described in *Chapter 7, Implementing NLP Applications*. In the training workflow, we have introduced the **Capture Workflow Start** node and the **Capture Workflow End** node to isolate the workflow snippet that we want to reproduce exactly in the deployment workflow.

This includes the following:

- The metanode named **Preprocessing test set**, including all required preprocessing steps
- The **Keras Network Executor** node to apply the trained network on the deployment transformed data
- The **Rule Engine** node, which decides on the positive or the negative class based on a threshold applied to the output class' probability

The workflow in *Figure 10.4* shows you this example based on the sentiment analysis case study. You can download the workflow from the KNIME Hub at `https://hub.knime.com/kathrin/spaces/Codeless%20Deep%20Learning%20with%20KNIME/latest/Chapter_10/`:

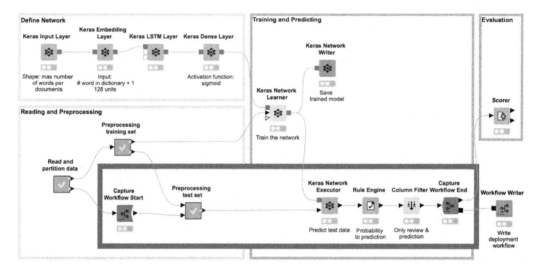

Figure 10.4 – Training workflow that automatically creates a deployment workflow using Integrated Deployment

The part in the thick box is the captured workflow snippet. The **Capture Workflow Start** node defines the beginning and the **Capture Workflow End** node defines the end of the workflow snippet to capture.

The start node doesn't need any configuration. *Figure 10.5* shows the configuration window of the **Capture Workflow End** node:

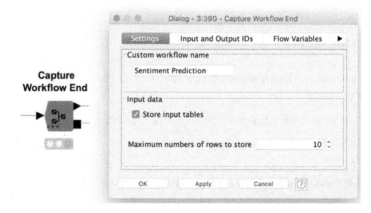

Figure 10.5 – Configuration window of the Capture Workflow End node

In the configuration window, you can set the name of the captured workflow snippet. You can also set whether the captured snippet should be stored with the data and, if yes, the maximum number of data rows to include. We will see in a second why it can be helpful to store some data in the captured workflow snippet.

The captured workflow snippet, with or without data, is then exported via the output port (the black square) of the **Capture Workflow End** node. In the workflow in *Figure 10.4*, the workflow snippet is then collected by the **Workflow Writer** node and written into the deployment workflow, with unaltered settings and configuration.

Figure 10.6 shows the configuration window of the **Workflow Writer** node:

Figure 10.6 – The Workflow Writer node and its configuration window

At the top, you can set the location of the folder of the destination workflow (**Output location**).

Next, you need to set the name of the destination workflow. The node automatically proposes a default name, which you can customize via the **Use custom workflow name** option. If the name you choose refers to a workflow that already exists, you can let the writer node fail or overwrite.

At the bottom, you can select the deployment option for the destination workflow: just create it, create it and open it, or save it as a .knwf file to export.

The next figure, *Figure 10.7*, shows you the automatically generated deployment workflow by the **Workflow Writer** node:

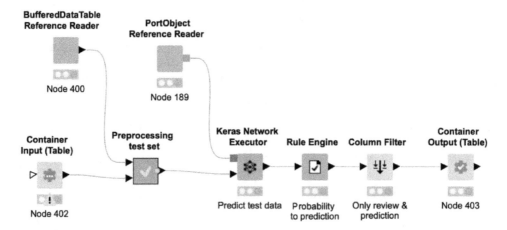

Figure 10.7 – Automatically created deployment workflow from the workflow snippet captured via Integrated Deployment

In the captured workflow you can see the **Preprocessing test set** metanode, as well as the **Keras Network Executor**, **Rule Engine**, and **Column Filter** nodes. Additionally, the whole Integrated Deployment process has added the following:

- Two **Reference Reader** nodes. They are generic reader nodes, loading the connection information of static parameters not found in the captured workflow snippet.

- A **Container Input (Table)** and a **Container Output (Table)** node in order to accept input data and to send output data respectively from and to other applications.

The execution of this deployment workflow can be triggered either by another workflow using the **Call Workflow (Table)** node or via a REST service if the workflow has been deployed on a KNIMEs Server. In the next chapter, we will talk about the REST calls and REST services in detail.

In *Figure 10.7*, the example deployment workflow reads two entities at the top of the workflow using the two reader nodes without an icon inside them. The left one provides the dictionary table based on the training data, and the right one provides the trained neural network.

In addition, you can see two more new nodes, which are the **Container Input (Table)** and **Container Output (Table)** nodes.

The **Container Input (Table)** node receives a data table from an external caller (that is, the **Call Workflow (Table Based)** node) and makes it available on the output port. A configuration parameter enables the external caller to send a data table to the **Container Input (Table)** node.

The **Container Input (Table)** node also has an optional input port (represented by an unfilled input port). If a data table is connected to the optional input, the node will simply forward this table to the next node; if a table is supplied via a REST API, then the supplied table will be available on the output port.

If no input is given, a default template table will be provided on the output of the node. Here, the **Store input tables** setting from the **Capture Workflow End** node comes in. If you select to store some data rows, they are used to define this default template table.

The **Container Output (Table)** node sends a KNIME data table to an external caller.

Let's now find out how the automatically created workflow can be used to predict the sentiment of new reviews during deployment.

Using the Automatically Created Workflow

Let's have a look now at how the deployment workflow can be consumed.

Figure 10.8 shows you an example of how the automatically created deployment workflow can be consumed to classify the sentiment of new movie reviews, and you can download it from the KNIME Hub to try it out, at `https://hub.knime.com/kathrin/ spaces/Codeless%20Deep%20Learning%20with%20KNIME/latest/ Chapter_10/`:

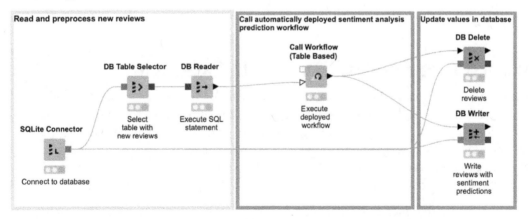

Figure 10.8 – Workflow calling the automatically created deployment workflow

The workflow connects to the database and reads the incoming new movie reviews.

Then, the **Call Workflow (Table Based)** node calls the deployment workflow (*Figure 10.7*), the one that was automatically built. The **Call Workflow (Table Based)** node indeed calls other workflows residing on your local workspace or on a mounted KNIME server. The called workflow must contain at least one Container Input node and one Container Output node to define the interface between the two workflows: the called and the caller workflows.

Via the **Call Workflow (Table Based)** node, we send the new movie reviews to the deployment workflow to feed the **Container Input (Table)** node. The deployment workflow is then executed, and the predictions are sent back to the caller workflow and made available via the output port of the **Call Workflow (Table Based)** node.

A great advantage of this strategy is the ensured consistency between the data operations in the training workflow and the data operations in the deployment workflow. If we now change any settings in the data operations in the training workflow, for example, the value of the threshold in the **Rule Engine** node (*Figure 10.4*), and we re-execute the training workflow, these changes are automatically imported into the new version of the deployment workflow (*Figure 10.7*) and used by any workflow relying on it (*Figure 10.8*).

> **Tip**
> Another great node of the **Integrated Deployment** extension is the **Workflow Combiner** node, which allows us to combine workflow snippets from different original workflows.

We have reached the last section of this chapter, which is on scalability and GPU execution.

Improving Scalability – GPU Execution

For the case studies described in this book, we have used relatively small datasets and small networks. This allowed us to train the networks within hours using only CPU-based execution. However, training tasks that take minutes or hours on small datasets can easily take days or weeks on larger datasets; small network architectures can quickly increase in size and execution times can quickly become prohibitive. In general, when working with deep neural networks, the training phase is the most resource-intensive task.

GPUs have been designed to handle multiple computations simultaneously. This paradigm suits the intensive computations required to train a deep learning network. Hence, GPUs are an alternative option to train large deep learning networks efficiently and effectively on large datasets.

Some Keras libraries can exploit the computational power of NVIDIA®-compatible GPUs via the TensorFlow paradigms. As a consequence, **KNIME Keras integration** can also exploit the computational power of GPUs to train deep learning networks more quickly.

In *Chapter 1*, *Introduction to Deep Learning with KNIME Analytics Platform*, we introduced how to set up Python for KNIME Keras integration and KNIME TensorFlow integration. In order to run the KNIME Keras integration on the GPU rather than on the CPU, you do not need to take many extra steps.

Of course, you need a GPU-enabled computer. TensorFlow 1.12 requires an NVIDIA GPU card with a CUDA compute capability of 3.5 or higher.

Besides that, most of the required dependencies (that is, CUDA® and cuDNN) will be automatically installed by Anaconda when installing the conda `tensorflow=1.12` and `keras-gpu=2.2.4`. packages

The only extra step at installation is the latest version of the NVIDIA® GPU driver, to be installed manually.

At installation time, by selecting **Create new GPU environment** instead of **Create new CPU environment**, an environment with `keras-gpu=2.2.4` is created.

When using the TensorFlow integration, it is also possible to execute on the GPU to read and execute TensorFlow's SavedModel.

> **Important note**
> The GPU support for the **KNIME TensorFlow integration** (which uses the TensorFlow Java API) is generally independent of the GPU support for the **KNIME Keras integration** (which uses Python). Hence, the two GPU supports must be set up individually. Due to the limitations of TensorFlow, the GPU support for the KNIME TensorFlow integration can only run on Windows and Linux, and not on Mac.

At the time of writing, the following GPU configuration is recommended by KNIME.

The KNIME TensorFlow integration uses TensorFlow version 1.13.1, which requires the following NVIDIA® software to be installed on your system:

- NVIDIA® GPU drivers: CUDA® 10.0 requires 410.x or higher.
- CUDA® Toolkit: TensorFlow (≥ 1.13.0) supports CUDA® 10.0.
- cuDNN (version ≥ 7.4.1): Select cuDNN v7.6.0 (May 20, 2019) for CUDA® 10.0.

For detailed instructions and the most recent updates, please check the KNIME documentation (`https://docs.knime.com/2019-06/deep_learning_installation_guide/index.html#tensorflow-integration`).

Summary

In this chapter, we have covered three different topics. We started with a summary of the many options for reading, converting, and writing neural networks.

We then moved on to the deployment of neural networks, using the sentiment analysis case study from *Chapter 7, Implementing NLP Applications*, as an example. The goal here was to build a workflow that uses the trained neural network to predict the sentiment of new reviews stored in the database. We have shown that a deployment workflow can be assembled in two ways: manually or automatically with Integrated Deployment.

The last section of the chapter dealt with the scalability of network training and execution. In particular, it showed how to exploit the computational power of GPUs when training a neural network.

In the next and last chapter of this book, we will explore further deployment options and best practices when working with deep learning.

Questions and Exercises

1. Which network conversions are available in KNIME Analytics Platform?

    a) Keras to TensorFlow network conversion

    b) TensorFlow to Keras network conversion

    c) ONNX to Keras network conversion

    d) Keras to ONNX network conversion

2. Which statements regarding Integrated Deployment are true (two statements are correct)?

    a) Integrated Deployment allows us to retrain a model during execution.

    b) The execution of the automatically generated workflow can be triggered by another workflow.

    c) The execution of the training workflow is triggered by the deployment workflow.

    d) Integrated Deployment closes the gap between training and deployment.

11
Best Practices and Other Deployment Options

In *Chapter 10, Deploying a Deep Learning Network*, we introduced the concept of deployment and we showed how to build a workflow to apply a network to new data. In this chapter, we will focus on two more deployment options using the KNIME software.

In the first section of this chapter, you will learn how to deploy a deep learning model as a web application so that end users can execute, interact with, and control the application via a web browser. In order to implement a web application, we need to introduce the KNIME WebPortal, a feature of KNIME Server. Components play a central role in the development of web applications since they are used to implement the interaction points according to the **Guided Analytics** feature of the KNIME software. In this chapter, you will also learn more about components.

Another deployment option to consume a deep learning model is a web service, through a REST interface. Web services have become very popular recently because they allow you to integrate and orchestrate a number of applications seamlessly and easily within the same ecosystem. In the second section of this chapter, you will learn how to build, deploy, and call workflows as REST services with the KNIME software.

We will conclude this chapter with some best practice advice and tips and tricks for working with both neural networks and KNIME Analytics Platform. These best practices and tips and tricks originate from our own experiences of many years of working on deep learning projects, some of which have been described in this book.

The chapter is organized into the following topics:

- Building a Web Application
- Building a Web Service with the REST Interface
- KNIME Tips and Tricks

Building a Web Application

In this section, we will show you the few steps needed to build a **web application** using the KNIME software.

After a short introduction to **KNIME WebPortal**, we will show how to create composite views, how to include them to create interaction points, and how to structure the application into a sequence of web pages as interaction points, following the **Guided Analytics** principles.

As an example, we will apply what we have learned to build a web application around the deployment workflow of the case study on cancer cell classification described in *Chapter 9, Convolutional Neural Networks for Image Classification*.

Introduction to KNIME WebPortal

The first step in building a web application is to design and implement the sequence of web-based interaction points within the workflow. In a case study on the classification of cancer cells, our data scientist could build a deployment workflow with two interaction points: one to allow the end user to upload a histopathology slide image, and one to display the results on the final web page. In between those two interaction points, the workflow ingests the new image and executes the trained model to classify it.

Once the workflow is ready, it will be transferred onto the production **KNIME server**. From now on, the workflow can be accessed on-demand through **KNIME WebPortal** via any web browser. This web-based interaction allows the pathologist to control the process without being familiar with KNIME Analytics Platform or the deep learning algorithm. *Figure 11.1* shows you what this web-based application could look like:

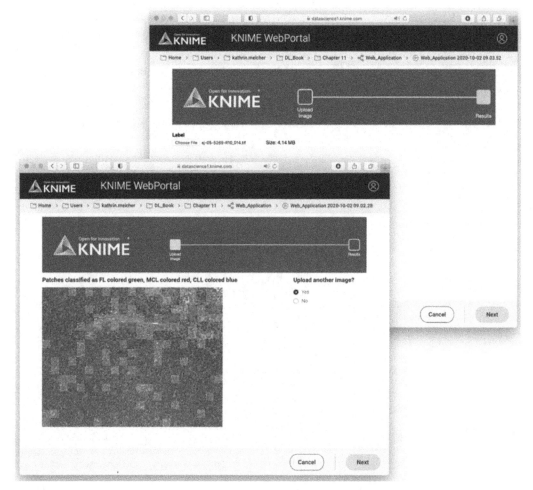

Figure 11.1 – A web application implemented by a KNIME workflow, running on KNIME Server, and called via KNIME WebPortal from any web browser

In this example, the web application is a very simple one. It has only two interaction points – that is, two web pages: the first one for the image upload and the second one to inspect the results.

More complex web applications can be developed codelessly using this combination of KNIME Analytics Platform, KNIME Server, and KNIME WebPortal. Some examples of quite complex and very beautifully designed web applications, such as Guided Visualization, Guided Labeling, and Guided Automation, are available for download from the KNIME Hub (`https://hub.knime.com`).

In contrast to KNIME Analytics Platform, KNIME Server contains no data operations or model training algorithms. However, it contains the whole IT infrastructure to allow collaboration among team members, on-demand and scheduled execution of applications, a definition of the access rights for each registered user or group of users, model management, auditing features, and, of course, deployment options, as we will see in this chapter. Also, in contrast to KNIME Analytics Platform, KNIME Server is not open source but rather needs a yearly license. *Figure 11.2* shows the login page for KNIME WebPortal:

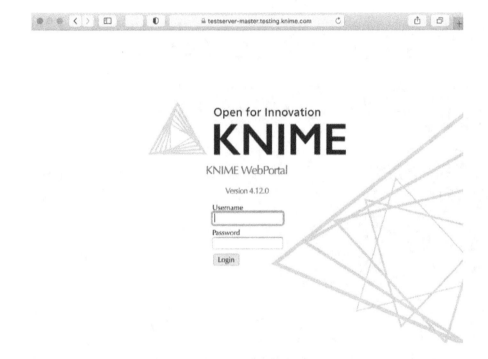

Figure 11.2 – Login page for KNIME WebPortal

Among the many IT features available with KNIME Server, KNIME WebPortal allows you to see and manage workflows from any web browser. This seems a simple feature, but it can be the missing link between the data scientist and the end user.

> **Important note**
> The end user is an expert in their domain and usually has neither the time nor the inclination to open KNIME Analytics Platform and investigate workflows and nodes. All the end user needs is a comfortable web-based application running on a web browser and showing only the information they need to see; at the very least, the page for the data upload and the final page summarizing the results.

WebPortal does not need any special installation. It comes already pre-packaged with the installation of KNIME Server. However, its appearance can be easily customized through dedicated *CSS style sheets*. KNIME WebPortal only accepts registered users and requires logging in (*Figure 11.2*).

After a successful login, the starting page appears with the folders you have been granted access to. Navigate to the workflow you would like to start and then press **Run** (*Figure 11.3*):

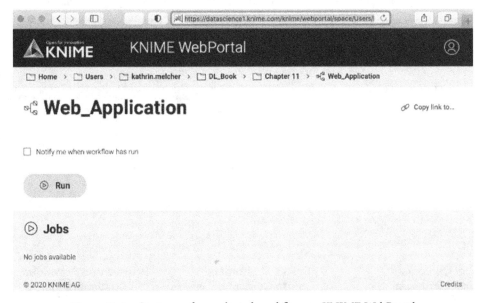

Figure 11.3 – Start page for a selected workflow on KNIME WebPortal

> **Important note**
> KNIME Server is the complementary tool to KNIME Analytics Platform.
> While KNIME Analytics Platform has all the algorithms and data operations,
> KNIME Server provides the IT infrastructure for team-based collaboration,
> application automation, model management, and deployment options.

Let's find out how a workflow must be structured to create a sequence of pages on KNIME WebPortal with defined interaction options.

Creating a Workflow to Run on KNIME WebPortal

The execution of a workflow on KNIME WebPortal moves from one web page to the next. These pages, also called wizard steps, offer the end user the possibility of visually guided actions to move and interact with the process.

Now, it would be long and complicated if we had to build all those pages/steps from scratch. Luckily, there are **components**. Each page/step just visualizes the content of the **composite view** of a component in the underlying workflow. So, implementing a sequence of web pages for WebPortal in reality corresponds to just implementing a sequence of components with the required composite views.

The upper part of *Figure 11.4* shows three web pages from an application running on KNIME WebPortal: a form to import customers from a database; a scatter plot and a table, connected to each other, to select some customers; and finally, a page displaying the information for the selected customers. The lower part of *Figure 11.4* shows the underlying workflow with the corresponding three components. The composite view of each component produces one page during the execution of the workflow on KNIME WebPortal:

Figure 11.4 – Top: step execution of an application on KNIME WebPortal. Bottom: the corresponding workflow generating the web pages for the step execution

The workflow in *Figure 11.4* is used as an example for a step execution of a workflow from a web browser and refers to a customer dataset. We will use only this dataset for this section since it allows us to show many different features used in component construction. This web application has been designed to allow the end user to inspect customer data and select customers with a high risk of churn to be contacted by a team member.

The first component, **Get Customers from Database**, creates the first page on the left. Here, the end user must provide their username and password to connect to the database.

After clicking on the **Next** button in the lower-right corner, the workflow is executed until the next component, **Select Customers to Contact**, is reached and the corresponding web page is created. On this page, the end user gets an overview of the customer data via a scatter plot and a table and selects the customers to contact. For the selection, the view provides two interaction options: select a product via the radio buttons in the upper-left corner or change the churn score using the range slider in the lower-left corner. The scatter plot and table are automatically updated according to the new selection parameters. Once the end user is happy with the selection, they click **Next** again to get to the last page of the web application.

The final page is created by the **Browse and Download Customers List** component. Here, the data of each selected customer is reported in a tile view and can be exported into an Excel file. The workflow is available on the KNIME Hub: `https://hub.knime.com/kathrin/spaces/Codeless%20Deep%20Learning%20with%20KNIME/latest/Chapter_11/`.

> **Tip**
> To open the interactive view of a component already in KNIME Analytics Platform, after execution, right-click the component and select **Interactive View: <name of the component>**.

To summarize, again each of these pages is created by one component in the workflow and displays its interactive view. Components and their composite views are then the key elements to build workflows for web applications.

Let's now see how a composite view can be created and customized.

Creating Composite Views

The composite view of a component collects all interactive views from the **View** and **Widget** nodes contained inside.

> **Tip**
> To create a new component, you must select the nodes to include inside the component, then right-click and select the **Create Component...** option.

Before looking deeper into the **View** and **Widget** nodes, let's have a look inside the **Select Customer to Contact** component (*Figure 11.5*):

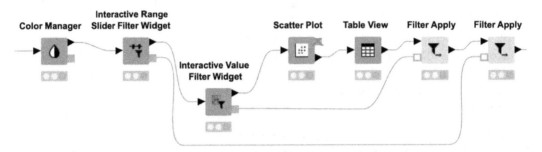

Figure 11.5 – Contents of the Select Customers to Contact component

In the lower-left part of the corresponding page, the end user has the option to define a threshold for the churn score via a slider. This interactive slider is created by the **Interactive Range Slider Filter Widget** node.

In the upper-left corner, the option to select the product is created by the **Interactive Value Filter Widget** node.

In addition, the page shows an interactive scatter plot and an interactive table. Those two views are created by the **Scatter Plot** node and the **Table View** node, respectively.

As you can see, each widget/view node adds one piece to the final composite view and therefore to the corresponding page in WebPortal.

> **Tip**
> In KNIME Analytics Platform, the view of each widget/view node is visible by right-clicking the node and selecting **Interactive View:<name of node>**.

The nodes that can contribute pieces to a composite view can be categorized into three groups:

- **Widget nodes**
- **View nodes**
- **Interactive widget nodes**

Let's have a look at each category in detail.

Widget Nodes

Widget nodes produce a view with an interactive form for setting parameters. The newly set parameters are then exported as **flow variables** and can be used by other nodes down the line in the workflow.

> **Tip**
>
> In *Chapter 2, Data Access and Preprocessing with KNIME Analytics Platform*, we introduced the concept of flow variables and how they can be used to overwrite setting options.

Each widget node is specialized in producing one specific input or interaction form, such as string input, integer input, selecting one or many values from a list, and more. You can find all the available widget nodes in the Node Repository under **Workflow Abstraction | Widgets**, as shown in *Figure 11.6*:

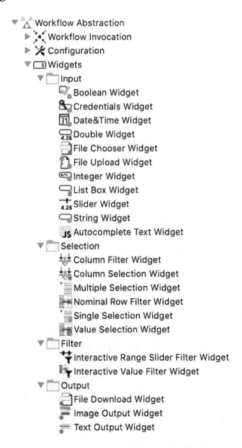

Figure 11.6 – Available widget nodes in the Node Repository

The widget nodes themselves can be divided into three subgroups:

- **Input widget nodes**: The widget nodes in the *input* category produce an input form on a web page, which allows you to input values of different types into the workflow – integers, strings, Booleans, doubles, or lists – as well as data in other formats, such as date&time or credentials.

- **Selection widget nodes**: The widget nodes in the *selection* category produce web forms to select values from a list, such as choosing a specific column from a data table, including/excluding multiple columns from a dataset, or selecting one or more values to filter data from a table.

- **Output widget nodes**: These widget nodes add custom text, links, or images to the composite view.

As an example, *Figure 11.7* shows the **Single Selection Widget** node and its configuration window:

Figure 11.7 – The Single Selection Widget node and its configuration window

Most of the widget nodes share some important settings, such as **Label**, **Description**, and **Variable Name**:

- **Label**: This creates a label on top of the form created by the widget node.

- **Description**: This value is shown as a tooltip on the widget form.

- **Variable Name**: This gives the name of the flow variable created by the node.

Let's have a look at the additional configuration settings for the **Single Selection Widget** node (*Figure 11.7*):

- **Selection Type**: Defines the objects used for the selection: a drop-down menu, vertical or horizontal radio buttons, or a list

- **Possible Choices**: Defines the list of available values to choose from

- **Default Value**: Assigns an initial default value to the selection operation

The standard widget node produces either some flow variables or a table as output, which can be used in the downstream nodes in the workflow. A special set of widget nodes are the interactive widget nodes.

View Nodes

View nodes visualize data through interactive charts, plots, and tables.

Figure 11.8 shows you an overview of the available view nodes in the Node Repository:

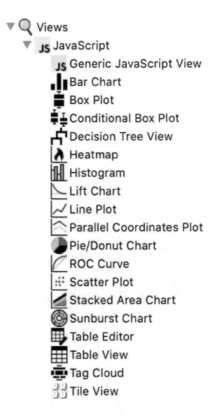

Figure 11.8 – Available view nodes in the Node Repository

If multiple view nodes are present inside a component, their views interact with each other in the resulting component view; for example, via selection, data points selected in the view of one node can be selected or even isolated in the view of another node.

> Tip
> The **Plotly** nodes and the **JavaScript** nodes in the **Labs** category offer even more interactive options to visualize your data in composite views. Views from (local) nodes in the **Local (Swing)** category cannot be integrated into the composite view of a component.

Interactive Widget Nodes

Interactive widget nodes are special widget nodes. They implement filter events and feed view nodes. During execution, changes in the interactive widget nodes are reflected immediately in the views of the subsequent view nodes.

At the time of writing, KNIME Analytics Platform offers two interactive widget nodes: the **Interactive Range Slider Filter Widget** node and the **Interactive Value Filter Widget** node.

These nodes can be used to trigger updates in the composite view. In the configuration window of downstream view nodes, we can set whether or not this node should listen to the filter events from previous interactive widget nodes. If yes, the view produced by the view node is immediately updated when settings in the filter event of the previous interactive widget nodes change.

In comparison to the standard widget nodes, these two nodes trigger direct filter events in the open composite view or web page. The flow variable created by a standard widget node can be used by a subsequent node but doesn't trigger direct changes in the open page or composite view.

Now that we have an overview of the nodes available to build a composite view, let's customize the composite view of a component through some layout options.

Defining the Layout of a Composite View

You can define a layout for the composite view of every component containing at least one widget or view node.

> **Tip**
> To open a component in a new tab in the workflow editor, you must press *Ctrl* + double-click the component or right-click the component and select **Component | Open**.

The layout in a composite view is set via the **layout editor** from inside the component. After opening the content of the component in a new tab in the workflow editor, click the layout editor button at the rightmost side of the top toolbar, as shown in *Figure 11.9*:

Figure 11.9 – Toolbar with layout editor button to the far right

Upon clicking on the layout editor button, the visual layout editor (*Figure 11.10*) opens:

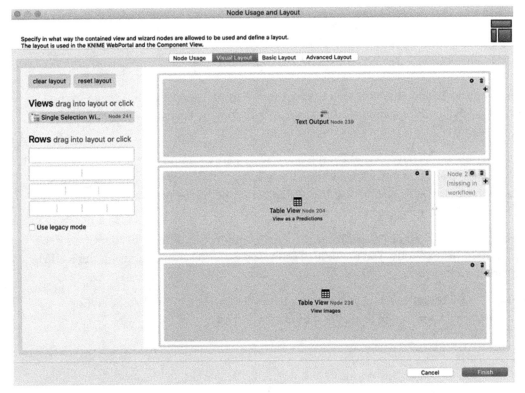

Figure 11.10 – Visual layout editor

The layout editor uses a grid structure with rows and columns.

On the left, there are row templates with different numbers of columns and a list of all the still-unplaced views. On the right, there is the layout editor itself.

You can change the layout by adding new row templates via drag and drop from the template list on the left to the layout editor on the right. To add a new empty column, click the + button in the layout editor. Columns inside a row can be manually resized.

Empty cells in the layout editor can be populated by dragging and dropping views from the list of unused views into the cells in the layout editor.

The default layout consists of one column only and all views from the widget and view nodes are placed in it from top to bottom. To start from a blank canvas, click the **clear layout** button in the upper-left corner of the layout editor. This clearing action adds all views to the list on the left.

> **Tip**
> Node labels (the text below the node) are used in the layout editor to identify the views. It is best practice to change the node labels to meaningful descriptions, to easily recognize the views in the layout editor.

If you want to exclude the view of a node from the composite view, you can go to the first tab of the layout editor, called **Node Usage**, and disable the node view for the WebPortal/composite view.

It is also possible to have nested components, which are a component inside a component. If the nested component has a view, this shows up as a node view in the layout editor. Thus, you can integrate the view of the nested component into your layout as you would do for any other node.

A composite view can be easily beautified – for example, by adding a header or a sidebar and styling the text body. You are in luck as there are shared components on the KNIME Hub to do that.

Figure 11.11 shows the web page before and after the introduction of some styling elements using some of the available shared components:

Figure 11.11 – Web page without (left) and with (right) a header, sidebar, and additional information in the body of the page

You will see some shared components in action at the end of this section when we build the cancer cell classification example.

Let's first find out more about shared components.

Shared Components

In the previous section, *Creating Composite Views*, we discussed how to use components to create composite views and then pages for WebPortal applications. Components can also bundle up functionalities that can be reused and shared with others via the KNIME Hub and KNIME Server. These functionalities range from simple repetitive tasks, such as entering credentials into a database, to more complicated tasks, such as optimizing parameters.

In comparison to metanodes, components have their own configuration window. They can be configured without touching the individual nodes inside – providing a handy way to hide configuration complexity. Of course, if needed, you can still open the component, dive into the details, and make any adjustments relevant to your use case.

To add settings in the configuration window of a component, you can use the **configuration nodes**. They work similarly to widget nodes but at the level of the configuration window instead of the composite view. You can find them in the Node Repository under **Workflow Abstraction | Configuration**. Components can have a description in the **Description** panel like any KNIME node. From inside a component, you can edit the description by clicking on the pen in the upper-left corner of the **Description** panel in KNIME Analytics Platform.

For components to become like all other KNIME nodes, they have to be shared.

To share a component, you right-click on it and select **Component | Share…**.

Then, you decide where to save the template: either on your local workspace, on the KNIME Hub, or on KNIME Server.

Next, you can select the link type to link the component instance to the component template. The link type defines the location of the component template when checking for updates. After choosing the destination of the component template, a dialog opens asking you for the link type:

- **Create absolute link**: The workflow uses the absolute path when looking for the component template.

- **Create mountpoint-relative link**: The workflow uses the relative path starting from the selected mountpoint when looking for the component template.

- **Create workflow-relative link**: The workflow uses a relative path starting from the current workflow folder when looking for the component template.

- **Don't create link with shared instance**: A component template is created but is not linked to the current instance.

> **Tip**
> When you deploy a workflow to KNIME Server, make sure that all link types on the component instances also work when on the server.

To create an instance of a shared component, simply drag and drop the component template from the KNIME Hub or KNIME Explorer to the workflow editor. Newly created instances are read-only and link to the corresponding shared component.

Each time the workflow is started, KNIME Analytics Platform searches for possible updates of the component template and if there are any, proposes to also update the instance. This has the advantage that if something changes in the component template, the changes are automatically reflected in the instances.

> **Tip**
>
> Being read-only, new instances cannot be edited. You need to disconnect the instance from the template first in order to change its content. To do that, you need to right-click on the component instance and select **Component | Disconnect Link**.

There are a lot of public shared components on the EXAMPLES Server or the KNIME Hub. You will also find some shared components in the workflow group for this chapter on the KNIME Hub.

Now that you are familiar with shared components and the WebPortal, let's have a look at the deployment example of cancer cell classification.

Building a WebPortal Application for Cancer Cell Classification

Let's go back to the cancer data and the workflow for cancer cell classification described in *Chapter 9, Convolutional Neural Networks for Image Classification*. In this section, we will show how to deploy a trained deep learning model as a web application using KNIME WebPortal.

The goal here is to produce a web application for pathologists who are not familiar with KNIME Analytics Platform and data science in general. It should help them in their daily routine by suggesting a cancer classification during the analysis of histopathology images. An additional requirement is the option to upload multiple images in sequence without restarting the application. *Figure 11.12* shows you the workflow implementing the application. You can download the workflow from the KNIME Hub: `https://hub.knime.com/kathrin/spaces/Codeless%20Deep%20Learning%20with%20KNIME/latest/Chapter_11/`.

Let's focus first on the middle part of the workflow: the loop body inside the annotation box:

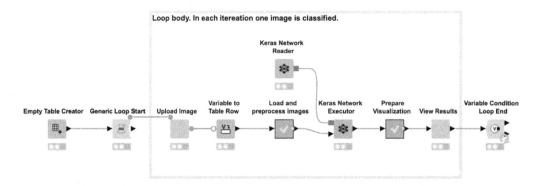

Figure 11.12 – Deployment workflow to score new histopathology images from a web browser

At each iteration, one image is uploaded, the classification is produced, and two web pages are presented to the pathologist. The loop takes care of the iterations and the two components in the loop body – the **Upload Image** component and the **View Results** component – of the web pages:

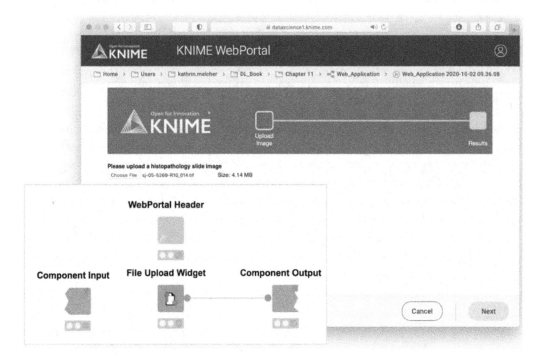

Figure 11.13 – Workflow inside the Upload Image component and the webpage created by it

The loop body starts with the **Upload Image** component, which creates the first web page of the web application. You can see the created page as well as the inside of the component in *Figure 11.13*.

The header of the web page, with the KNIME logo and the navigation path, is created by the shared component named **WebPortal Header**. For WebPortal applications with many steps, a header like this helps the end user to get an overview of the current step (in frame), the steps already covered (yellow boxes or light-gray boxes), and the steps yet to come (gray boxes).

The little green arrow in the lower-left corner of the **WebPortal Header** component indicates that this component instance is linked to a shared component template. The **WebPortal Header** component comes with a configuration window (*Figure 11.14*), resulting from configuration nodes in it. In this configuration window, you can define the step labels and whether to outline the current step with a yellow frame:

Figure 11.14 – Configuration window of the WebPortal Header component

The web page for the **Upload Image** step includes just one item to upload the next image. By clicking on the **Choose File** button, the pathologist uploads the file with the histopathology slide image to a temporary local folder. This item is created by the **File Upload Widget** node. The output variable of the node contains the file path to the selected image in a temporary folder.

In the workflow in *Figure 11.12,* the flow variable is written into a table using the **Variable to Table Row** node. The **Load and preprocess images** metanode performs the same preprocessing steps as for training, as described in *Chapter 9, Convolutional Neural Networks for Image Classification.* That is, it loads the image, normalizes it, splits it into patches of 64 x 64 pixels, and swaps some dimensions to fit the VGG16 model used as the starting point for the transfer learning approach.

Next, the workflow reads the trained deep learning network using the **Keras Network Reader** node and applies it to the image patches with the **Keras Network Executor** node.

In the **Prepare Visualization** metanode, the image patches are assigned a color, according to the probability of belonging to one of the three cancer classes.

Finally, the results are visualized using the last component, named **View Results**. *Figure 11.15* shows you the workflow inside the component and the corresponding web page obtained when executing the workflow in the web browser:

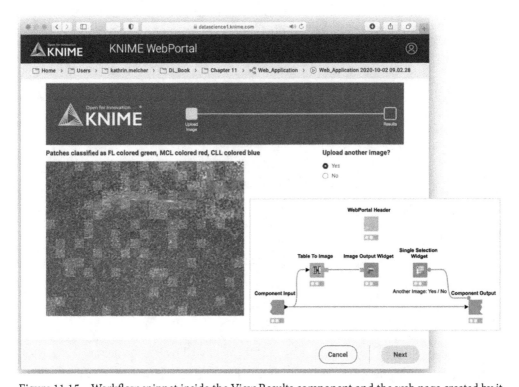

Figure 11.15 – Workflow snippet inside the View Results component and the web page created by it

In the **View Results** component, we again find the shared **WebPortal Header** component, to create the page header, this time with the **Upload Image** box in yellow (past steps) and the **Results** box with the yellow frame (current step).

The **Table to Image** node converts the image contained in the first row of the selected column into an image object. This image object is then fed into the **Image Output Widget** node to display it inside a composite view.

Lastly, the pathologist must decide whether to upload another image. This selection part is implemented in the web page via radio buttons and in the workflow by the **Single Selection Widget** node.

This node produces a flow variable at its output port with the selected option:

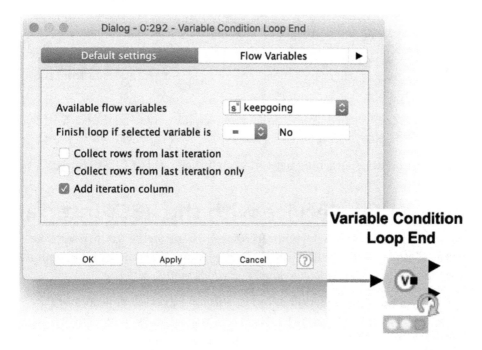

Figure 11.16 – Configuration window of the Variable Condition Loop End node

This whole snippet, from **Upload Image** to **View Results**, is wrapped in a loop, to meet the additional requirement to give the pathologist the option to upload multiple images. The last radio button selection is used as the loop stopping criterion.

> **Tip**
> Remember that a loop always needs a loop start and a loop end node. In between these two nodes, there is the loop body, which is executed at each loop iteration.

There are many different loop start and loop end nodes available. Some, for example, use only a subset of rows at each iteration (**Group Loop Start** and **Chunk Loop Start**) and some only a subset of the columns (**Column List Loop Start**).

The workflow in *Figure 11.12* uses the **Generic Loop Start** node to start the loop and the **Variable Condition Loop End** node to close the loop. The two nodes allow us to build a loop with a custom stopping criterion that can be defined in the configuration of the **Variable Condition Loop End** node (*Figure 11.16*). According to these settings, the loop stops if the flow variable named keepgoing – created by the **Single Selection Widget** node – has the value No. As the **Generic Loop Start** node always needs an input table, an empty table is created with the **Empty Table Creator** node to feed the node.

After deploying this workflow to a KNIME server and running it on KNIME WebPortal, the pathologist can easily upload new images and get the result from the automatic classification.

In this section, you have learned how to build a web application using the KNIME software and how to deploy a deep learning network as a web application.

Let's now discover how deep learning networks can be deployed as REST services.

Building a Web Service with the REST Interface

In this section, you will learn how to build **REST** services using the KNIME software. As a practical example, we will walk through the deployment workflow of the sentiment analysis example of *Chapter 7, Implementing NLP Applications*.

The KNIME Server REST API offers an interface for non-KNIME applications to communicate with KNIME Server via simple HTTP requests. The main benefit of **RESTful web services** is the ease of integration of the application into the company IT landscape. Self-contained and isolated applications can call each other and exchange data via the REST interface. In this way, it becomes easier to add new applications to the ecosystem.

Any workflow uploaded on KNIME Server is automatically available via the **REST API**. This allows you to seamlessly deploy KNIME workflows as web services via the REST API and integrate them into the infrastructure of your data science lab.

In the sentiment analysis example, we want to deploy the deep learning network as a **REST service**. In this way, external applications – for example, a website or a mobile app – can send some text to the REST service and get back the predicted sentiment.

Let's quickly look at the steps required to build a deployment workflow as a REST service in KNIME Analytics Platform.

Building a REST Service Workflow

In the example of sentiment prediction, the goal is to build a REST service with an input, the new movie reviews, and an output, the sentiment predictions.

When building a REST service with an input and an output, we need to define the structure of the inputs and outputs. In KNIME Analytics Platform, this can be done via the **container** input and output nodes.

> **Important note**
>
> Not every REST service has inputs and outputs. For example, a REST service that connects to a database to get the most recent data only has outputs. A REST service that concludes the process by writing the results to a database does not need to output any results.

KNIME Analytics Platform has a variety of input nodes that can be used to define the structure of the input to the REST API. You can find these nodes in the Node Repository under **Workflow Abstraction | Workflow Invocation** (*Figure 11.17*):

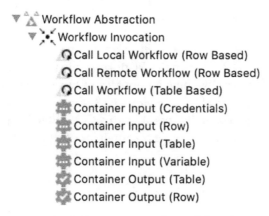

Figure 11.17 – Available container nodes to define the REST API

As you can see in *Figure 11.17*, there are four **Container Input** nodes – for credentials, for one data row only, for a data table, or for flow variables. A table input allows you to send either a single data row or multiple data rows to the web service. On the other hand, a row input sends only one single data row.

The **Container Input (Row)** and **Container Input (Table)** nodes have an optional input port. This port receives a template data table and based on that table, defines the input structure. This template serves two purposes: first, if no input table is provided when the workflow is called via the REST API, the values from the template are used as default input to execute the workflow. Second, the table is used to define the input structure that the web service expects. If the structure of the current input differs from the template, the web service will produce an error message. The advantage of this template technique is that the input is parsed automatically and converted into the specified types.

Similarly, to define the output of the REST service, you can use one of the **Container Output** nodes: either the **Container Output (Row)** or the **Container Output (Table)** node.

For our deployment workflow, to classify one movie review at a time, we used a **Container Input (Row)** node to define the input structure and a **Container Output (Row)** node to define the output structure to the REST service. In order to classify one or more movie reviews at a time, the **Container Input (Table)** node and the **Container Output (Table)** node could be used.

There are two ways to create a workflow that can be deployed as a REST service:

- Automatically with the **Integrated Deployment** feature
- Manually by building the workflow from scratch

In *Chapter 10*, *Deploying a Deep Learning Network*, we introduced the **Integrated Deployment** extension of KNIME Analytics Platform, which allows you to capture parts of the training workflow and deploy them automatically. Even there, as an example, we used the sentiment analysis case study. In *Figure 11.18*, you can see the automatically created workflow via **Integrated Deployment**, with a **Container Input (Table)** node and a **Container Output (Table)** node to define the input and output data structures:

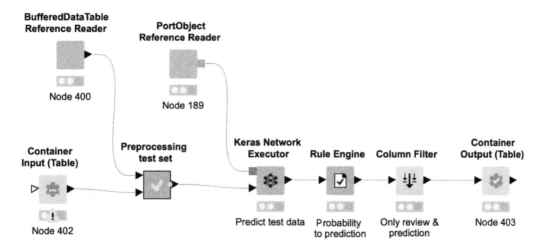

Figure 11.18 – Automatically created deployment workflow from Chapter 10, Deploying a Deep Learning Network

In *Chapter 10, Deploying a Deep Learning Network*, we saved this automatically created workflow locally and we triggered its execution through a **Call Workflow (Table Based)** node. Instead of saving the workflow locally, we could deploy it on a KNIME server.

The other option is to build a REST service manually from scratch. In this case, we have to provide the dictionary and the trained model (*Figure 11.19*):

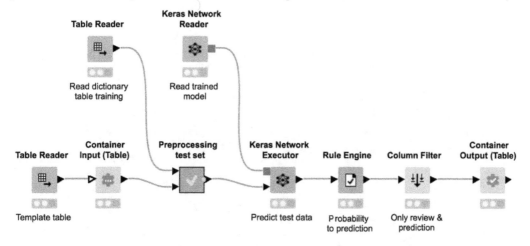

Figure 11.19 – Manually built REST service deployment workflow

As you can see, it looks really similar to the previous workflow in *Figure 11.18*, with the only difference that it uses a **Table Reader** node and a **Keras Network Reader** node to read the dictionary and the trained model. In addition, a template table has been inserted to define the input data structure to the REST API.

We have the REST service. Let's see how we can call it.

Calling a REST Service

To call the deployed workflow as a REST service from an external application, you need to know the path to the REST service and the expected input data structure. KNIME Server can show you the API definition in your browser. Simply right-click the deployed workflow on the server and select **Show API definition**. A browser window opens showing the REST API definition for this specific workflow (*Figure 11.20*):

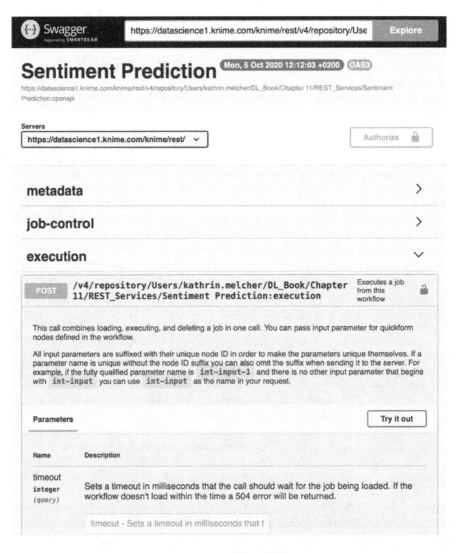

Figure 11.20 – Documentation of the REST API using Swagger

This web page is created using an open source framework called **Swagger**. Swagger has been integrated into KNIME Server to document the REST API, to easily explore the different HTTP requests and test them.

For example, you could test how to trigger the execution of the REST service with a **POST** request. By selecting the POST request, Swagger shows you an overview of the possible parameters, the schema for the input data, and the URL to call. You can also try it out by clicking on the **Try it out** button.

You can also trigger the execution of the REST service from another workflow using the **Call Workflow (Table Based)** node. This node calls local or remote workflows, sending the provided input table and outputting the REST service response.

The workflow in *Figure 11.21* shows how to trigger the execution of a REST service on KNIME Server:

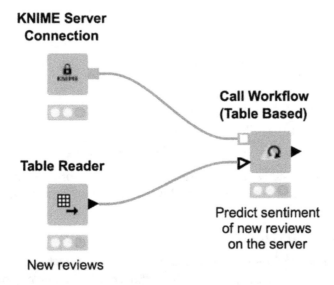

Figure 11.21 – This workflow triggers the execution of a REST service on KNIME Server

If you want to run a workflow on KNIME Server, you have to ensure that the **Call Workflow** node is connected to the server. To connect to a KNIME server, you can use the **KNIME Server Connection** node. In its configuration window, you need to provide the address to the server by either typing it in manually or by selecting a mountpoint and entering the credentials.

In the configuration window of the **Call Workflow (Table Based)** node, you get the list of all the workflows deployed on KNIME Server by clicking on the **Browse workflows** button. After selecting a workflow, in the advanced settings, you can assign the input table to the input of the called workflow and the output table to the output of the called workflow. This feature comes in very handy when the deployed workflow has many input nodes.

In this section, you have learned how to deploy a workflow as a REST service on KNIME Server. Let's now conclude with some tips and tricks from our own experience.

KNIME Tips and Tricks

Throughout the book, we covered many case studies, implemented using KNIME Analytics Platform. In the KNIME Hub space of this book, you can find these workflows and you can use them as a starting point for your deep learning projects: `https://hub.knime.com/kathrin/spaces/Codeless%20Deep%20Learning%20with%20KNIME/latest/`. In this last section, we want to share some tips and tricks to work with deep learning in KNIME Analytics Platform.

Let's start with data shuffling for training.

Shuffling Data during Training

When training neural networks, for faster convergence of the training process and to avoid overfitting, it is recommended to shuffle the training data before each epoch.

To do that, make sure you activate the **Shuffle training data before each epoch** checkbox in the **Advanced** tab in the configuration window of the **Keras Network Learner** node.

Using Batch Normalization

Batch normalization is a technique that standardizes the data in each batch. This has the effect of stabilizing the learning process and dramatically reducing the number of training epochs required to train deep networks.

To add batch normalization to your network, you can use the **Keras Batch Normalization Layer** node.

Keeping Your Workflow Clean and Structured

To make it easy to maintain your workflows, it is important to document and structure them in logical, easy-to-understand blocks:

- **Use metanodes and components**: To keep large workflows tidy and clean, it is recommended to hide the implementation details and some of the complexity inside metanodes or components. Indeed, to make a workflow easily understandable at first glance, you can create one metanode or component for each step in the project, such as data access, data preprocessing, model training, and model evaluation. Inside each metanode/component, you can have further metanodes and components for different sub-steps, such as, for example, different preprocessing steps or network layers.

- **Documenting a workflow**: KNIME Analytics Platform offers you three ways to document a workflow:

  a) **Node labels**

  b) **Annotation boxes**

  c) **Workflow description**

Node labels and annotation boxes help you and other users to understand at a glance the workflow's tasks and subtasks easily.

It is also possible to add meta-information to your workflow through the **Description** panel. To do so, click anywhere in the workflow editor (not on a node). The **Description** view changes to a workflow description with meta-information about the workflow: the title, description, and related links and tags.

Using the GroupBy Node and Pivoting Node to Avoid Loops

The execution of loops can be slow as the nodes must be executed at each iteration. Often, however, no doubt due to our programming background, we overdo the use of loops and use them even when more efficient alternatives are available.

For example, some loops could be avoided by simply using the following aggregation nodes: **GroupBy**, **Pivoting**, **Ungroup**, and **Unpivoting**. **Aggregation** nodes often perform the same task as a loop and are much more efficient in terms of execution speed.

Specifying the Execution Order

When you have parallel branches in a workflow, it is sometimes important to define an execution order. *Figure 11.22* shows you a very simple example where the order of writing tables into Excel sheets is enforced:

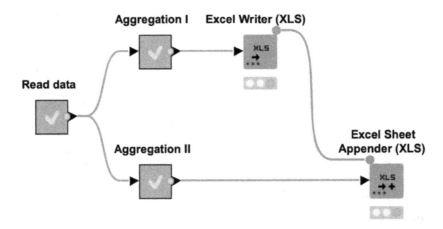

Figure 11.22 – In this workflow, the execution order is forced by using a flow variable connection

Of course, the **Excel Sheet Appender (XLS)** node should be executed after the **Excel Writer (XLS)** node. By using a flow variable connection from the flow variable output port of the **Excel Writer (XLS)** node to the flow variable input port of the **Excel Sheet Appender (XLS)** node, we force the execution of the **Excel Sheet Appender (XLS)** node to start only after the execution of the **Excel Writer (XLS)** node is finished.

Summary

In this chapter, you learned about two more options to deploy your trained deep learning networks: web applications and REST services. We finished the chapter – and the book – with some tips and tricks to successfully work with deep learning in KNIME Analytics Platform.

In the first section of this chapter, you learned how to build web applications using KNIME WebPortal of KNIME Server so that end users can execute their workflows and interact with the web pages comfortably from a web browser.

Next, you learned how to build, deploy, and call REST services using KNIME Server to integrate your deep learning networks into the company's IT infrastructure. You learned about the many options to define the input and output data structure of the REST service, how to inspect the REST API using the open source Swagger tool, and how to trigger the execution of a REST service from within KNIME Analytics Platform.

In the last section, we collated some tips and tricks from our own experience that might turn out to be helpful when working with deep learning in KNIME Analytics Platform.

At this point, we think that you are well equipped to start building and deploying your own workflows to train and use deep learning networks suitable to your own business cases and data with the KNIME software.

Questions and Exercises

1.   Which kind of nodes can you use to add input fields to a composite view?

   a) Configuration nodes

   b) Widget nodes

   c) View nodes

   d) Container input nodes

2.   How can you create a composite view?

   a) By selecting some nodes, right-clicking, and selecting **Create Metanode**

   b) By selecting some view or widget nodes, right-clicking, and selecting **Create Metanode**

   c) By selecting some view or widget nodes, right-clicking, and selecting **Create Component**

   d) By right-clicking anywhere in the workflow and selecting **Create Component**

3.   How can you define the layout of a composite view?

   a) Right-click on a component and select **Component | Layout**.

   b) Double-click on a component and go to the **Layout** tab in the configuration window.

   c) Go inside a component and click on the **Layout** button in the toolbar.

   d) Right-click on a component and select **Layout**.

4.   Which node can be used to define the input and output of a REST service?

   a) Configuration nodes

   b) Widget nodes

   c) View nodes

   d) Container nodes

Other Books You May Enjoy

If you enjoyed this book, you may be interested in these other books by Packt:

Hands-On Mathematics for Deep Learning

Jay Dawani

ISBN: 978-1-83864-729-2

- Understand the key mathematical concepts for building neural network models
- Discover core multivariable calculus concepts
- Improve the performance of deep learning models using optimization techniques
- Cover optimization algorithms, from basic stochastic gradient descent (SGD) to the advanced Adam optimizer
- Understand computational graphs and their importance in DL

Applied Deep Learning and Computer Vision for Self-Driving Cars

Sumit Ranjan, Dr. S. Senthamilarasu

ISBN: 978-1-83864-630-1

- Implement deep neural network from scratch using the Keras library
- Understand the importance of deep learning in self-driving cars
- Get to grips with feature extraction techniques in image processing using the OpenCV library
- Design a software pipeline that detects lane lines in videos
- Implement a convolutional neural network (CNN) image classifier for traffic signal signs
- Train and test neural networks for behavioral-cloning by driving a car in a virtual simulator
- Discover various state-of-the-art semantic segmentation and object detection architectures

Leave a review - let other readers know what you think

Please share your thoughts on this book with others by leaving a review on the site that you bought it from. If you purchased the book from Amazon, please leave us an honest review on this book's Amazon page. This is vital so that other potential readers can see and use your unbiased opinion to make purchasing decisions, we can understand what our customers think about our products, and our authors can see your feedback on the title that they have worked with Packt to create. It will only take a few minutes of your time, but is valuable to other potential customers, our authors, and Packt. Thank you!

Index

D

E

T

www.ingramcontent.com/pod-product-compliance
Lightning Source LLC
La Vergne TN
LVHW081330050326
832903LV00024B/1105